Research Methods in Human Resource Development

Valerie Anderson

Chartered Institute of Personnel and Development

Published by the Chartered Institute of Personnel and Development,
151 The Broadway, Wimbledon, London SW19 1JQ

First published 2004
Reprinted 2004, 2005

© Chartered Institute of Personnel and Development 2004

Design by Fakenham Photosetting, Fakenham, Norfolk
Typeset by Fakenham Photosetting, Fakenham, Norfolk
Printed in Great Britain by The Cromwell Press, Trowbridge, Wiltshire

British Library Cataloguing in Publication Data
A catalogue of this publication is available from the British Library

ISBN 0 85292 982 X

The views expressed in this publication are the author's own and may not necessarily reflect those of the CIPD.

The CIPD has made every effort to trace and acknowledge copyright holders. If any source has been overlooked, CIPD Enterprises would be pleased to redress this for future editions.

Chartered Institute of Personnel and Development
151 The Broadway, Wimbledon, London SW19 1JQ
Tel: 020-8612 6200
E-mail: cipd@cipd.co.uk   Website: www.cipd.co.uk
Incorporated by Royal Charter.   Registered Charity No. 1079797

Research Methods in Human Resource Management

Valerie Anderson

Valerie Anderson is a lecturer in Human Resource Management at the University of Portsmouth Business School. She has extensive experience of teaching research methods and supervising research projects, dissertations and management reports. Prior to her career in higher education, she undertook a range of HR roles both in the public and private sectors.

The Chartered Institute of Personnel and Development is the leading publisher of books and reports for personnel and training professionals, students, and all those concerned with the effective management and development of people at work. For details of all our titles, please contact the Publishing Department:
Tel: 020–8612 6204
E-mail: publish@cipd.co.uk
The catalogue of all CIPD titles can be viewed on the CIPD website:
www.cipd.co.uk/bookstore

Contents

List of Figures and Tables

Acknowledgements

I am grateful to a number of publishers who have given permission to reproduce extracts from copyright material and these are acknowledged individually in the text itself.

A further acknowledgement is due to those students who permitted me to include their experiences as 'case illustrations' within the text. Only their first names have been given so as to ensure the anonymity of their employing or workplacement organisations. I should like to thank, Gurinder, Kate, Lyn, Maria and Sarah, who studied at Westminster University and Shirley, Anna, Grace and Mark, students at the University of Portsmouth.

My experiences as an HR practitioner, student, supervisor and research methods tutor have informed the ideas in this book. In particular, my thinking about the value and potential of enquiries undertaken by practitioner-researchers has been developed as a result of working with, and learning from, John Bowden at Westminster University.

This book would certainly not have come to fruition without the expertise of the publishers, the advice and feedback provided by colleagues and reviewers and the help, encouragement and patience of my family. I should like to thank them for their significant contributions.

Valerie Anderson

Foreword

The ability to complete a successful research project has been a central component of Master's degrees in Human Resource Management for many years. Many students struggle with this part of the Master's programme because they have not received sufficiently good training in research methods and too often they are left to work it out for themselves. Now that the CIPD Professional Development Scheme has firmly been established at postgraduate level, a well-executed project with a clear critical base is also required for everyone who wishes to gain graduate status with the CIPD.

In the light of this background, Valerie Anderson's new book is not only timely but also extremely relevant and comprehensive for all postgraduate students who are undertaking a dissertation or project in human resource management. The book is written in a very systematic and logical way, and it will undoubtedly help all students, but especially those who are doing a postgraduate project for the first time. There are stacks of examples in the text, plus mini-questions and opportunities to review one's understanding as the text develops. A key feature of the book is its attempt to link together the practitioner and the academic requirements in the area, and construct a paradigm that develops the notion of the 'thinking performer' – itself a central component of the CIPD Standards. In short, the book provides an excellent text that should become required reading on postgraduate programmes in HRM.

The book divides into three broad sections: planning; acting and observing; and reflecting. The planning section of the book provides essential knowledge and understanding in what is perhaps the most vital part of any project – making sure the terms of reference and objectives are clearly thought through, relevant and achievable. Valerie Anderson stresses that this must be done carefully and offers a number of suggestions about how to choose an appropriate project, including the very obvious but often overlooked notion of examining previous work In the subject. It is critically important for students to get this stage right, because otherwise, examiners are often left with the 'So what?' impression when assessing their work, and questions are raised about focus and direction, as well as value.

The acting and observing section of the book provides an introduction to different methods of data collection, broadly differentiated into documentary analysis, qualitative and quantitative approaches. This section offers a wealth of advice about how to undertake research and provides pointers to the major benefits and shortcomings of different methods of data collection. Hopefully, it should help students understand that there is less to fear about quantitative approaches than they often think, and that with certain projects this is the most appropriate method by which to collect relevant and useful data.

Finally, the reflecting section of the book provides students with guidance about how to communicate their research findings to different audiences in a clear and systematic manner that has relevance to practitioners and to academics. This section also advises them that they need to reflect on what they have learned from the process – this is often where the better students excel as they undertake a critical analysis of their performance, indicating ways in which they would have improved their current project as well as suggesting ways in which it could be done differently next time. Learning and self-reflection is something that everyone should be practising throughout their entire careers.

The key focus in my role as Chief Moderator, Standards, is to ensure that management reports, from whatever route into entry to the profession, are all at postgraduate level. At present, the sort of guidance students receive from their tutors is bound to vary, and the lack of a dedicated textbook makes it hard for students to ensure that they are going in the right direction. Although there is a single chapter in *People Management and Development: HRM at Work* on research and change management skills, this can do no more than scratch the surface of what is a massive area. Thankfully for students, Valerie Anderson's book is set at precisely the right level to encourage them to engage in research with a systematic and critical approach, using both theory and practice to develop our understanding of human resource management.

Professor Mick Marchington

Professor of Human Resource Management, UMIST
and Chief Moderator, Standards, CIPD
October 2003

Introduction

The nature of research in HR, and how to use this book

CHAPTER 1

Chapter outline
How to use this book
What is research in HR?
The research process
The nature of research
Requirements for student projects
The links between change and research in organisations
Summary
Further reading

LEARNING OUTCOMES

This chapter should help you to:

- **define what is meant by research in HR and recognise the different ways in which research contributes to effective HR practice in organisations**

- **identify the different components of an effective research project and compare different approaches to HR research**

- **assess the distinctive features of organisational research and comprehend the implications of being a 'practitioner-researcher'**

- **plan the best way to use this book to help you complete your project successfully.**

HOW TO USE THIS BOOK

This book has been written primarily to meet the needs of those who are undertaking an HR research project as part of a qualification-related course. Many will be part-time students who are working on a project as a 'practitioner-researcher'. Others will be full-time students for whom there are particular challenges in doing organisational research into an HR issue, but for whom the issues of working as a practitioner-researcher are still relevant. Some readers may be undertaking some form of assessment of professional competence in order to gain a qualification. In focusing on the issues of being a practitioner-researcher, this book is also relevant for those who plan to undertake an investigative enquiry for their employer or for a client that is not linked to a qualification.

The ability to undertake investigative enquiries that lead to valuable and worthwhile practical outcomes is an important part of the toolkit of effective HR practitioners at all levels and in all types of organisation. This book seeks to present the research process in an accessible and practical way. It is not a substitute for regular communication with the reader's supervisor, tutor or adviser. It is best regarded as a resource to help the reader develop the knowledge, understanding and practical skills that will help him or her to undertake worthwhile and valuable investigations and to communicate what he or she has learned in an appropriate way.

USING THE BOOK

Most people who make use of this book are likely to be first-time researchers. Investigative enquiries are rarely completed in a short space of time and they often compete for attention with many other important and urgent matters. The chapters in this book each aim to provide an introduction to the different stages on the journey from initial project idea to submission of the final project report in the most time-effective way. Different chapters of the book are relevant at different stages of the project process.

Research really can be a win/win activity. Organisation(s) in which your investigations take place can benefit from what you find out. In addition, you will find that you gain valuable personal development in a wide range of areas. The ability to reflect on different learning needs as they arise throughout the research process can be a key factor in achieving a successful outcome. Each chapter ends with questions for review and reflection that can help you to identify areas where you would benefit from further development and appropriate ways of meeting those needs. Your responses to these questions can also form part of a Continuous Professional Development log or portfolio. Some ideas about additional reading are also included at the end of each chapter to enable you to go further or deeper as you think necessary.

Case illustration

EOC urges local authorities to confront lack of senior women

The Equal Opportunities Commission (EOC) has criticised local authorities for the continuing under-representation of women in senior management positions. Julie Mellor, chair of the EOC, has written to the Society of Chief Personnel Officers in Local Government (Socpo) calling for 'urgent action' over the low number of women in senior roles. Mellor's letter notes that only 28 per cent of elected councillors, 12 per cent of council leaders and 10 per cent of local authority chief executives are women. It continues: 'The evidence that women are not adequately represented in local authorities should in our view lead to urgent action by those involved in leading local government . . .'

People Management 13 June 2002. Reproduced with permission of *People Management*.

DISCUSSION QUESTIONS

Imagine that you work in the HR department of a local authority. You are studying part-time for an HR qualification and have to undertake an investigative project in addition to a number of taught modules. You are already struggling to keep up with all the assessments. Your work is demanding, and although your employer sponsors your studies you are still expected to fulfil all the requirements of your full-time role.

You have to decide what to do for your project. The chief executive of the local authority for whom you work is keen to show that the 'urgent action' referred to in the news article above is being undertaken in your authority. Your manager thinks this would be a good project for you to undertake.

1 Identify three benefits of tackling a project like this from your own perspective and three benefits from the perspective of your employer.

2 What problems might you foresee if you were to undertake this project?

Feedback notes

There are a number of benefits that may have occurred to you. Undertaking this sort of high-profile project might be good for your career prospects. Equal opportunities might be an area you are personally interested in. There should be a good level of support for you from women who aspire to senior positions. You know the organisation and can have access to a considerable amount of information. Most of the work could be undertaken in work time rather than at home at weekends.

The organisation also stands to benefit from such a project. Public and political interest in equal opportunities issues is high. 'Women's issues' are towards the top of management's HR agenda. There may be a perception that the potential contribution of female managers is not fully recognised throughout the authority. This may also be an opportunity for the HR department to enhance the credibility of its 'strategic contribution'.

In spite of some benefits there are also some problems that would probably occur to you in this sort of situation. Practical issues such as your own time constraints may be of concern as well as the extent to which this would be a project that is interesting to you personally. Other questions you might pose may include:

■ Over what timescale would the employer expect you to work on this project?

■ Is it possible to satisfy both your employer and the requirements for your qualification?

■ In that you are (probably) not a senior manager, how would you go about identifying 'urgent action' for senior people in the organisation?

■ Is the organisation genuinely interested in this project?

Perhaps these concerns might be summed up with three more questions:

■ What exactly would this project involve?

■ Is it feasible as a topic for a student project?

■ How would it add value to HR practice in the organisation?

The purpose of this chapter is to explore these general questions from the perspective of both full-time and part-time students of HR so that the reader is in a better position to understand the contribution of research to real organisational situations and to consider the role of the 'practitioner-researcher'. This should help the reader to work out how to use this book to plan and execute his or her own research project.

WHAT IS RESEARCH IN HR?

There are many different ideas about what 'research' actually is (see, for example, Easterby-Smith et al, 2002; Walliman, 2001). A useful and simple definition to start with is:

> **finding out things in a systematic way in order to increase knowledge.**

Such a definition takes account of scientific enquiries that occur in laboratory situations and relate to the physical world as well as enquiries into the nature of human interactions and processes, the context of which is the 'real world'.

One way of expressing what management research is, therefore, might be

> **finding out things in a systematic way in order to increase knowledge about people and processes involved in the management of work organisations.**

This is both a broad and a narrow definition. It reflects how HR practices occur in the 'real world' and the way in which the provision of accurate information can contribute to effective decision-making in organisations. It does not, however, differentiate HR research from other areas of research in business and management.

There are many different ways of understanding and explaining the nature and purposes of HRM/D (see, for example, Fombrun et al, 1984; Beer et al, 1985; Legge, 1995; Storey, 2001). It is possible to state some of its components as:

- seeing the people of the organisation as a 'strategic resource' for achieving competitive advantage
- ensuring that HR activities and policies are linked with organisational strategy
- designing and implementing personnel systems based on a coherent approach to managing the employment relationship
- planning to ensure that the organisation has the people and skills it needs to achieve its objectives.

In order to undertake effective HR in the organisation it is important that information of good quality underpins decisions and approaches to solving problems, but it would be unfortunate if investigative enquiries relevant to HR were wholly confined to the management arena. Indeed, research in HR can be undertaken to enhance the actions and decisions of others involved in the employment relationship, such as trade unions, individual employees and professional organisations (Hodgkinson et al, 2001; Whitley, 1984).

A more appropriate definition of research in HR, therefore, might be:

> **the systematic enquiry into HR issues to increase knowledge and underpin effective action.**

HR research – pure or applied?

Many writers about research distinguish between 'pure' and 'applied' research (see, for example, Gibbons *et al*, 1994; Starkey and Madan, 2001; Hedrick *et al*, 1993). The distinction, however, is not always clear-cut and corresponds better to a continuum that relates to the purpose and context in which the enquiry process occurs. The main focus of pure research, for example, tends to be on gaining knowledge, finding causes, examining the relationships between variables, and developing and testing generalisable theories. Applied research, by contrast, is more concerned with solving problems, predicting effects, and developing actions and interventions in discrete organisational contexts.

Most HR research – particularly that which is done as part of a qualification-based programme and which involves an enquiry process that is undertaken within one organisation – falls towards the applied research end of the continuum. Such research may not always be accorded high academic prestige but it requires a significant level of skill to undertake in an effective way. Indeed, applied research may require greater skills across a broader range of areas than pure research demands.

This book works from the position that in HR, certainly, applied research is at least as valuable as pure research. HR research that is carried out in a rigorous way can lead to more effective practice than decisions based mainly on intuition, common sense, or personal preferences. Common sense tends to take many features of organisational situations for granted. A systematic process of research, however, makes it possible to challenge taken-for-granted assumptions and so generate new ways of understanding situations that can form the basis for different approaches to solving complex problems. A key capability for effective HR practitioners, therefore, is the analysis of HR situations and the use of investigative techniques to underpin decision-making and problem-solving.

The basis of this book is that HR research is about 'advancing knowledge', but also it addresses organisational issues and provides a process for solving HR problems and contributing to the development of the organisation.

At the same time, the prospect of undertaking research is not something that many HR practitioners are particularly keen on. They think that research is too academic and remote from the real world. Research is perceived as the realm of complex theory that gets in the way of intuitive, commonsense approaches to managing human resources. It is to be

Applied research	*Pure research*
problem-solving	gaining new knowledge
predicting effects	establishing causes
concern for action	assessing relationships between variables
time/cost constraints	'as long as it needs'
client orientation	academic orientation

Figure 1 *The spectrum of pure and applied research*
Sources: Robson, 2002; Easterby-Smith *et al*, 2002; Saunders *et al*, 2003

regarded as something that is essentially broad-ranging whereas most practitioners are concerned with the pragmatic and practical level of solving organisational problems. Researchers, it is argued, can never be familiar with the unique culture of different organisations and the nature of problems faced by HR practitioners (Kearns, 2002).

Common objections to doing research
Research is:

- just a way of proving what you already know
- best left to academics or to experts
- just a way of justifying what the CEO wants to do anyway
- too difficult
- too time-consuming
- removed from reality
- unable to change anything
- too scientific and statistical
- boring.

(Blaxter *et al*, 2001; Jankowicz, 2000)

Such objections, however, stem in part from a misunderstanding of the research process and its potential role and contribution to the effective practice of HR in organisations.

WEB-BASED ACTIVITY

Visit the website of an HR periodical such as *People Management* (peoplemanagement.co.uk) or *Personnel Today* (personneltoday.com). Run a search using the word 'research'. If you can, limit the dates of the search to the most recent one or two calendar months.

Feedback notes
An activity such as this demonstrates how much of HR practice and opinion is informed, in some way or other, by what is claimed as 'research'. Research is used to justify why certain HR practices are beneficial and is also used to evaluate the success (or otherwise) of HR initiatives and activities. A study of the list of articles that the search word 'research' generates suggests its contribution to HR at strategic, policy and operational levels. It also indicates a variety of topics for research, a range of different types of research, and a wealth of opinions about how research should be undertaken and for what purpose.

THE RESEARCH PROCESS

ACTIVITY – A DIFFICULT PROBLEM

Imagine that you are mid-way through a course of study for a Chartered Institute of Personnel and Development (CIPD) qualification. For a variety of reasons it is necessary for you to leave the centre you are currently registered with and transfer your studies to a centre in a different part of the country. Consider and write down how you might find out what centres in your new area offer CIPD courses and which would be the most appropriate one for you.

Feedback notes

In order to find an appropriate centre there are a number of questions that you must find the answers to. These include:

- Which centres offer CIPD programmes in the new part of the country?
- What modes of study are offered? How much time is spent in a 'classroom'?
- How good are the courses?
- What facilities does each centre have to offer?
- How well do the modules offered fit with what you have already undertaken?
- What are the cost implications?
- What mode of study would be most appropriate for you in your new situation (distance learning, day-release, block release, full-time)?

To answer these questions there are a range of sources of information that you might draw on. These include:

- CIPD website/information services
- college, university brochures/publicity materials
- the opinions of other people in the new area who have studied for the same (or even different) qualifications
- the recommendations of your current tutors
- discussion/information provided by tutors in centres that you may be interested in.

Clearly, the more sources of information you can draw on, and the greater the variety of types of information you can gather (opinions as well as sales brochures, statistics as well as recommendations), the more confident you are likely to feel in your ultimate decision. Merely enrolling at a centre because it is cheap and it was the first one you stumbled across is less likely to result in a good decision. To enhance the fact-finding process you must first be clear what it is you are really looking for (part-time, full-time, which area of the country, etc). Then it is necessary to find out what you can about the transfer process (what the transfer points are, what the CIPD regulations are, etc). Next, you search for further information, obtaining as many different types of data as possible. Finally, you make sense of all the information – and make your decision.

The activity above is, at basic level, a small and personal research activity. It involves the systematic enquiry into an issue to increase knowledge and underpin effective decision-making. The activities it would involve are, however, indicative of the components of any systematic enquiry or research process (see Figure 2).

Often research is represented as a series of discrete and linear stages, and indeed this book is structured in a similar sort of way. However, the reality of organisational research is that each stage is often interrelated with the others, and experiences in later stages frequently lead to reconsideration of earlier ones (Saunders *et al*, 2003).

Each of these stages is considered in more detail in subsequent chapters of the book, but a brief introduction to some of the elements of the process is provided now.

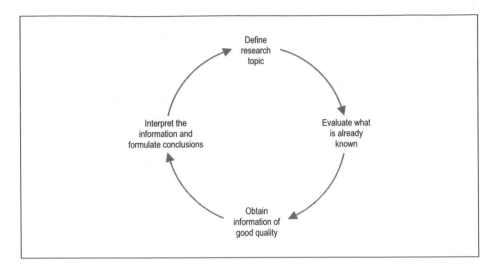

Figure 2 *Components of the research process*

Theory and practice in organisational research
Case illustration

Researching into survivor syndrome

Lyn is a student in a hurry. She fulfils a demanding role in a dynamic organisation that provides IT services. In the four years in which she has been employed with her firm she has seen it grow rapidly during the dot.com boom to 2,000 employees based in a number of different countries. More recently there has been a significant downturn in business. Although the firm has survived, it has shed large numbers of staff and currently employs 800 people in only a few countries. Lyn has been responsible for the HR features of the organisational downsizing process, which has occurred in two major phases. In her role as HR manager in the organisation she is concerned about the effect of the downsizing process on those employees who remain in employment. She has decided to undertake research into 'survivor syndrome' for her project. As a result of this project she hopes she will be better able to help the organisation to move forward and develop and maintain a level of business performance that will not require further staff cuts.

Lyn is under a lot of pressure at work. She does not have much time to devote to her project. The focus of her project is on producing practical recommendations for her organisation. She wants to know why she should have to spend time considering 'theories' as part of her enquiry.

DISCUSSION QUESTIONS

1   Identify and discuss the reasons why Lyn is resistant to using theories in her enquiry.
2   In what ways might 'the literature' add value to Lyn's project?

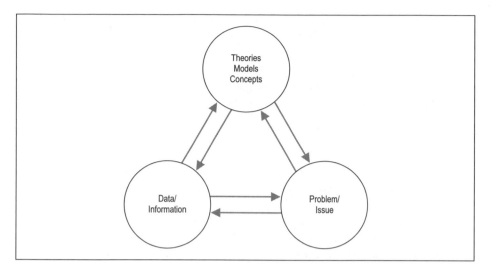

Figure 3 *Theory and practice in research*

Feedback notes

Reading up on her topic will expose Lyn to a range of theories and models. Theories and models seek to explain things, to make things intelligible, to suggest why things are the way they are, or to describe why they happen in the way that they do. Concepts are the building-blocks of theories and models. Concepts are abstract: they do not exist in reality. 'Labour market' and 'business strategy' are examples of common concepts referred to in HR. You cannot actually touch concepts, but we need them to provide a structure to the way we think about particular subjects or issues.

Many HR practitioners are suspicious of theories, models and concepts, seeing them as remote from the real world, difficult to understand and problematic to apply easily in practice. Time spent in understanding abstract explanations, it is argued, is a distraction from the 'real business' of getting information about particular situations and resolving specific problems.

Nonetheless there are two main reasons why reading around the topic will add value to Lyn's project. First, Lyn wants to investigate survivor syndrome. What does this mean? What does it involve? Engaging with theories of motivation, stress, the effects of redundancy, and so on, will help her to formulate and clarify her research topic. Second, once Lyn has collected information about the 'survivors' in her organisation she will need to interpret or analyse her data in order to formulate meaningful and valuable conclusions. Here again, concepts, theories and models may provide a framework through which she can understand and explain her findings and so enable her organisation to fully benefit from her enquiry.

Obtaining information

Clearly, useful research involves more than theoretical evaluation, and in addition to the contribution of theories, models and concepts, it is also important to obtain and analyse as much information as possible. Many different sources of information contribute to research processes. There are two main types of information, depending on the purpose for which the data has been generated: primary and secondary data.

- *Primary data* is information that is collected by the researcher, usually for the purposes of a particular research project. Primary data might include information from

11

interviews conducted as part of an enquiry. Similarly, the responses to a questionnaire which forms part of your study would be primary data.

■ *Secondary data* is that which has been generated elsewhere for other purposes. It may be published data (government statistics, trade body survey data, labour market data, etc) or it may be data that has been generated within the organisation (payroll data, HR data sets, minutes of meetings, budget records, etc).

Case illustration

An investigation into the effectiveness of the reward system for secretarial staff in a financial services organisation

Kate was an HR student whose project was designed to investigate and analyse the effectiveness of the reward system for secretarial staff within the investment banking part of a large financial services organisation. Much of the literature about pay and benefits advocates performance-related pay structures, although Kate had also read studies that detailed the difficulties with such ideas in practice. Kate wanted to find out if the current reward system in her organisation was achieving the company's stated objective, which was to link pay for all staff with their individual contributions and with business results as a whole. Three components underpinned the current system of pay for secretaries in this organisation: base pay, performance-related pay, and bonus payments. Overtime payments were also payable for secretaries.

DISCUSSION QUESTIONS

1   What sources of data will enable Kate to investigate the effectiveness of the reward system for secretaries?

2   Having obtained her information, what will Kate need to do to analyse the effectiveness of the current system?

Feedback notes

For a study of this type there is likely to be a wealth of information (secondary data) already existent within the organisation. In this case Kate was able to obtain numerical data relating to base salaries, overtime payments and performance-related pay from the payroll department and from the HR information system used in the organisation.

Kate also wanted to assess the extent of any relationship between performance appraisal processes and pay, so she studied the paper-based appraisal records to estimate the likelihood that appraisals took place for secretarial staff.

In addition Kate needed to assess the extent to which pay was related to business performance as a whole. She obtained data from the payroll department about the bonus pool for secretaries in two contrasting (but recent) years. One of the years she chose reflected the most profitable year to date, and the other – as a result of problems in financial markets overseas – was a more difficult year for business results.

Kate was keen to try to compare the practices of her own organisation with those of others in similar sectors, and so she also utilised labour market surveys and other market data relating to the financial services sector.

Secondary data was not sufficient to enable Kate to analyse the effectiveness of the current system, and she also gathered primary data through a questionnaire that she sent to all the secretaries in her part of the organisation and through semi-structured interviews with line managers and HR managers.

This case illustrates the wide range of data that is available within organisations and which can contribute to an investigation. Yet different types of data require different skills of analysis and different approaches to analysis. Numerical data about pay and bonuses, for example, can be analysed through a process of calculation and quantification. To some extent, questionnaire data can be analysed in a similar way. Interview data where the respondents have been allowed scope to express their thoughts, feelings and experiences in a less structured way is, on the other hand, less amenable to such processes but is still valuable as a way of 'getting beneath' the generalised findings of numerical analysis. However, it may not be possible to draw generalised conclusions based on data that reflects the more subjective features of the experience and opinions of people in organisations.

THE NATURE OF RESEARCH

Positivist and interpretivist understandings of research

Discussion about different types of data is also linked with an important distinction in thinking about the nature of research and how it should be conducted. Although the distinction may be overstated (see, for example, the discussions in Gill and Johnson, 2001; Robson, 2002), it is an important element in thinking about the most appropriate way to conduct an enquiry.

Positivist research

Positivist researchers emphasise the importance of an objective 'scientific' method (Remenyi et al, 1998). They see their role as collecting facts and then studying the relationship of one set of facts to another. They analyse quantitative data (data that can be counted) using statistically valid techniques and so produce quantifiable and, if possible, generalisable conclusions. This approach stresses the importance of studying social and organisational realities in a 'scientific' way that mirrors, where possible, the research processes used in the natural sciences.

Interpretivist research

Interpretivist researchers, by contrast, are more concerned to access and understand individuals' perceptions of the world. This is because they see social phenomena ('facts') as the product of human interactions that, because they are the product of shared understandings and meanings, are not always predictable or even formally rational (Remenyi et al, 1998). The less quantifiable and the subjective interpretations, reasoning and feelings of people (qualitative data) are seen as a more relevant line of enquiry in order to understand and explain the realities of HR situations. The focus of interpretivist research, therefore, is not so much on facts and numbers but on words, observations and meanings (Cresswell, 1994).

Although there are groups of researchers who find the positivist approach to be unrealistic, others are concerned about the subjective nature of the interpretivist approach. The argument in this book is that the investigation of organisational issues can be carried out from either a positivist or an interpretivist perspective.

The diversity and richness of HR research

The process of managing people in employing organisations is complex and dynamic. A range of different factors, both external and internal to the organisation, influences the way that people act and behave. As a result, features of HR research (positivist and interpretivist) may be informed by, and contribute to, disciplines such as economics, sociology, psychology, law and politics, as well as the more general discipline of 'business and management'.

HR research contributes to knowledge in a diversity of ways, at many different levels, and from a range of perspectives, and these are briefly outlined now.

Descriptive research

This type of research sets out to provide an accurate profile of situations, people or events. It focuses on 'what?', 'when?', 'where?' and 'who?' Publications from Incomes Data Services and the Work Foundation (*Managing Best Practice*) are examples of descriptive, practitioner-oriented research.

Although some descriptive research is worthwhile in its own right, in most cases researchers will want to go further and ask, 'So what?' They will want to analyse the data and draw relevant conclusions. Both qualitative and quantitative data are useful in descriptive studies.

Explanatory research

Here the purpose is to explain a situation or problem, usually in the form of causal relationships. The focus is on 'why?' and 'how?'. Many consultancy reports, for example, seek to explain organisational problems and, through assessment of the causes, to recommend changes for improvement. Cost-benefit studies of training interventions are also examples of research that seeks to explain the relationship between different variables in an organisation. Again, both qualitative and quantitative data may be useful.

Exploratory research

The purpose of exploratory research is to seek new insights and find out what is happening. There is an attempt to ask questions and assess phenomena in a new light. A more qualitative approach often underpins this sort of enquiry and the focus is on obtaining new insights into current situations and issues.

Case illustration

Better training needed for older jobseekers

Older jobseekers who are long-term unemployed may not be getting all the training opportunities they deserve, accorded to recently published DfEE research. To help this group find and retain work, the study calls for changes to the funding of work-based learning for adults (WBLA) programmes. It also recommends:

- more attention to age in monitoring equal opportunities policies for clients
- improvements to the services offered by guidance organisations and jobcentres, and
- greater use of programme centres and work trials.

The findings support the need for the government to continue to discourage age discrimination in employment.

The study looked at the effectiveness of WBLA, programme centres and work trials for jobless people aged over 50 who had been long-term unemployed – ie out of work for more than six months. It examined their participation and achievements, the impact of the programmes' current funding arrangement, and equal opportunities.

Cause for concern

Long-term unemployment is more prevalent among people aged over 50 than other groups. The figure below indicates the length of time that unemployed people tend to remain jobless. It shows that 34% of claimants aged over 50 had been unemployed for over a year. This can be compared to 27% of those aged 25 to 49.

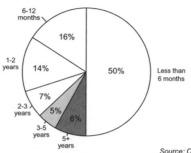

Duration of Unemployment for Claimants aged 50+

Source: Claimant unemployment data for Great Britain, February 2000

Yet this group is not especially homogenous. The study revealed wide variations in their job histories, skills, qualifications and attitudes to work.

Work-based learning

Despite being over-represented in long-term unemployment, the group is under-represented among the long-term jobless on WBLA programmes. In November 1999, the share of those aged 50+ was 17%, compared with 25% of all long-term unemployed claimants aged over 25.

Older trainees are less likely than their younger counterparts to find work after leaving WBLA. Differences between the two groups in terms of their ability and previous length of employment may be a factor, along with ageism by some employers.

But other factors could apply. In some areas, the range of occupations available on WBLA programmes is rather limited and may not meet the needs of older jobseekers. There is a lack of employer placements on the programme generally. And funding arrangements may be a constraint.

Programme centres

Programme centres are popular among older jobseekers for the helpful approach of staff, the availability of training and job search resources, and the opportunity for social contact with peers. Those who use the programme centres find work at the same rate (38%) as younger participants aged 25–49. But the share of older people using the centres is low.

Work trials

Older people are also under-represented on work trials. Yet they are just as successful in finding work as younger participants aged 25–49. Several factors affect take-up levels in work trials: their perceived unpopularity among jobseekers, a hesitancy by some jobseekers in suggesting a work trial during employer interviews, and the infrequent promotion of work trial to clients or employers by Jobcentre staff.

DfEE, Skills and Enterprise Executive, May 2001.
Crown copyright material is reproduced with the permission of the Controller of HMSO and the Queen's Printer for Scotland.

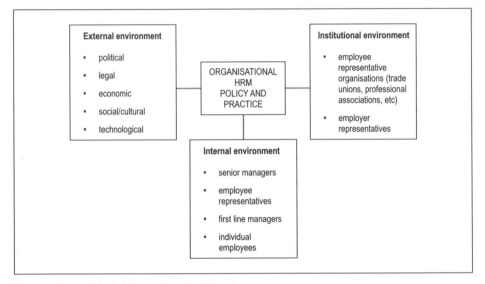

Figure 4 *Factors that affect the employment relationship*

Feedback notes

This case illustration shows how the different types of research are not mutually exclusive and how, as noted already, it is quite possible that a particular study may be concerned with more than one purpose. The purpose of the research underpinning this article is mostly descriptive, but in order to make recommendations an attempt has been made to explain the experiences of older jobseekers. Quantitative, numerical data has been used here to describe features of the current situation. Some qualitative data (about preferences and so on) has also been utilised in the analysis and has informed the conclusions. The article makes very little reference to theories, models or concepts.

The audiences for HR research

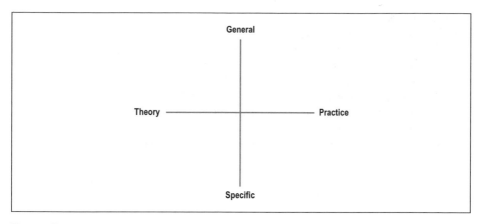

Figure 5 *The orientation of different research outputs*

Feedback notes

Your list of likely audiences for HR research might include individual practitioners, individual managers, members of trade unions, central government, local government, specialist organisations/pressure groups (eg EOC, HSE), professional associations, academics, employer/trade bodies, leaders of trade unions, and students.

When finding out about research, there is an equally wide range of publications and opportunities that different groups might use. These include:

- newspapers
- specific reports (internal or external)
- books
- trade journals
- professional journals
- academic journals
- unpublished research (dissertations, projects, etc)
- conferences/seminars.

Each of these different vehicles for communicating knowledge does so in a different way in order to meet the needs of its audience. As a result they engage to different extents with both theory and practice and with the general and the specific.

ACTIVITY – ASSESSING DIFFERENT RESEARCH PUBLICATIONS

Study one copy of the following types of HR publication:

- academic refereed journal (eg *Human Resource Management Journal* or *Personnel Review*)
- professional journal (eg *People Management* or *Personnel Today*)
- practitioner report (eg *IDS Report* or *Managing Best Practice*).

Skim-read the publications and try to plot each of the features of the research articles/reports on the two axes shown in Figure 5.

Feedback notes

It is likely that different articles from each of the first two types of publications may need to be plotted differently. Some studies, even within one publication, are very concerned with one specific situation and others are more general. What is easier to characterise is the different levels of engagement with theories and models. Those in a refereed academic journal, such as *HRMJ*, will be significantly concerned with evaluating theories as well as with practically focused investigations. Practitioner reports, by contrast, are more concerned with describing practice than with explicitly locating it within any conceptual framework. Feature articles in practitioner journals vary somewhat here, although the extent of 'theory' is never great. This is a factor of the 'audience' or readership of these publications.

REQUIREMENTS FOR STUDENT PROJECTS

The use of literature, theories and frameworks

As can be seen already in this chapter, a large volume of published HR research does not engage explicitly with theories, models and frameworks. This may be because its readers are often not themselves interested in such features. In reality, however, this sort of research is based on a theory, model or framework, but the theoretical or conceptual basis of the enquiries are implicit. Articles about performance-related pay (PRP), for example, are often based on the assumption that there is a link between motivation and PRP. Articles about employee involvement are often grounded upon a model that adopts an individualistic approach to managing people rather than a pluralist or collectivist approach (Gennard and Judge, 2002).

Research found in academic journals, by contrast, seeks to make the theoretical assumptions explicit so that the theory can be evaluated and judged along with the information that has been generated.

Projects carried out as a part of qualification-bearing programmes of study are, of course, written primarily for an academic audience. An engagement with theory is part of the expectations of such work. You will be required to demonstrate a critical awareness of the current state of knowledge in the area you have chosen to investigate so that you can consider how your project fits into the wider context. The extent to which this is required will vary depending on the nature of the qualification (undergraduate, postgraduate, diploma or master's, etc) as well as on the assessment criteria used by different centres of study. It is worth finding out, at an early stage in the project process, the expectations of your institution as regards the balance between theory and practice.

Primary and secondary data

All projects undertaken as part of a course of study are likely to include the appropriate use of secondary data. Most investigative enquiries in HR will also contain primary data. In many cases this will be generated in one organisation (sometimes in more than one). In a few cases it will involve accessing secondary data and carrying out an analysis of it, the product of which would then be primary data.

Pure or applied?

Although 'pure' research is not ruled out of a qualification-bearing programme of study in HR, it is much more likely that your project will be focused on an enquiry into a specific HR problem, opportunity or issue. It is to the specific requirements of applied, organisational, research that this chapter now turns.

THE LINKS BETWEEN CHANGE AND RESEARCH IN ORGANISATIONS

As an integral part of employing organisations, HR is inevitably involved with organisational change. Much change is gradual, incremental and adaptive, although increasingly organisations need to achieve a more fundamental, radical and transformational type of change. Whether incremental or transformational, organisational change processes have significant implications for HR. The ability to contribute to and manage change is seen as a key issue for effective HR.

Case illustration

Changing routes – Levi Strauss

It is easy to convince people of the need for change when things are going wrong, but when Levi Strauss embarked on a major re-engineering of its European operations in 1994 there was no immediate crisis. With the business dominating the market, many within the organisation saw little need for change.

Before the re-engineering could begin, therefore, we had to persuade people that while Levi Strauss was a healthy company, there were areas that required improvement. Customer service, for example, was not performing as well as marketing or manufacturing.

The re-engineering programme went well beyond the methods used to satisfy customer demand. The aim was to change all our business processes, from sales and retail relations to marketing and development, and from manufacturing and sourcing to forecasting and logistics.

Some companies might have attempted to do all this without involving their employees. But for us this was not an option. Levi Strauss is a privately-owned company with a value-driven culture and a long history of employee involvement. Our mission and aspiration statements talk about a commitment to responsible commercial success and respect for employees, as well as customers and suppliers.

Because the company has these very strong people-centred values, those of us who work in human resources played a key role in supporting the re-engineering process. We were the custodians of the change, overseeing the people aspects of the process and providing a measure of consistency across an organisation that operates in 30 European countries.

In performing this role, we found the company's culture both an advantage and a disadvantage. Our preferred way of making decisions through consensus undoubtedly slowed the process down. Yet the advantage of having an empowered way of working was that many of our employees were able to come to accept the inevitability of the changes, even when they did not much like the nature of some of the changes affecting them.

The changes themselves were driven by a steering committee made up of senior people from all parts of the business in Europe. Their role was to direct and

---

challenge the thinking of the teams that were designing, and later implementing, the re-engineering process.

To support this process, a wide-ranging communication and education programme was developed, targeting a number of different audiences: the steering committee, managers and employees. Led by the HR team, the education aspect of the programme included workshops to help managers prepare for change, and lead themselves and others through times of uncertainty. For employees there were workshops on managing themselves through change.

We also tried to keep people informed of what was happening at the organisational, local and individual levels, although I have to admit that we often had no answer to the question: 'What does all this mean for me?'

Towards the end of the design phase, it became clear that business process re-engineering would have a significant impact on many individuals, and the communication programme was stepped up. So too was the involvement of the HR function, since the staffing issues we were now facing were massive.

Many roles connected with re-engineering business processes changed significantly. For example, in Northampton the company turned what had been a traditional warehousing environment into a high-tech distribution centre. The new facility needed only half the number of people employed in the old warehouse, while those who remained had to adapt to a completely new way of working.

Where roles had changed significantly as a result of re-engineering, we felt the fairest way to fill what were in effect new jobs was to ask people to apply for them, and we provided some very specific training to help them to do this. Some employees chose not to take up these opportunities, preferring instead to accept the fairly generous redundancy terms we were offering.

I believe those who decided to stay are pleased they made that decision. But neither they nor anyone else in the organisation can expect things to remain as they are. Growing competition in the clothing industry and an over-capacity in European manufacturing have led to some factory closures.

Levi Strauss has now moved into a new period of change even more profound than the still ongoing business process re-engineering. We are developing a new management structure aligned to our various brands and are adopting yet more new ways of working. But that's another story.

G. Rutherford, 'Changing routes', *People Management*, 8 April 1999.
Reproduced by permission of the author.

DISCUSSION QUESTIONS

1   What phases formed part of the change process that has been described here?

2   What contributions did the HR function make to the change process at Levi Strauss?

3   What sort of information would the steering committee need to underpin the decisions it took with regard to managing the change process?

4   To what extent is it possible to evaluate the effects of the business process re-engineering process?

Feedback notes

You probably noted that the change process described in this case illustration involved a 'design' stage followed by one of implementation. The HR function was able to contribute in different ways to both processes. In the design stage the contribution was through training, educating and involving employees in thinking about and preparing for change. In the implementation stage it involved managing a change in headcount, implementing changes to organisational structures and systems and more training to cope with the processes of change.

It is clear that decisions about major change processes cannot be made in a vacuum and information is required. Here information about organisational features (culture, policies, etc) is required as well as data about headcount and skill-sets. Before moving from design to implementation it is also important to find out how successful the involvement and education processes have been.

The difficulty with evaluating the overall change process is one of separation. Before the conclusion of one major change, further changes are being undertaken to cope with developments in the external competitive environment. In this way it seems that the effects of a change process will, of necessity, impact on the design and implementation of newer processes.

Action-focused organisational research

The Levi Strauss case illustration demonstrates how, in reality, change is a continuous process rather than a discrete event. The effects of one change often lead to the identification of areas for further improvement. In addition, the dynamic nature of the organisation's environment stimulates the need for further change before the initially conceived actions have been completed.

Most HR research undertaken within an organisation occurs in the context of change processes stimulated by external and/or internal factors. It involves investigating HR problems or issues and making recommendations for change and improvement. In turn, any changes that are undertaken will themselves be evaluated, and further changes and recommendations are likely to result.

Action research

The particular issues identified here are, of course, not confined to research in employing organisations and apply equally in other action-oriented disciplines such as education and welfare (health, social services, etc), where the contribution of a researcher is perceived to

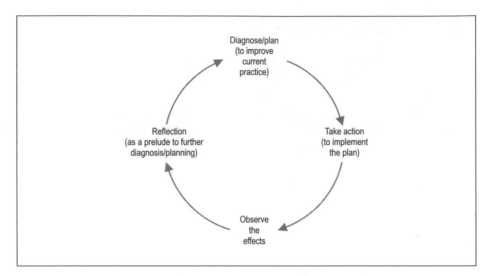

Figure 6 *A model for organisational research*

involve understanding and promoting change. Key features of such research are diagnosis of problems or issues, considering how to solve them, taking action, and then evaluating the effectiveness of the action.

The term 'action research' was first used by Kurt Lewin (1946), a researcher and writer in change management. He suggested that effective organisational research should involve a continuous and interrelated process of planning, acting, observing, and reflection.

Within this approach, planning involves fact-finding leading to a diagnosis and a plan to solve or improve a particular problem or issue. The plan is then implemented, and it is important to observe (investigate and gather data about) the effects of the action in order to evaluate it. The conclusions, or reflections from this process, then inform further planning as part of a continuous improvement process.

The action research model also highlights the inter-relationship of the different stages. Thus the action stage has implications and is interrelated with the process of data collection involved in observing the effects, and also influences, on a continuous basis, the diagnosis of issues and problems. In addition to being a continuous cycle, therefore, action research involves smaller cycles of planning, acting, observing, and reflection during each of the stages. Planning is thus not a static activity, and the outcome of it (diagnosis and an action plan) is itself the result of observation and reflection.

Since the 1940s many researchers have developed and modified the concept of action research (see, for example, Kemmis and McTaggart, 1981; Rapoport, 1970; Carr and Kemmis, 1986), but the basis on which it was first developed remains central in that:

■ researchers are (and should be) involved in the situations they are researching
■ researchers are (and should be) part of a cycle of improvement.

The model of action research embodied by planning, action, observation, and reflection is used throughout the rest of this book. The chapters in Part 2 relate to the planning stage of a

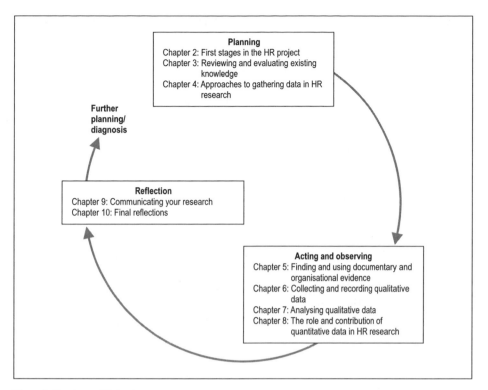

Figure 7 *How to use this book*

project. Part 3 is concerned with action and observation (in practice, the separation of these would be artificial within this book). And Part 4 is concerned with reflection (see Figure 7).

Each chapter also follows this structure. The early part of each chapter focuses on planning issues for each topic before a progression to activity and observation. Finally, each chapter concludes with a summary and/or a checklist as well as opportunities for reflection on practice.

It is likely that most investigative enquiries will be undertaken within a specific organisational context and will be focused on the solution of a particular HR problem or issue. In this sense an action orientation is more likely, and the implications of this for the practitioner-researcher are now explored.

Being a practitioner-researcher

A 'practitioner-researcher' can be defined as someone who is employed in a job and who at the same time carries out a research project which is of some relevance to his or her current role as a practitioner. In the context of this book this definition embraces three types of people:

■ part-time students undertaking research within their employing organisation – In this case the student may be a regular employee or, alternatively, may be someone who is undertaking some form of consultancy assignment in the organisation. Of course, a practitioner-researcher may also be someone who is undertaking an investigative enquiry within his or her organisation (or that of a client) for which there is no link with the attainment of a qualification

- full-time students who have a part-time job in an organisation in which they undertake their research project

- full-time students for whom a work placement forms part of their course, and who will be undertaking a research project within the placement organisation.

In all cases carrying out the research is normally, but not always, undertaken in addition to the normal duties and responsibilities.

There are advantages and disadvantages of being a practitioner-researcher. The difficulties that are often encountered relate to:

- time – When the project has to be undertaken in addition to normal workloads, it is difficult to give it the attention it deserves.

- preconceptions – When you are a part of the very organisation that you are researching, you may have formed many preconceptions about situations that someone from outside would not be influenced by.

- status issues – Often practitioner-researchers are not in senior positions within the organisation. This can make it difficult for their project to be taken seriously. Alternatively, they may have high status within the organisation. This can make it difficult for subjects of the research to express themselves freely.

- being critical – Although undertaking a research project involves adopting a critically evaluative approach to both theory and practice, in some organisations taking a critical approach is not encouraged.

- being instrumental – A further danger, from the perspective of the organisation, is that where projects are linked with gaining a qualification, research can become more of a vehicle to achieve the student's purposes than a motivation towards the resolution of a problem or issue.

There are also significant advantages to being a practitioner-researcher:

- 'insider' opportunities – If you know the organisation and are a part of it, you have access to a range of knowledge and experience that someone from outside would find difficult to achieve.

- practitioner opportunities – As an experienced practitioner within the organisation it is more likely that actions that you recommend can and will be implemented.

- synergy between theory and practice – As a researcher who engages with theory and also knows the context of the organisation, it is more likely that you will be able to design and carry out useful studies that contribute to enhancements in both knowledge and practice.

In summary, undertaking research projects in organisational situations provides a number of advantages, but there are also dangers. Key issues for students are avoiding the temptation to merely repeat established organisational mantras, and endeavouring to make sure that their project leads to new insights. Therefore practitioner-researchers must endeavour to:

- explicitly consider the wider context of the problem or issue that is being researched, both within the organisation and with regard to practice and developments outside the organisation

■ critically engage with theories, models and concepts at all stages of the research process

■ encourage, where possible, the dissemination of the findings of studies so that they can inform the development of practice and understanding in other organisations and contexts.

Further ideas about how this can be achieved include:

■ Where possible, negotiate a time-allowance to carry out the research.

■ Be prepared to 'sell' the idea of the research within the organisation.

■ Try to establish a difference of procedure between activities connected with your research and your normal day-to-day practitioner activities. Be clear to yourself and to others about when you are wearing the hat of a researcher and when you are acting as a practitioner.

■ Be explicit in your thinking about methods, sources of information and so on. This will allow you to reflect proactively about its strengths and limitations (and so improve on it). It will also enable others to make an appropriate assessment of your work.

■ Ensure that your research procedures are systematic and can be justified by more than convenience. If you cut corners (and you probably will), you must be explicit about the impact of the short cuts on what you have found out and how you have interpreted your information.

SUMMARY

■ HR research involves systematically enquiring into HR issues to increase knowledge and underpin effective action.

■ Most HR enquiry can be characterised as 'applied research', being concerned with solving problems, considering effects, and developing actions and interventions.

■ Effective research processes involve: formulating a research topic, evaluating what is already known, obtaining information of good quality, interpreting the information, and formulating conclusions.

■ Engaging with theories, models and concepts helps to formulate a research topic and provides a framework through which to interpret information.

■ Primary data is collected for the purposes of an investigative project. Secondary data, which has been generated elsewhere and for different purposes, also contributes to an understanding of situations and issues.

■ Positivist approaches to research emphasise the importance of replicating, where possible, a traditional 'scientific' approach to gathering facts and analysing them in order to generate generalisable conclusions.

■ Interpretivist approaches to research emphasise the subjective nature of human interactions and focus enquiry on the meanings and understandings of those involved in social and organisational processes.

■ HR research is sponsored and utilised by a range of different individuals and groups who are involved with the employment relationship. HR research outputs focus to different extents on generalised patterns or specific situations and engage to different extents with theories, models and concepts.

■ Projects undertaken to fulfil the requirements of an academic qualification are expected to make appropriate use of theories, models and concepts as well as primary and secondary data.

■ Action-focused organisational research involves the interrelated processes of diagnosis/planning, action, observation, and reflection.

■ There are advantages *and* disadvantages to being a practitioner-researcher but organisational research, properly undertaken, can lead to new insights into HR issues, problems and situations.

Review questions

Carefully study the information your centre provides about the requirements for your project. Look closely at the assessment criteria that are provided. Study the indicative structure that may be described. Make sure that you can answer all the questions below. If you cannot, then make sure that you find out the answers from whoever is responsible for projects in your study centre:

1 What is the submission deadline for the final report?

2 What is the indicative word limit for the report?

3 Over what timescale should the project be undertaken?

4 What level of engagement with theories, concepts, frameworks of best practice etc is expected?

5 How important is it to gather primary data?

6 Does the research have to be based in an organisation?

7 Are implementable recommendations a requirement for the project?

8 What support is available to students when undertaking their project, and how can that support be accessed?

Questions for reflection

These questions are designed for two purposes: project planning, and demonstrating reflective practice.

Project planning

Answering these questions should help you to identify actions and priorities that will be important in undertaking your project. The answers you make to these questions may influence:

■ which chapters of this book you need to study particularly closely

■ which sources of further reading will be relevant to you

■ the extent to which you should seek further advice on features of the research process.

Demonstrating reflective practice

Students undertaking CIPD courses have to submit a Continuing Professional Development record that shows they have identified (on a continuous basis) their development needs; that they have undertaken appropriate actions to meet them; that they have applied their learning in practice; and that they have evaluated the success of the learning process they have undertaken. Carrying out an investigative enquiry is clearly a learning process for the practitioner-researcher. Written answers to some or all of these questions can form a part of your CPD portfolio or log, which you must submit in order to upgrade your level of CIPD membership when you have completed the qualifications process.

Taking stock

1   What are your anxieties about, or your objections to, undertaking a research project? What do you think lies beneath these anxieties? How might you overcome some of your objections?

2   How feasible is it for you to undertake research in one organisation? For how long do you expect to be a part of the organisation in which your research may be based? What other options may be open to you for your investigative enquiry?

3   What are your employer's priorities in the medium term? How might they impact on your choice of a topic?

4   How clear are you about a topic for your project? Who do you need to discuss your ideas with to decide about the feasibility of the project? (Chapter 2 is particularly useful to answer these questions.)

5   What resources of expertise and advice are available to you from your project supervisor/tutor/adviser? How can you make best use of these resources?

Strengths and weaknesses

1   How confident are you about the process of undertaking a literature search to enable you to critically evaluate what is already known about your topic? What are the skills you will need to search and critically review theories, models and concepts within the literature? (Chapter 3 is particularly relevant to these issues.)

2   How aware are you of sources of secondary data that would be relevant to your project? What skills will you need to obtain and analyse the secondary data you have in mind? (Chapter 5 is particularly helpful on these issues.)

3   What options might you consider to obtain primary data? What are the skill implications of the data-generation options that you are considering?

4   What skills and competences have you already developed that you can utilise in the process of undertaking your project?

Being a practitioner-researcher

1　What are the status or political issues within your organisation that may affect the process of undertaking your project? How might you be able to manage these effectively?

2　What are the timescales for your project that are required by: a) your study-centre, and b) your organisation? What are the implications of this for the process of doing your project?

3　What opportunities can you identify to sell your project ideas to: a) your manager and colleagues, and b) others in the organisation?

4　Finally, describe how you will feel when you have completed your project. Hold on to that feeling!

FURTHER READING

It is very important to carefully read any handbooks or guidance notes relating to project work provided by your study centre. Most students skim through these at the beginning of their project process and only read them carefully at the very end of the process, when it is almost too late.

One of the best ways to learn about research methods is to read and critique good-quality refereed, research-based articles. You can tell if a journal is a 'refereed' one by glancing at its notes for contributors, which will indicate that potential contributions go through a 'blind refereeing' process.

General business and management and social sciences research methods books include:

BELL, J. (2001) *Doing Your Research Project*. Buckingham, Open University Press.

COLLIS, J. and HUSSEY, R. (2003) *Business Research: A practical guide for undergraduate and postgraduate students*. Basingstoke, Palgrave.

EASTERBY-SMITH, M., THORPE, R. and LOWE, A. (2002) *Management Research: An introduction*. London, Sage.

GILL, J. and JOHNSON, P. (2001) *Research Methods for Managers*. London, Paul Chapman.

JANKOWICZ, A. D. (2000) *Business Research Projects for Students*. London, Chapman & Hall.

ROBSON, C. (2002) *Real World Research: A resource for social scientists and practitioner-researchers*. Oxford, Blackwell.

SAUNDERS, M., LEWIS, P. and THORNHILL, A. (2003) *Research Methods for Business Students*. London, *Financial Times*/Pitman.

Planning

First stages in the HR project

Chapter outline
How to use this chapter
Deciding what to research
Establishing the focus of the project
Approaches to research
Research design issues
Access to data
Ethical implications for research activities
Final preparations – project planning
Summary
Further reading

LEARNING OUTCOMES

This chapter should help you to:

■ **generate possible topics for a research project**

■ **evaluate your research ideas and select an appropriate research topic**

■ **formulate and justify a suitable approach to research for your topic and consider research design issues**

■ **identify potential sources of data for your project and consider how you may be able to access the data you need**

■ **consider, and take into account, the ethical implications of undertaking your project**

■ **draw up an outline project plan.**

HOW TO USE THIS CHAPTER

This chapter is particularly relevant if you are in the early stages of thinking about how to undertake an investigative enquiry in HR. At this stage you will have to make decisions about the overall focus and strategy for your project and the data you will need to obtain. You will have to incorporate a consideration of the ethical implications of what you plan to do into your thinking. As a part of this, some of the themes that were introduced in Chapter 1 are developed further, but with particular emphasis on their consequences for your project. You must determine whether a positivistic or an interpretivist approach is appropriate for your enquiry (see Chapter 1), and this chapter will enable you to explore those issues more fully. This chapter will also offer some further ideas on the particular opportunities presented by undertaking organisationally-based and action-oriented research (see Chapter 1).

If you are already sure of what you plan to research, you could go straight to the section of this chapter entitled *Establishing the focus of the project* and start from there.

Case illustration

Finding a topic

Maria worked for an IT services organisation experiencing rapid growth. The company was formed in 1999 and became a plc in 2000. As a result of its impressive organisational growth the company had initiated several subsidiary companies across Europe and had three sites in the UK. Responsibility for HR in each of the countries of operation was the responsibility of the respective country managers but a Group HR services function also operated from the UK, concerned with HR policies and procedures group-wide. Maria worked as the Group HR Administrator.

For some while the company had been interested in the possibility of investing in a group-wide HR information system, and Maria wondered if this would be a possible area for a project. At an early stage (about a year before the intended submission date) she discussed, with her manager and with her tutor, her intention to assess current HR information systems within the different parts of the organisation; to consider the potential offered by integrated HR information systems; to research into the implementation issues that would be involved in any such development; and to consider the potential contribution that such a system might make to the strategic development of the organisation.

Six months later Maria submitted a revised project suggestion to her study centre. She now wanted to evaluate the effectiveness of performance development plans (PDPs) at a large NHS Trust, focusing particularly on the contribution they had made to the achievement of the Trust and the NHS plans and goals.

DISCUSSION QUESTIONS

1. What factors may have caused Maria to change her project topic in such a radical way?
2. What problems might Maria experience with changing her topic idea mid-stream?
3. Imagine that you are Maria's tutor and you have to advise her on taking her revised project forward. What does Maria now need to do to make progress with her enquiry?

Feedback notes

The case illustration above highlights the different sets of stakeholders that have something to contribute as well as something to gain from the process of undertaking an enquiry (see Figure 8). The choice of a topic will be influenced by all of them.

In this case, just as Maria was about to begin her project in earnest (some weeks after she formulated her initial research idea), her employing organisation downsized significantly, making both her and her project redundant. Similar difficulties can also occur for full-time

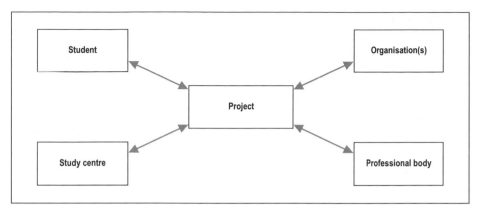

Figure 8 *Stakeholders in the research project*

students who may have obtained permission to undertake a project involving one or more organisations. As business situations change, so the ability of organisations to support the research process may also change. As far as Maria was concerned, once she was in employment again, the priorities of the new organisation were very different, and so the topic selection process had to begin again.

Changing a topic was not too difficult in this situation, because the submission date was still six months away. Things are more difficult when there is less time available before completion – hence the importance of starting the process as early as possible, just in case.

Although Maria now had a revised project, with organisational support, there were further issues to be considered and decisions to be made to focus and refine the project topic (to make it do-able) as well as decisions about what data would be needed and how it might be obtained in an ethical and rigorous way. It is these issues that this chapter will address.

DECIDING WHAT TO RESEARCH

For some students, the choice of a topic for a research project is relatively straightforward. However, for many it can be a slow and frustrating process. Selecting an appropriate topic can lead to a better submission at the end, and will certainly result in a more fulfilling process for the student and have a better chance of evoking a practical application and organisational improvement.

Generating ideas for projects

Some people have a fairly clear idea of their intended project at an early stage in their studies. Others are given a topic to research by their organisation. Most people, however, when faced with the necessity of choosing a topic for a piece of independent enquiry, find it difficult to pick out different possibilities.

Deciding on a topic to research can be psychologically as difficult as writing the first few sentences of an assignment. However, it is possible to structure the process in order to generate some ideas. Once ideas are generated it is possible to evaluate them, choose the most appropriate topic, and then clarify its focus and objectives.

Starting with the organisation

As the case illustration above on *Finding a topic* demonstrates, for many HR researchers the organisational context in which they are working is very significant to the choice of a project topic. Yet the identification and selection of an issue for research in such a situation can be a complex process. One reason for this is the interrelatedness of many features of organisational experience. Thus trying to isolate an issue for research while knowing that it is embedded in other related issues can be problematic. Nonetheless, practitioner-researchers have to make choices about boundaries, taking into account available time and resources.

In the topic-generation process, therefore, if you are undertaking your investigation in an organisation where you already work, it is worth standing back from the organisation to enable you to discern possible issues for an enquiry. Where possible, and where appropriate, part of this process should involve discussions with relevant managers and colleagues. Many of the suggestions they offer may well not suit you – but listening to these people, and considering how you might enquire into the issues or activities they suggest, will get you thinking.

Key questions that are worth asking in this way are:

- What is currently bothering me/my boss/my department/my organisation?
- What changes may be occurring in the near future?
- What HR developments may impact on the organisation in the next few weeks and months?

In addition, customers and clients as well as your friends and family may be of assistance in discussing things with you. They may not work in HR but the very activity of talking through issues with outsiders may help you to identify areas of interest and possible research topics.

Starting from journals

If you still have no idea what you would like to enquire into, the following activity may be useful.

ACTIVITY – GETTING RESEARCH IDEAS FROM JOURNALS

Browse through a recent edition of an HR journal such as *People Management* or *Personnel Today*.

Make a list of the main news articles and features. Record their titles and summarise what they are about in no more than one sentence. Generate a list of at least 12 articles/features.

Each of these articles/features could act as a trigger to the identification of one or more possible topics for your research. Work through the summaries you have made and list the topics they highlight. Give each of the topics a rating for the following characteristics if you were to consider them as an idea for an enquiry:

- your level of interest in the topic
- its likely value to you
- its likely value to your department/future career prospects
- its feasibility as a project.

Starting from past assignments

Another way of generating some research ideas is to look back on work you have already done as part of your course. It is very likely that you have previously studied a number of areas of HR practice as part of the assessment requirements of your course. Perhaps it would be worth re-reading coursework that you have undertaken and recalling which topics you found to be most interesting. Is there a potential topic for a fuller enquiry within your previous assignments? Alternatively, it may be that you have been involved in a particular project at work, or on a work placement, that has excited your sense of curiosity, or which you realise you and/or your organisation would benefit from knowing more about.

Starting from past project titles

If all of these suggestions have so far generated no ideas, then you might also review a list of past projects undertaken by students to stimulate your imagination enough to come up with some possibilities. Your study centre should be able to provide such a list. An indicative list of project titles is shown below. It is intended to stimulate your thinking, rather than to suggest that particular topics are more appropriate than others.

Examples of research topics

- Post-acquisition harmonisation of recruitment and selection: an evaluation of recruitment and selection processes used by [a company] in comparison with those of its French parent company
- An investigation into the role of human resources in not-for-profit organisations
- Bullying in the workplace
- The contribution of management development processes to organisational change at [company namc] plc
- The role and contribution of the personnel department to strategic HRM at [company name] plc
- Diversity awareness training within retail organisations: a case study
- An evaluation of the Investors in People process in a public transport company
- An evaluation of the use of psychometric testing for career planning at [company name] plc.
- Disability discrimination in non-profit-making organisations: an investigation into the experience of employment discrimination in a housing association
- An evaluation of the contribution of cross-cultural coaching to the management of international projects
- The 'glass ceiling': an investigation into equality of opportunities for women managers in the Philippines
- How flexible is the flexible organisation? An investigation into the development of flexible working in the financial services sector
- Operating internationally: the learning process in newly internationalising smaller businesses.

Deciding between alternative topics

Having identified two or three possible topics it is important to select the one that is most likely to lead to a successful project submission. Here again the expectations of the different sets of stakeholders must be taken into account – the student, the study centre or academic institution, the professional organisation, and the organisation(s). It is worth thinking through these requirements as you decide which topic to choose. You may also find that you start to modify and amend your proposed topic somewhat as you take account of these different features.

Issues to consider are listed below, linked with their importance to different stakeholders in the enquiry process.

Your perspective

- personal interest – Choose something that is interesting to you. There is little point in doing a project that has been selected because you were unable to think of anything else. You will have to work independently on your project for a number of months. If you start on it without much motivation, interest and enthusiasm, there is little chance that you will feel positive about it by the end of the process.

- career plan – Your motivation will also be enhanced if you can find a topic that has value to you in the medium or long term. Choose a topic that might make you more 'marketable', increase your knowledge in a specialised area, or improve your skills and experience.

- time – The project must be achievable within the specified time limit and in addition to other work and commitments. Avoid any topic that is so large that it cannot be completed on time or to a sufficient standard.

- skills – Good research topics are 'stretching' to the practitioner-researcher, but they must also be within your capabilities and/or realistically allow for appropriate development. A project studying the difficulties of communication in a multilingual organisation would be difficult to undertake, for example, if you can yourself read and communicate in only one language.

Your study centre's perspective

- links to theory/potential for fresh insight – To achieve academic credit, projects must be capable of being linked in some way to theories, models and frameworks of practice. Which of the topics that you are thinking about have the most potential for this?

- regulations and expectations – Each study centre and/or academic institution will have clear guidelines about what is expected from a research project or management report. Some institutions require that primary data is gathered and forms part of an enquiry, for example. It is also important to be clear about the expected wordcount, the relative importance of different features within the project (the marking scheme) and the format for presentation. If you are taking a course in HR, you will be expected to research an issue related to this field (and not principally concerned with marketing or finance, for example). Make sure that you choose a topic that enables you to meet these expectations. The advice of your supervisor or adviser is very important as you consider the suitability of your proposed topics.

- scope – This relates to whether the project has the opportunity to increase or confirm current thinking about HR policy and/or practice. Avoid choosing a topic that merely replicates a certain form of HR practice and does not provide an opportunity to critically evaluate existing assumptions.

- wider context – Even if your project is going to be undertaken within one organisation, an appropriate topic will also have some value beyond that organisation – perhaps to the business sector, to the HR profession, to other HR managers, and so on.

- professional institution – If the course of study you are taking is linked with a professional institute (such as the CIPD), choose a topic that meets the criteria the institute has established.

The organisation's perspective

- organisational relevance – A project that has clear potential value to the organisation that permits the enquiry to be undertaken is more likely to be completed successfully.

- access to data – A topic for research will only be feasible if the data, or sources for the data, that you need exist and if you are able (politically and logistically) to access them within your time and budget constraints.

- resources required – Although basic IT and other resources are likely to be available, requirements for specialist software or other resources (such as particular training) must be checked out before a topic is selected.

Clearly, any evaluation you make as part of the decision process when choosing a topic must take account of all the relevant stakeholders. It is important to identify which projects might be ruled out as a result of the criteria above, and which seem more likely to succeed.

Having decided on the broad area of your research, it is important to establish a focus for the study.

ESTABLISHING THE FOCUS OF THE PROJECT

Arriving at a research idea is a big step forward, yet it is also important to refine and focus the topic. People tackle this process in different ways but the aim of the focusing process is to clarify the scope and purpose of the enquiry, to identify the main questions to be answered, and so to identify the key issues of interest.

One approach to establishing the focus is to begin by writing down all the possible questions that might follow on from the research idea and then to refine and examine each of them until you arrive at four or five that are most relevant and interesting for your project.

Case illustration

Disability sidelined in firms' social reports

Only 12 per cent of 50 leading UK and global companies mention disability as part of their strategy for corporate social responsibility (CSR), the Employer's Forum on Disability has found.

The forum's first-ever analysis of firms' social and ethical reports shows that few refer directly to disability in their strategy for this area – even though more than one-third mention recruitment, retention and personal development of their disabled employees elsewhere in the report.

As part of the research – aimed at establishing where disability sits on the CSR agenda – the Forum this week published a list of 13 areas in which social reports

---

produced by firms should mention disability (see www.peoplemanagement.co.uk/efd). It found that only one company currently refers to disability in all 13 areas.

'Many organisations promoting disability awareness have a great deal of ground to make up if they are to ensure that they are not left behind on this issue,' said Susan Scott-Parker, the Forum's chief executive.

'It appears that, for far too many, disability is simply not on their radar screen. This puts them at serious legal, financial, reputational and competitive risk.'

Scott-Parker believes that HR professionals have a key role to play in ensuring that disability is seen as a business issue – but that they must work hard to do so.

'They can do a better job of communicating with their CSR counterparts,' she said.

Mike Emmott, CIPD Adviser, Employee Relations, agreed that many firms fail to appreciate the issue's importance.

'People who deal with CSR might not see disability as central to the debate, but it is part of the corporate responsibility strategy,' Emmott said. 'This is about the extent to which fair employment policies are followed. This is part of CSR and should be included.'

The Forum used the research to calculate a 'disability global inclusion benchmark'. Firms scoring well included BT, the Co-operative Bank, Centrica, B&Q and IBM.

Roy Gardner, chief executive of Centrica, believes that the business case for working with disabled people as employees, customers and partners is compelling. 'There are 8.6 million disabled people in the UK with a combined spending power of £50 billion,' he said.

The Forum plans to work with employers to help them adopt its 13-point guide to good practice.

K. Higginbottom, *People Management*, 11 July 2002.
Reproduced by permission of *People Management*.

DISCUSSION QUESTIONS

Imagine that you work for a large services-oriented organisation. You have to undertake a research enquiry for your course and are unsure what to tackle. You have read this news report and are quite interested in the areas of both corporate social responsibility and disability.

1 Compile a list of between six and eight questions that might flow from your interest in the issues raised in this article.

2 Refine and evaluate your questions to see if you can narrow them down to four or five that would underpin a study you might want to undertake that originated from issues raised in this article.

Feedback notes

The main problem you would face in tackling this enquiry is to work out what data to gather in order to answer what question. Clearly, in a fairly limited project you cannot enquire into everything related with corporate social responsibility in your organisation or, indeed, disability issues. So it is important to narrow down the enquiry and focus on key issues of interest.

Questions that might be posed in relation to this article include:

- What is meant by 'disability'?
- What is meant by 'corporate social responsibility'?
- How does my organisation (or a range of organisations) deal with social or ethical issues?
- Do we have a social and ethical strategy?
- How many organisations make social and ethical reports of this type?
- In what ways is disability a business issue?
- How does HR relate with corporate social responsibility in my organisation?
- What do disabled employees in my organisation expect from the HR function?

A glance at these questions suggests that there are probably at least three different projects that might be undertaken. It is possible that some of the questions may themselves lead you to ask further questions. Others are less relevant to your interest or may themselves be sub-questions of a larger issue. At this stage, therefore, it is important to refine, narrow down, and formulate about four or five questions that are relevant for your enquiry.

Reading around the subject

Part of the process of refinement from a general idea to a researchable topic is the definition of key concepts, issues and contexts that are relevant for your enquiry. To do this it is necessary to do some initial reading. Two students following up ideas from the case illustration above, for example, might decide to focus on disability and would need to read around this topic. As a result of some this reading the two students might choose to focus on different issues within the 'disability agenda'. Another student might pursue corporate social responsibility, necessitating different reading – and so on.

Research aims, objectives and questions

Once you have identified the main issues, concepts and contexts that are relevant to your enquiry, you are in a position to generate an initial statement of the aim of your enquiry and the main research questions you wish to address or the research objectives you wish to achieve.

Opinion is divided about whether research objectives are preferable to research questions in expressing the focus of any study (see, for example, Black, 1993; Cresswell, 1994; Werner and Schoepfle, 1987; Janckowicz, 2000; Saunders *et al*, 2003). Some study centres may have particular preferences, but many accept research questions, research objectives, or both. Indeed, the distinction between the two can be over-stated in that both are derived from a questioning process as a result of the refining and focusing process.

ACTIVITY – RESEARCH QUESTIONS OR RESEARCH OBJECTIVES?

Imagine that you are going to undertake some research on corporate social responsibility within your organisation. You have come up with a list of questions you would like to answer:

- Why do organisations report on corporate social responsibility issues?

- How does HR relate to corporate social responsibility in my organisation?

- How can the effectiveness of corporate social responsibility policies be measured?

- To what extent has corporate social responsibility impacted on my organisation?

- How effective has corporate social responsibility been for my organisation?

- How might HR and corporate social responsibility be better integrated in my organisation?

Try to express each of the research questions above as research objectives.

Discuss whether you think research objectives or research questions are preferable.

Feedback notes

Research objectives that you might formulate might look something like:

- To identify organisations' objectives for introducing reports on corporate social responsibility issues

- To identify the ways in which the HR function relates to corporate social responsibility issues at [company name] Ltd

- To establish appropriate criteria for considering the effectiveness of CSR policies

- To determine the extent to which the criteria for the effectiveness of CSR have been met at [company name] Ltd

- To identify the implications of CSR policies at [company name] Ltd for the HR department.

It is interesting that although research questions at this stage seem more specific, their formulation in a more generalised form as research objectives allows for more relevant alternatives to be explored. So, for example, with the first research objective it might be that many organisations have unclear (or no) objectives for CSR. This in itself is an important and worthwhile finding. The final objective also prompts for evaluation of current HR contributions and the formulation of conclusions and recommendations that are action-focused.

The formulation of effective research objectives can also help to avert a common danger in action-oriented organisational projects. The danger here is the temptation to formulate questions that you think you already know the answer to, and which will merely serve to reinforce existing personal and/or organisational assumptions or activities. As you formulate objectives (or questions) it is therefore worth making explicit what you think the answers may be to your questions – but also what alternative answers may exist.

Case illustration

The value of potential outcomes

Gurinder worked for a large multinational organisation that was engaged in the provision of a range of outsourced services, ranging from the finance to the telecommunications sectors. Each time an outsourcing contract was secured, a number of employees from the client organisation would be transferred to Gurinder's company. These transferred staff had therefore to adjust to a different culture and working environment because, although their work remained broadly similar, they now worked for a different organisation. Attitude surveys undertaken by Gurinder's company had indicated that there might be low morale amongst such transferred employees. This was typified by a growing 'them' and 'us' attitude between long-term company employees and those who were transferred, by high absenteeism and by high employee turnover.

For her project Gurinder decided to investigate the company's largest outsourced account to test a hypothesis that 'unmet employee expectations lead to low employee commitment and poor performance'.

DISCUSSION QUESTIONS

1   What is the likelihood that Gurinder will be able to establish whether or not unmet employee expectations lead to low employee commitment and high employee turnover?

2   What are the implications for Gurinder's project if she cannot prove that there is a causal relationship between these variables?

3   How valuable is a hypothesis in action-oriented organisational research of this kind?

Feedback notes

If Gurinder could show that 'unmet employee expectations' *always* caused 'low commitment' and high turnover, the project would have had a worthwhile outcome. However, given the complexities of the concepts of 'employee expectations' and 'employee commitment', and the interrelationship of these issues with a range of other organisational and environmental factors, it is likely that the relationship could not be unambiguously proven. As a result her findings would be less interesting, and also have little practical relevance to the organisation. This is an example where there is a lack of *symmetry of potential outcomes*. In fact, Gurinder went on to formulate a number of research questions that meant that her findings had value whatever the outcome. These were:

■   What were the employees' expectations of their new employer before they officially transferred as part of the outsourcing contract?

■   Once transferred, to what extent were employee expectations fulfilled?

■   If the employee expectations were met, did it result in increased job satisfaction and commitment?

- In what ways can employee expectations be fulfilled or managed more effectively?
- To what extent can the lessons learned from the sample case be effectively applied across different types of outsourced accounts?

Gurinder's decision to base her research on the testing of a hypothesis also indicates the different approaches that are taken to understanding and enacting the research process – and it is to these issues that this chapter now turns.

APPROACHES TO RESEARCH

In Chapter 1 the differences between positivist and interpretivist approaches to research were introduced. The main differences between the two approaches are shown in Table 1.

To undertake a research project based on positivist principles therefore involves a structured process whereby you first evaluate what is already known about your topic. On this basis you would then formulate a hypothesis and gather data to test whether the hypothesis proves true or false.

The most popular definition of a hypothesis, produced by researchers in education and often quoted in business and management textbooks, is (Verma and Beard, 1981; p.184):

> *a tentative proposition which is subject to verification through subsequent investigation. ... In many cases hypotheses are hunches that the researcher has about the existence of relationship between the variables.*

Table 1 *Positivist and interpretivist principles*

Positivist principles	Interpretivist principles
- Work from scientific principles. ✗ 1. - Analyse phenomena in terms of variables. - Start with theory and test/refine theory with data. - Data should be collected by 'dispassionate' researchers. [detached] ✗3. - A highly structured research process should be used. ✗ 2. - Theories can be used to predict future relationships and behaviours. - Quantitative data is preferred. - The validity and reliability of data are important for formulating generalisable conclusions.	- Knowledge is constructed by human beings as they make sense of their environment. ✗ 1 - Analyse phenomena in terms of issues. - Researchers cannot be wholly dispassionate – they are involved and will influence situations to various degrees (often unintentionally). ✗3. - Flexibility may be required to allow the emphasis of the research to change as the process unfolds. ✗ 2. - Qualitative data is preferred. - Generating 'rich' data is as important as (or more important than) the ability to generalise.

ACTIVITY – RESEARCHING INTO EMPLOYEE TURNOVER

Imagine that you are a full-time HR student who is interested in undertaking a project on employee turnover. You work part-time in a large store and have noticed that many employees stay in their jobs for only a very short period of time before leaving the organisation. Having read up on different approaches to research, you have decided to try to adopt a positivist approach to your research and are keen to undertake your project in as scientific and objective a way as possible. The aim of your project is to investigate patterns of employee turnover in the retail sector.

To begin the investigation you have first undertaken considerable reading to find out what is already known about the causes of high rates of turnover, and you have found that the literature suggests that turnover rates (in general) may be related to age, length of service, and the type of employment undertaken. You now need to investigate whether there is indeed a relationship between the variables of 'turnover', 'age', 'length of service', and 'type of employment' within the retail sector.

DISCUSSION QUESTIONS

What hypothesis or hypotheses might you formulate by which to test whether or not turnover from work in the retail sector is related to age, length of service and type of employment?
How would you measure 'age', 'turnover', 'length of service' and 'type of employment'?
What data will you need in order to test your hypothesis?
How will you obtain the data that you need?

Feedback notes

Although the wording may differ, it is likely that you might come up with something like the following hypotheses:

- 'Compared with the norm for the retail sector, a higher proportion of leavers are younger workers who are hourly paid.'
- 'Hourly-paid employees with a higher length of service are less likely to leave their employment in the retail sector than those with a shorter length of service.'

If you are committed to measuring issues like age, turnover, and so on in an objective way, it is also important that you operationalise your concepts. In this case, perhaps you might come up with something like:

- 'hourly paid': defined as relating to a permanent or temporary contract by which the person's rate of pay is calculated on an hourly basis
- 'young': defined as aged 21 years or less
- 'length of service': defined as the number of complete months within the current period of employment.

Having got this far you are now in a position to gather some data. If you are committed to a scientific method, you will want to ensure that the data-gathering process generates information that is objective, is measurable, and can be statistically analysed in a rigorous way. It will not be scientific if you affect the subjects of your research or are in any way affected by them.

There are a range of objective methods you could choose from – but perhaps the most likely choice, because it means you remain fully independent, is a postal survey to retail organisations, asking them to tick boxes that relate to questions about their patterns of employee turnover, the age of their leavers, and so on. It is important to get information that is relevant to all of the retail sector, not just the company you work for on a part-time basis, so perhaps you will find a sample of respondents from 100 different retail companies (small shops as well as large organisations). The larger the sample size that you can put together, the more generalisable, and therefore worthwhile, the results of your analysis of the data should be. You might also choose to survey employees in the retail sector and ask them to answer questions about their employment history, and so on.

If you were to undertake a project in this way, you would be able to analyse your data and form a conclusion related to your hypotheses. If the evidence you gather supports your hypotheses, the links are confirmed. If it does not, then a subsequent researcher will have to investigate other factors. If your company is interested in your research, on the basis of knowledge about these causes, it can, if it wishes, make some changes to the way the employment relationship is managed for young people on hourly-paid contracts.

Criticisms of the positivist approach

The *Employee turnover* Activity above shows that it is possible to undertake very creditable research utilising a positivist approach. However, the following reservations about it might also be expressed (Remenyi *et al*, 1998; Smith, 1983):

- the unanswered question 'why?' – Although the research in the Activity may show that there is a relationship between age, type of employment, and length of service, it does not explain *why* this phenomenon occurs. To answer the 'why' question requires an understanding of people's perceptions of their employment situation

- problems of categorisation – By categorising data as part of the operationalisation of the hypothesis, how sure can we be of the meaning of our findings and analysis? Is it reasonable to confine 'youth' to under-21s or to include temporary as well as permanent types of employment within the categories? How likely is it that respondents would accurately indicate their length of service in a job in 'months'?

- issues of the data – The use of quantitative data can provide for broad generalisations but it only answers questions posed in a fairly short questionnaire. Is this sort of data superficial? If we are concerned with the contribution of people in an employment situation, perhaps 'richer' (more qualitative) data is also required

- relevance for applied research – The purpose of a good deal of research in HR is to contribute to the solution of organisational problems. Although the research in the Activity would be interesting, it does not really relate to the management of the employment relationship, confining itself only to describing links between variables

- dealing with complexity – The basis of the positivist approach is to reduce situations and isolate discrete variables for analysis. However, most situations in organisations are more complex if not genuinely messy, requiring a more flexible and integrative approach to enquiry

- issues of detachment – In organisational studies it may not be possible to be as detached as the scientific method requires. Every researcher is a product of his or her culture and background. Although a practitioner-researcher might feel objective, therefore, it is possible that someone else tackling the same enquiry, but from a different organisational or societal background, would identify the issues differently.

Criticisms of the interpretive approach

This brief overview of the different approaches to research can lead to a perception of a no-win situation. On the one hand the positivist approach may underestimate real and significant features of organisational phenomena, and overestimate the level of objectivity that can be achieved by the researcher. On the other hand, there are also problems with the interpretivist approach (Bryman, 1988; Robson, 2002; Gill and Johnson, 2001).

- loss of direction – The flexibility of the interpretivist approach, whereby issues are explored rather than tested against a predetermined hypothesis, is attractive, but many researchers find that they have collected a huge volume of data and have no clear idea of what to do with it
- time and resource constraints – The closer link between data collection and data analysis (such that the interim outcome of some analysis might lead to a change of the research emphasis and the collection of different data in a subsequent stage of research) is attractive, but is often not practical within the time and resource limitations of a student project.

Many students therefore find themselves drawing, to some extent, on both traditions. The benefits of this have been highlighted by a number of authors in the social sciences and business fields (Bryman, 1988; Gill and Johnson, 2001), who suggest that both understandings of research can generate enquiries that complement each other in providing an analysis of organisational issues that incorporates a range of perspectives.

Whatever approach you opt for, however, it is important to be clear about the aim and purpose of your enquiry. A hypothesis may be useful (although symmetry of outcomes must remain possible) or broader research objectives may be more appropriate. Whatever your decision, make sure you can answer the questions in the list below.

Clarifying the topic of an enquiry
- What is the aim of my research?
- What are the research objectives or questions?
- What do I think the answers will be to my questions?
- What alternative answers might there be?
- Where do I fit into the situation I will be researching?
- What will other members of the organisation think of my working on this issue?
- What opposition will I encounter?

RESEARCH DESIGN ISSUES

Research design is about turning your research ideas into a project. It involves deciding on the overall research strategy (how you propose to try to answer your research questions) and the details of how you will implement your strategy. Books about research methods highlight a range of generic research strategies. Opinion differs about how many strategies there are and what they should be called (see, for example, Saunders *et al*, 2003; Robson, 2002; Bell, 2001). Here the strategies that are most appropriate to students undertaking an HR project are described.

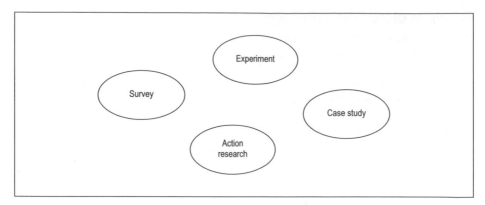

Figure 9 *Some generic research strategies*

Experimental research

Many books on research methods include the experiment as a possible research strategy. The Hawthorne experiments of the 1920s are a well-known example of such a research strategy in an organisational context where changes to work environment and conditions were applied to one particular group of workers, and the effect on their productivity was studied and compared with the productivity of workers who had not experienced these changes (Roethlisberger and Dickson, 1939; Landsberger, 1958). As a research strategy, therefore, the experiment involves measuring the effects of one variable (perhaps a new appraisal scheme) on a group of people by subjecting them to it, measuring its effects, and comparing these results with equivalent measures for a 'control' group who were not part of the new scheme.

For a small-scale investigative enquiry, however, it is difficult – if not impossible – to achieve such controlled situations (Neuman, 2003; Barber, 1976). Indeed, even when it is possible to introduce one variable to one group and withhold it from another, it might still be difficult to determine if changes in behaviour in one group were the result of the variable (the new appraisal scheme) or the result of a combination of different factors (as was the case with the Hawthorne experiments). As a result, in organisational studies the experiment is rarely selected as a research strategy.

Other research strategies that are appropriate for relatively short-term projects undertaken in organisations are:

- survey
- case study
- action research.

The following case illustrations provide examples of enquiries that highlight particular features of these strategies, after which the advantages and disadvantages are summarised.

Survey research

Case illustration

Survey research:
Employee induction in licensed retail organisations

... Work on labour turnover reveals that where labour turnover is high, it occurs within a few months of the initial appointment. Survival curve analysis frequently identifies an 'induction crisis' where new employees leave within a few weeks or months of joining the organisation. Typically, where high labour turnover exists, 70 per cent of leavers have been with the organisation for less than three months (Lashley, 2002). While staff turnover can be due to a range of factors, a failure to ensure that new employees are 'eased' into their new jobs is an important one.

This research explores current practice for the induction of new employees within a sample of licensed retail organisations. The research focused on employee induction, though the recruitment and induction of managers is a subject worthy of further research. The research identifies the general approach to staff induction and highlights examples of best practice. ...

... Models of best practice (Lashley, 2000; Boella, 1996) suggest that induction programmes contain features that are inclusive and meet the wide needs of both parties. All new employees – irrespective of whether they are working full-time, part-time, temporarily or on a casual basis – need an induction programme. As individuals they still have the same need to be accepted quickly by the organisation, and as new employees the organisation needs to assist them to be effective as quickly as possible. When planning the induction programme it is necessary to consider the information and experiences required to help them settle in and then how best the information should be given. Generally, induction programmes are best planned over a period of time. It is a mistake to provide too much information on the first day. Good induction programmes occur over a period of time. This may commence before the employee formally starts work, and cover the first day, week and months.

Some sort of induction seems to be taking place in most firms in the licensed retail sector. A total of 86 per cent of employers trained their staff in the sector and 70 per cent offered formal training beyond induction (HtF, 2000). However, the findings give little insight into the degree of formality or informality of the approach. Given the size and ownership patterns where a small number of large firms control significantly high proportions of the pub estate, this study explores the extent that induction systems are planned and structured from the 'centre' and the degree of uniformity that is delivered across all units in the estate. Also the research studies the aims, extent and scope of the induction training. As we have shown earlier, this can vary considerably. The most intensive and broad approach shows that all employees go through an induction programme irrespective of their job level or tenure. These programmes cover a wide range of issues, including the social needs of the new employee, and introduce the recruit to a programme of skill and career development.

Research approach
The research aimed to:

- establish the approach to staff induction, current practices and the management of induction in a sample of licensed retail organisations, and
- highlight examples of best practice in the induction of new staff within the sector.

Key issues
Based on the discussion above, the key issues to be explored follow the themes outlined below:

- the aims of the induction process – To what extent is the aim to meet the new recruit's social needs, or is the aim merely to familiarise the recruit with the relevant job role and rules? Is there a probationary element to the process?
- the form, structure and management of induction programmes in place – This will help explore the extent to which induction provision is a formal element of the new recruit's early experience and is managed to ensure uniformity of standards
- the length of time that the induction process takes
- the inclusiveness of the process – Do all recruits get a similar programme, or are there significant differences in the programme depending on job-holder status or tenure of employment?

Research methods
Given that the research is chiefly concerned with exploring induction practices in the pub estate that is directly owned and managed by multi-unit companies, the research was chiefly concerned with three types of firms: local brewer retailers, licensed retailers with a single brand estate, and national retailers with a multi-branded estate.

Lucas (1999; p.7) says that the survey method of research 'is about searching and looking in order to ask a question, or series of questions', in this case gaining an impression from those who represent firms operating pub properties in a managed format. The study was not concerned with the induction practices in tenanted, leased or freehold pubs. The *Publican* (2000) survey listed the top 100 firms operating 15,089 licensed retail properties in this directly-managed format as at 7 January 2000. Researchers conducted telephone interviews with a cluster of companies and then conducted semi-structured interviews with four licensees and 11 staff at pubs from one organisation that appeared, on the basis of the telephone interviews, to have a good approach that could usefully be explored in practice ...

Extracts from C. Lashley and W. Best (2002) *International Journal of Contemporary Hospitality Management,* 14 (1) 6–13.
Reproduced by permission of Emerald (MCB), Bradford.

DISCUSSION QUESTIONS

1 How many firms would you wish to include in the telephone survey described in this article?

2 Who would be the most appropriate person to answer the questions in the telephone survey?

3 What are the limitations of this approach in relation to achieving the aims of the research?

Feedback notes

As noted in the extract above from a much longer article, the survey approach involves the collection of data in a standardised form from groups of people. Postal, telephone or e-mailed questionnaires may be used to obtain data and, as in this case, structured interviews may also be used. Some form of sampling is required to obtain information from a representative selection of respondents. The aim of a survey is therefore to generate data for analysis so that patterns can be extracted and comparisons can be made.

In the research described in this article the following (rather limited) sample frame was used:

Licensed retail organisation	Phone interviews	Semi-structured interviews		
		senior managers	pub managers	staff
Local brewery retailer	4			
Single brand retailer	4	1	4	11
Multi-brand retailer	3			

Here, then, 11 firms out of a total of 100 large operators were contacted, who were responsible for the operation of over 15,000 licensed retail properties. With all but one retailer, however, there would be only one (head office) respondent to the telephone questionnaire, which might have restricted the representativeness of the responses. In order to probe more deeply into practice, as well as policy, the researchers undertook semi-structured interviews with 16 people, at different levels in one of the organisations. This organisation was chosen as likely to provide some evidence about 'good practice'.

The aim of this research was to establish the approach to staff induction, current practices and the management of induction in a sample of licensed retail organisations, as well as to highlight examples of good practice. The sample had to take account of constraints of time and access to organisations. It is likely that the responses to questions from the telephone survey provided more of an official view about what *should* happen than an accurate account of what *actually* happens in practice. The researchers probed this possibility in the semi-structured interviews, where they discovered that induction processes were often limited in scope and informally organised. Further, there were inconsistent patterns of practice across the different sites because many managers were not trained to deliver induction and there did not seem to be a robust system in place to check whether induction had been received by all employees (Lashley and Best, 2002).

Survey-based research design – advantages and disadvantages

Both advantages and disadvantages of survey based research are highlighted in this illustration and are summarised in Table 2.

Table 2 *Advantages and disadvantages of survey-based research*

Advantages	Disadvantages
■ It is relatively cheap to organise ✗ ■ It can achieve a broad coverage for comparisons ✗ ■ It can be undertaken within a relatively short time-frame ■ It produces a high volume of information ■ It is relatively easy to present the data in order to make comparisons ✗ ■ A survey can be repeated again at a different location or at a different time to allow for further comparisons ✗	■ 'Depth' is sacrificed for 'breadth' ■ Poor questionnaire design leads to poor-quality data ■ A poor level of responses may make data unrepresentative ■ There is no control over who responds to the questions ■ Questions may not necessarily be interpreted in the same way by all the respondents ■ The responses of some respondents may follow from private agendas ■ There is no knowing what do those who do not reply think (and it may or may not matter anyway)

Sources: Groves (1996), Neuman (2003)

The case study

This involves a detailed investigation into a situation in a single 'case' or a small number of related 'cases'. It is a strategy that allows for a problem or issue to be studied in some depth, within the context of the case(s), and that therefore seeks to investigate the interaction of different factors and events that contribute to the focus of the enquiry. A range of types of data (such as observations, interviews and the analysis of documents) contribute to the enquiry to provide the basis for a rounded analysis of the issue or problem. 'Historical' research can also be undertaken whereby the researcher endeavours to find out all about, say, the development of the organisation, or of a particular problem, as part of the data-gathering process (Yin, 2003; Eisenhardt, 1989).

Case illustration

Strategic HRM and the gendered division of labour in the hotel industry: A case study

There exists a considerable body of literature about the sexual division of labour in Britain (Knights and Willmott; 1986; Hansard Society Commission, 1990; Firth-Cozens and West, 1991). Though authors may at times differ as to the circumstances under which such a division has developed, countless studies and surveys demonstrate how work is divided, if not segregated, along gender lines. Segregation of women and men is both horizontal and vertical. Women are concentrated in service roles within organisations and in the lower levels. Women represent, for example, 80 per cent of hairdressers, cleaners, caterers and clerical workers, yet only 0.8 per cent of surgeons, 12 per cent of solicitors, 16 per cent of secondary head teachers and at most 22 per cent of managers (Faludi, 1992;

Spencer and Podmore, 1987; Al-Khalifa, 1988; Hirsch and Jackson, 1989). Additionally, women typically have different patterns of work from men. They are more likely to take career breaks, to work part-time and on average are paid considerably less than men (Metcalf and Leighton, 1989). ...

The hotel industry is a fertile environment in which to study issues surrounding women's experience of work. Traditionally, the hotel industry belongs to that group of industries classically segregated by gender (Bagguley, 1991; Hicks, 1990; Guerrier, 1992). Typically, large numbers of women are employed particularly on the non-managerial side of the organisation where work is semi- or unskilled, low-paid, and classically segregated by gender. Women occupy the low-status roles such as chambermaids, and men occupy the more prestigious roles such as managers and chefs. Indeed, there appears to be an unspoken understanding within the industry that women are not really 'cut out' for the more prestigious roles such as that of hotel manager (Hicks, 1990; Guerrier, 1992). The hotel industry is an area well researched and documented in many directions – eg pilferage and employment and HIV/AIDS (Mars, 1985; Adam-Smith and Goss, 1993). Any real attention to gender, however, has focused on the female hotel manager 'dilemma' (Guerrier, 1992), with a few notable exceptions (Bagguley, 1991; Fine, 1987; Whyte, 1948). ...

The study

From the above literature review a number of research questions emerged. These were:

- What roles are women in hotel work expected to fit into?
- Do women adopt coping strategies to enable them to deal with these roles?
- What career aspirations do female hotel workers have?
- What views do hotel workers hold about gender segregation within their industry?

In order to address these questions, a case study methodology (Eisenhardt, 1989; Gummesson, 1991; Hartley, 1994) was chosen in order to gain an in-depth understanding of one particular hotel. A selection of qualitative research methods including interviewing and observation were the techniques adopted to elicit the data. The aim was to gain a proper 'feel' and 'understanding' of the culture of the organisation. Semi-structured open response interviews (King, 1994) were conducted to generate information around the issue of gender without explicitly inviting the interviewee to talk solely of gender. General questions were asked of all employees interviewed about their length of service, position in the organisation, age, qualifications, career path to date and general information about the nature of their duties. The research took place over a period of three months. A total of 23 full-time members of staff were interviewed: 15 females and eight males. All the members of the management team were interviewed, of whom three were men and three were women. The longest interview lasted for over two hours; the shortest was 30 minutes. All interviewees were volunteers and had given up their own time for the research.

Extracts from R. Biswas and C. Cassell (1996) *Personnel Review*, 25 (2) 19–34.
Reproduced by permission of Emerald (MCB), Bradford

DISCUSSION QUESTIONS

1   What other types of data might also have been utilised within this research?

2   Identify three advantages of this research strategy, and also three limitations.

3   What influence might the researcher have on the information people divulged during the interviews, and on the behaviour of employees when they were being 'observed'?

Feedback notes

The case study research strategy uses a mixture of methods, including observation and interviews, but also contemporary documents, archival records, 'participant observation' (working alongside chambermaids, for example) and physical artefacts (Yin, 2003). It is particularly useful when the issue being examined is difficult to separate from its context.

The case study is, in many ways, the most obvious research strategy for HR students in some form of employment, undertaking a project over a limited timescale. Even for full-time students the case study is attractive because it may be easier to obtain access to a single organisation (often where they already have some form of contact) than to seek responses from many companies.

However, the very ease of access is also a significant limitation of the case study method in these circumstances, because in such a situation a practitioner-researcher is already influenced by the culture and practices of the organisation – and, indeed, influences the culture and practices of the organisation. In this sense, 'objective detachment' is not realisable.

Even in the research undertaken in this illustration, where the researcher was not an employee, there was an impact on the research process, as this further extract illustrates:

In this kind of in-depth qualitative work, it is important to consider the impact the researcher has on the research process. One of the authors conducted this research, and it is interesting to consider how the participants responded to her as a relatively young woman. A general observation was that men treated her with contempt or caution, and that the women treated her as a soul-mate. Clearly, it would be interesting to speculate how the interviewees would have responded differently to a male interviewer. Beyond this one must consider the impact the researcher has on an organisation during the research and after the event. By asking questions and conducting interviews, a researcher brings issues to the fore that may not otherwise have been the case. As previously acknowledged, the whole issue of gender is generally neglected – yet, when openly researching it as a topic over a period of three months, in a relatively small organisation, the issue inevitably becomes heightened in people's minds. It is impossible to quantify the extent of the impact, but the following scenario provides insight into the fact that some impact occurred.

> While waiting to interview a member of the restaurant staff the researcher was standing for a couple of minutes (unseen) just inside the entrance to the restaurant. A male restaurant supervisor was talking to a female junior restaurant supervisor. As she turned away from him he smacked her on the bottom with a menu. As he did so he looked up, saw the researcher and hastily said, 'Oh dear! That was a bit sexist!'

A summary of the main advantages and disadvantages of the case study approach are shown in Table 3.

Table 3 *Advantages and disadvantages of case-study-based research*

Advantages	Disadvantages
■ One issue can be studied in depth ■ The interaction of factors and events can be taken into account ■ Breadth in the methods of data collection ■ Access to one organisation (or a small number of cases) ■ The case study can focus in depth on one department or group	■ A huge volume of qualitative data may be difficult to analyse ■ Potential difficulty in cross-checking information ■ Generalisation is not possible ■ The researcher may individually influence and be influenced by the case

Sources: Ragin and Becker (1992), Neuman (2003), Yin (2003)

Action research
Case illustration

Achieving organisational collaboration in the non-profit sector: An action research approach

In 1998, eight independent voluntary organisations working in the field of HIV/AIDS in the UK commissioned a research team, including two of the authors of this article, to conduct a study into options for working together more closely. ...

In effect what was commissioned was a piece of action research (Argyris *et al*, 1984; Elden and Chisholm, 1993; Hart and Bond, 1995; Lewin, 1946) in that the 'independent study' had three key features:

■ It was focused on issues of practice.

■ The work was to be carried out by the researchers in collaboration with the agency CEOs who had commissioned it.

■ It was intended that the study itself would be part of, and would facilitate, a process of change.

The action research

For the HIV/AIDS project, the research team ... collected data in five ways.

1   We examined a range of documents generated by the eight participating agencies as well as other documents relating to public policy on HIV/AIDS.

2   We conducted semi-structured interviews with the CEOs of the eight participating agencies. Our accounts of these interviews were fed back to the interviewees who were able to modify them as they wished. The final 'cleared' documents were eventually shared with the other participating CEOs in an appendix to the final report.

3   We conducted semi-structured interviews with nine representatives of external stakeholders – people with practical and/or policy knowledge of the HIV/AIDS sector and with an interest in possible organisational collaboration by the participants.

4   We reviewed research-based and 'grey' literature on previous experience of organisational collaboration in the UK and US voluntary/non-profit sectors with a view to uncovering possible organisational models.

5   We also interviewed two senior practitioners who had been involved in institutional alliances in the voluntary sector.

The final output from the work was a consolidated report. This included an account of the perceived advantages and disadvantages of a 'multiple agency institutional alliance' based on our five data sources. It also suggested possible organisational models for closer collaboration between voluntary agencies working in the HIV/AIDS field in the UK – ranging from full merger through various forms of federation to a loose alliance in which each participating organisation remained organisationally and legally autonomous.

We developed these models on the basis of our interview findings plus our literature search. Although we were fortunate in that we were able to draw on a body of existing theoretical knowledge about mergers and organisational structure, the literature that dealt explicitly with voluntary agencies was sparse. Thus, we developed existing generic theory by adapting the models that were available into a format, which demonstrated the possible benefits or disadvantages of each for voluntary agencies.

Following delivery of our report to the commissioning consortium, we facilitated a group discussion with the CEOs of the eight participating agencies. This discussion led to ... a full merger of five (later six) of the original eight commissioning organisations. ...

Facilitating organisational change
Three aspects of our action research method seemed to be particularly helpful in facilitating organisational change in this case.

First, since the research process included feeding back interview notes to participants and sharing cleared accounts with others, it enabled participants to understand each other's hopes and fears and to identify both the commonalities between them and the potential stumbling-blocks. We were building on some shared feelings of trust, but the research process helped to develop that further. It was made clear to us by some of the participants themselves that being presented with the views of others in this format gave them greater insight into the problem of how to effect a form of change to which they could collectively agree. This in turn enabled them to make a decision on how to move the change process forward.

Second, our own written report provided the basis for a group discussion that helped the participants to reflect on their own views and on the models with which they were presented. The fact that the participants had confidence in the independence of the researchers was a critical factor in allowing them to be open and honest with one another, in an environment which they perceived to be safe.

In addition to these two features, a third element ... was the development of organisational models or 'scenarios'. Our research report provided several possible models for a new organisation, and this enabled study participants to envisage what the realities of closer collaboration, and even a new national organisation, might be. This both diffused some anxieties, since some participants had not been able to conceptualise a changed organisation, and provided a foundation for negotiation within the consortium of eight agencies.

Extracts from M. Harris and J. Harris (2002)
Organization Development Journal, 20 (1) 28–35.
Reproduced with permission of the *Organization Development Journal,*
The O.D. Institute, 11234 Walnut Ridge Road, Chesterland, Ohio 44026, USA.

DISCUSSION QUESTIONS

1   In what ways does this example of action research differ from the case-study-based research in the previous case illustration?

2   Identify three or four objections that a positivist researcher might have to the action research that has been described in this article.

3   How might some of these objections be overcome?

4   To what extent can action research be undertaken for most student projects?

Feedback notes

There are similarities and differences between the case study and action research strategies. Both utilise a range of different types of data (qualitative and quantitative) to inform the research process although the main emphasis is likely to be on qualitative data. Both strategies are also situationally specific.

The main areas of difference are that action research is firmly grounded in problem-solving, the aim of the research being to understand and to promote change. The researcher is thus part of a continuous cycle of planning, taking action, observation and reflection. As such the researcher is involved in the situations being researched and is part of a cycle of improvement that may continue indefinitely.

Criticisms of action research (see, for example, Gummesson, 1991; Adelman, 1989) highlight the potential influence of the context of a problem or opportunity such that researchers may uncritically accept the dominant assumptions, theories and ways of thinking within the organisation(s). Action research is also seen as being descriptive and exploratory, and does not explain why things are the way they are (Neumann, 2003). Like the case study approach, action research is centred in the organisation and is even involved in the organisational change process, so it is almost impossible to refute or critique. It is therefore difficult to assess its value. Could there have been a better outcome? Were the most appropriate decisions actually made?

Practical disadvantages of action research

- time duration – The action research methodology requires continuous involvement in planning, taking action, observing the effects, and reflecting (often two or three times round the complete cycle). It is unlikely that a student project, as part of a taught qualification-based course, would extend over a sufficient period.

- transparency of research process and outcomes – A major reason for undertaking research in HR is to expand knowledge and understanding of particular organisational phenomena. If the way that action research is undertaken tends to be limited to the pragmatic and commonsense level, it may be difficult to communicate the outcomes of the project outside the organisation.

Planning to implement your research strategy

It is important to be clear about the overall strategy of your project, but as the brief overview of different strategies indicates, there may be considerable overlap and it may well be that some combination of strategies is most appropriate for your project. The broad approach that you adopt, however, will influence the decisions you go on to make about what sort of data to try to gather and where to obtain it.

Before making a final decision about a research topic and strategy, therefore, the questions below might be usefully answered.

- Will you be able to access the data that you need to implement your strategy?
- Do you have the skills (or can you develop the skills) required to collect the data you need, and to analyse it?
- How will your strategy and methods affect the answers that you get?
- How will you (your position in the organisation, preconceptions, etc) affect the research?

ACCESS TO DATA

HR research involves gaining access at three main levels. First, you have to get access to an organisation (or group of organisations). Then you need access to relevant people in the organisation to enable primary data to be gathered. Third, you require access to sources of secondary data from those organisation(s). (See Chapter 1 for definitions and explanations of primary and secondary data.)

Access is a critical aspect of all projects, the difficulty of which is often underestimated by many students. It is important to gain access to participants who are really willing to co-operate, rather than to those whose initial interest fades away rather quickly. It will also be differently undertaken depending on the current position of the researcher, who may be:

- a part-time HR student in employment in the organisation to be investigated
- a full-time HR student who also works part-time in one or more organisations
- a full-time HR student using a work placement organisation for his or her research
- an HR student (full- or part-time) with no current employing organisation
- an experienced practitioner undertaking a form of assessment of professional competence.

Access as an outsider

'Cold calling'

Although difficult, this is not impossible – but access may be time-consuming to achieve and may take many weeks to arrange. Most students find that written requests for access go unanswered and that several telephone calls or e-mail messages, once you have established who is the appropriate person to contact, are required.

Using your networks

Contacting an organisation with which you already have some form of connection is more likely to be successful. Gaining access to organisations through the employers of colleagues on your course, or members of the local branch of the CIPD, for example, is often possible. Sometimes it is necessary to ask your existing contact to introduce you to a more relevant contact within his or her organisation.

Before attempting contact with an organisation it is important to be clear about the aims and purpose of your project and what sort of data you might be seeking to collect (interviews, surveys, observation, etc). Once contact has been established you should also be prepared to negotiate on issues like sample size, interview structure, and so on.

ACTIVITY – GETTING PERMISSION

Imagine that you are the HR manager of a medium-sized organisation. You have been contacted by someone who is the friend of one of your employees. He is an HR student and he wants to undertake his research project on the reward management strategy of your organisation.

Write down a list of about five objections that you might have to allowing him access to your organisation.

Feedback notes

It is very possible that you could list far more than five concerns you might have in this situation. Such concerns might include:

- What would this project involve?

- Would you have to release sensitive data?
- How much 'poking around' would this person want to undertake?
- What disruption might there be to normal operations?
- Could employees be unsettled if the report was critical of your organisation's approach?
- Are there any public relations issues?
- How confidential would the information be?
- Would employees expect enhanced pay as a result of a project like this?
- How competent is the person to undertake such a project?

It would be difficult to gain access to this organisation unless most of these concerns can be allayed. It is therefore important to sell the idea of the project in an effective way. Some ideas on how to go about achieving this are listed below.

- Communicate clearly the purpose of your project, the type of access that you want and the sort of data that you are hoping to gather.
- Indicate the time commitment of those in the organisation who might contribute to your research (how many interviews? of what duration? who with? how many people to be surveyed? what documents to be analysed?)
- Be aware of organisational sensitivities – if management think you are going to highlight all the weaknesses in the organisation's approach and none of its strengths, they are unlikely to let you in.
- Be clear about how you propose to ensure confidentiality and anonymity of the organisation and individuals within it.
- Sell the benefits of the research – how it will help the organisation cope better with HR issues in the future, the useful feedback (copy of your report, and so on) that you will provide for the organisation.
- Use the language of business, rather than the language of academics.
- Be prepared to develop access on an incremental basis. Perhaps get permission for a short questionnaire first. Provide some feedback based on this and then get agreement for some structured interviews of key people. Then indicate how helpful it would be to be able to read the notes of relevant meetings, and so on. If you undertake the first stage in a sloppy way you are unlikely to be allowed to continue. Once your credibility is demonstrated, however, and you are successful in building good relationships within the organisation, there is more chance that you will be granted further access.

Access as an insider

Many people will undertake their projects in the organisation of which they are already a part, whether on a full- or a part-time basis. In this sense, physical access is easier, although what is really required for an effective project is support and acceptance.

The main advantage for insider researchers is, of course, that they already know the politics of the organisation, and who best to approach for different types of data. Hopefully they will also have some organisational credibility. There are a number of difficulties, however, that practitioner-researchers have to take into account:

- detaching yourself as a researcher from your role as a practitioner
- the dynamics of interviewing colleagues who know you and are known by you
- handling confidential disclosures that may affect your future working relationships
- living with the consequences of any mistakes that you make.

Planning and preparing for an enquiry in your own organisation requires just as much thought as for one with which you have limited contact. Important elements of the access process are listed below.

- Establish appropriate points of contact (not just your manager).

- Produce an outline of your proposed project and get it cleared at all necessary levels in the organisation (you don't want your questionnaire blocked by the MD just two days before you plan to issue it).

- Be honest with yourself and others about the purpose of the study and the data you need in order to achieve your objectives.

- Discuss your project with 'gatekeepers' (heads of department, managers, union reps, etc) and try to anticipate possible sensitive issues and areas.

- Discuss your study with participants. They will be more likely to co-operate if you inform them what is to be done with the information they provide.

- Be aware of the needs of those in the organisation with regard to politics, confidentiality and sensitivity. Decide what you mean by 'anonymity' and 'confidentiality'.

Many of the issues raised with negotiating access also relate to issues of ethics in research – to which this chapter now turns.

ETHICAL IMPLICATIONS FOR RESEARCH ACTIVITIES

There are a range of ethical issues that have to be taken into account when considering HR research. Ethics has been defined as a 'code of behaviour in relation to the rights of those who become the subject of your work or are affected by it' (Wells, 1994; p.284). All research enquiries, whatever discipline they are based in (marketing, medicine, etc), need to work within general principles of acceptable behaviour and practice. For those interested in the HR implications of organisational issues, there are particular tensions to be taken into account. With applied research, for example, the researcher will be closely involved with individuals in a range of organisational 'real-life' situations. In addition, HR practitioners have to take the power relationships of the organisation into account. Whereas the enquiry process may be a 'project' for the researcher, those who have been 'researched' will have to live with the consequences of it in the longer term.

The CIPD has a general Code of Professional Conduct for all members that includes some important ethical principles relevant to HR research:

- accuracy of information
- confidentiality of personal information
- equal opportunities and non-discriminatory practices
- fair dealing in the treatment of individuals.

All HR research projects should include an explicit explanation of the way in which ethical issues have been considered throughout the duration of the project. Five ethical principles, that build on the CIPD Code, should underpin the process from the beginning to its conclusion.

HR research should be undertaken in a way that:

■ is professional and responsible (takes account of privacy and confidentiality)
■ collects data in an appropriate way
■ involves informed consent by those being researched
■ does not involve deception
■ is carefully interpreted.

Three stages of the research process have ethical implications (Saunders *et al*, 2003):

■ the consideration of initial research design and access issues
■ obtaining information of good quality
■ interpreting the information and formulating conclusions.

Research design and initial access

The main issues here are of consent and privacy. It is inappropriate to put undue pressure on intended participants to grant access. If you are an internal practitioner-researcher, managers will be able to give or withhold permission for your project. However, it is important not to subject colleagues or subordinates to pressure to co-operate. It is also important to consider issues of privacy if you plan to approach them to request their co-operation outside normal working hours. Privacy issues also come to the fore where you plan to make use of secondary data held within the organisation.

It is also essential to make sure, from the research design process onwards, that participants are able to give informed (rather than implied) consent. This involves clearly communicating the scope and intention of the project to participants so that they are clear about:

■ the nature of the research – its purpose and progress
■ expectations of participants – the type of data to be collected and the methods of collection
■ the implications of participating – the possibility of withdrawing at any time from what is entirely voluntary participation; the approaches to be taken with regard to anonymity and confidentiality
■ the subsequent use of data – who will have access to it, how results will be communicated, and what will happen after the project has been completed.

The data-collection process

In addition to principles described with regard to research design and initial access there are further ethical issues to consider when undertaking data collection.

■ objectivity – How will you make sure that your data is collected accurately and that the possibility of subjective bias is minimised as far as possible?

- confidentiality and anonymity – If you are gathering qualitative data, how will you ensure that the data is not only accurate but untraceable to individuals?
- fair treatment – In interview situations it is important not to ask questions that might put a participant under undue pressure or might diminish his or her self-esteem.
- privacy – If you are undertaking observation, what permissions will you first obtain? Perhaps after the observation processes it would be appropriate to undertake a debriefing with the participant(s).

When thinking through these issues it is important to consider the level of trust and confidence that your intended participants will have in you. This will be affected by the nature of the power-relationship you have at present with them, as well as the organisational culture and management style of the organisation in which your research is to be conducted.

Interpreting data and formulating conclusions

Key issues here are accuracy and objectivity, as well as confidentiality and anonymity. This may apply to individuals who participated in the research but also to the organisation(s) in which it was based. Can you use the organisational name(s) in your project report? To what extent might your analysis be used to adversely affect the collective interests of your participants?

Ethical issues for practitioner researchers

Clearly the issues described above are pertinent to all types of projects, but ethical concerns can be rather less clear-cut for practitioner-researchers undertaking action-oriented projects. Key principles that may be helpful in this context are:

- Make sure that all relevant permissions have been gained before commencing the project.
- Involve participants – encourage them to shape the form of your enquiry.
- Be prepared to negotiate access with individuals – don't assume it will be given.
- Be open about your progress so that any concerns can be taken into account.
- Never undertake observation without the explicit permission of the observed.
- Get permission before you examine or copy files, correspondence or other organisational documents.
- Report back to participants your accounts of interviews and observations of them, and allow them to suggest amendments which enhance fairness, accuracy and relevance.
- Take responsibility for maintaining confidentiality.

FINAL PREPARATIONS – PROJECT PLANNING

Unlike many other features of taught courses in HR, the research project or management report is a piece of independent work, undertaken with the benefit of the guidance and advice of a supervisor, tutor or adviser. Responsibility for planning your project so that you can be sure to submit work of appropriate quality, on or before the submission date, remains with you. There is more chance that this will be achieved if an effective 'project management' approach is adopted (Marchington and Wilkinson, 2002).

The main skills of project management, of course, once the project has been designed, are those of breaking the project down into a series of tasks and milestones in order to establish

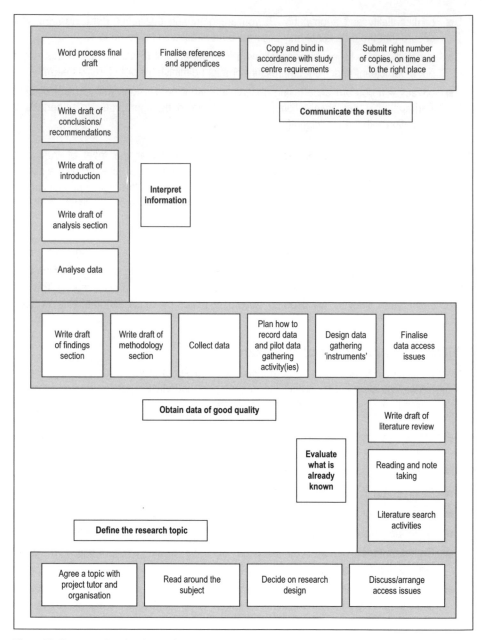

Figure 10 *The research project 'journey'*

an outline plan. Because you will be working independently, you will have more control over the tasks and the way they are carried out. The disadvantage of this is that many elements of the project cannot be carried out in parallel, and so linear time planning is required.

As a result a process of estimating time requirements for different stages of the research project process, and scheduling in activities to achieve elements of it, is necessary. It is important that estimates of time and effort are both honest and reasonable. Experience of writing up a coursework assignment might be used to estimate the time required for writing up one section of your final report, for example.

A typical list of tasks that comprise the 'journey' to a completed research project is shown as Figure 10.

Having identified the various tasks it is important to allocate appropriate time slots in which to carry them out. At this stage it may become clear that other activities, both at home and at work, may be affected, and you will need to discuss this with those involved in order to overcome any potential difficulties. Some tasks can be undertaken in parallel (such as the initial drafting of the literature review and drafting a questionnaire or carrying out some initial interviews), and this is a good opportunity to work out how you wish to proceed.

Monitoring progress

As with all projects, it is important to go public with the project plan in order that any significant errors of estimation can be discussed, any logistical oversights can be incorporated (your sister's wedding – no study that weekend!), and so that those around you, at your study centre, your workplace (where appropriate) and your family and friends, are aware of your commitments. Progress meetings with your manager (where the project is organisationally-based) and your project tutor or adviser will also be an important way to gauge whether you ought to revise the plan.

SUMMARY

- Studying recent HR journals, reviewing past assignments, assessing topics that other students have studied and (where appropriate) identifying key HR issues for your employing organisation are all ways to trigger initial ideas for an enquiry.

- An appropriate research topic will meet the different expectations of: the student, the employing organisation(s) involved, the study centre, and, where appropriate, relevant professional institutions.

- Investigative enquiries must be focused so that the aim and purpose of the project are clear and research questions or research objectives are formulated accordingly.

- There are advantages and disadvantages to both positivist and interpretivist approaches to research. Most, but not all, organisationally-based HR projects tend to work from more of an interpretivist approach.

- Research design involves deciding on an overall research strategy as well as considering how to implement it.

- Most HR organisationally-based enquiries adopt either a survey, case study or action research strategy (or a combination).

- HR research involves gaining access at three levels to organisation(s), people and documents. In addition to physical access, support and acceptance is important for effective research to be undertaken.

- Ethics in research involves following codes of behaviour in relation to the rights of those who may be subjects as well as those who may be affected by the research. Ethical issues must be considered at the research design stage as well as the data-collection, analysis and communication stages.

- HR research should accord with ethical principles of privacy, confidentiality, anonymity, accuracy, objectivity and fair treatment.

- Outline project planning involves breaking the research process down into stages and tasks, scheduling those tasks, and monitoring progress on a regular basis.

Questions for review/reflection

As with Chapter 1, these questions are designed to enable you to identify key areas for development with your project. The answers to them can also form part of a CPD portfolio or log. This is a requirement of the CIPD for those wishing to upgrade their membership status.

Taking stock

1 How much time is left until your project must be completed and submitted? What are likely to be the main stages of your project? How long will you have to complete each of them? How, and with whom, will you monitor your progress?

2 If you have not yet determined your project, identify three possible research ideas. For each of them write down **three** advantages/disadvantages. Make sure you take account of the perspective of yourself, your study centre and (where appropriate) your employing organisation, in the advantages and disadvantages that you identify. Who might you also consult in the process of identifying a research idea?

3 Write down the main features of positivist and interpretivist research approaches. Which approach seems the most appropriate for you, and why? What are the implications of this for your choice of a research strategy?

4 Write a summary (no more than three sentences for each) of the four research strategies (experiment, case study, survey, action research). Which strategy is most attractive to you, and why?

Strengths and weaknesses

1 How clear are you about the aims of your potential project? What do you need to read in order to identify key concepts, issues and contexts? Who might you discuss your research ideas with?

2 What will be the main challenges for you with regard to access to organisation(s), people and documents? What skills and behaviours will you need to develop to overcome those challenges? What opportunities does your current situation afford for access to people and data?

Being a practitioner-researcher

1 How might your position in the organisation affect, and be affected by, the research project you plan to conduct? What are the implications of your role for the research strategy that you are considering?

2 What ethical issues must you consider with regard to obtaining informed consent, ensuring privacy for potential participants and maintaining confidentiality of sensitive documents? How will you communicate the outcome of your reflections about ethical issues to those involved (as sponsors or subjects) of the research?

FURTHER READING

BELL, J. (2001) *Doing Your Research Project*. Buckingham, Open University Press.

BELL, J. and OPIE, C. (2002) *Learning From Research*. Buckingham, Open University Press.

BRYMAN, A. (ed.) (1988) *Doing Research in Organisations*. London, Routledge.

COGHLAN, D. and BRANNICK, T. (2001) *Doing Action Research in Your Own Organisation*. London, Sage.

CUNNINGHAM, J. B. (1995) 'Strategic considerations in using action research for improving personnel practices', *Public Personnel Management*, 24 (2) 515–29.

GILL, J. and JOHNSON, P. (2001) *Research Methods for Managers*. London, Paul Chapman.

JANKOWICZ, A. D. (2000) *Business Research Projects for Students*. London, Chapman & Hall.

MCNIFF, J. (1988) *Action Research: Principles and practice*. Basingstoke, Macmillan.

NEUMAN, W. (2003) *Social Research Methods: Qualitative and quantitative methods*. Boston, Wiley.

OJA, S. N. and SMULYAN, L. (1989) *Collaborative Action Research: A developmental approach*. London, Falmer.

ROBSON, C. (2002) *Real World Research: A resource for social scientists and practitioner-researchers*. Oxford, Blackwell.

SAUNDERS, M., LEWIS, P. and THORNHILL, A. (2003) *Research Methods for Business Students*. London, *Financial Times*/Pitman.

ZUBER-SKERRITT, O. (ed.) (1996) *New Directions in Action Research*. London, Falmer.

Reviewing and evaluating existing knowledge

Chapter outline

How to use this chapter
Why read, when to read, and what to read
Different types of literature
Searching for and finding appropriate sources
Reading the literature and making notes
Evaluation and analysis
The structure of the literature review
Referencing your work
Summary
Further reading

LEARNING OUTCOMES

This chapter should help you to:

■ **identify what you need to read and find out where to get hold of it**

■ **undertake an effective literature search**

■ **establish an effective note-taking/recording system**

■ **read in a critically evaluative way**

■ **plan and structure your literature review.**

HOW TO USE THIS CHAPTER

This chapter focuses on the requirement in all projects linked to qualifications for a review of the literature to be undertaken. Many students struggle to find the time to keep up with their 'normal' coursework, let alone undertake the work for their research project. You may well feel that the literature review is a chore to be minimised as far as possible. This chapter sets out to show how a good review of 'what is already known' can add value to the enquiry you are engaged with. It also aims to help you to work in a time-effective way to find and read appropriate materials and to write up a literature review section of good quality for your final report.

Different parts of this chapter are relevant to different people and different stages of the research process. The second and third sections (see the list in the *Chapter outline* above) introduce the terrain. If you are not confident about paper-based and electronic literature search processes, the fourth section is helpful. If you find note-taking a challenge, then focus on the fifth section. If feedback on previous assignments has suggested that your work is too descriptive, the ideas about assessing materials in an analytical and evaluative way in the sixth section should help. The seventh section focuses on how to structure the literature review part of your report. This may well be a section that you skim through now, but come back to as you begin to draft that part of your report.

Case illustration

From topic to literature review

Grace was a full-time 'overseas' HR student, studying in the UK. She came from the Philippines. As a result of some coursework early in her studies she became interested in equal opportunities in management, and in particular in the concept of the 'glass ceiling' as it related to women managers. When the time came to choose a subject for her research project she wanted to investigate the extent to which the glass ceiling was an issue for women in management in the Philippines. Because she had some contacts already 'at home' who were managers in organisations, she decided to focus her investigation on the extent to which the concept of the glass ceiling adequately described the experiences and expectations of women managers in the Philippines.

DISCUSSION QUESTIONS

1 What topics would Grace need to read up on in order to make progress with this project?

2 What difficulties might she face?

Feedback notes

A person in Grace's position might feel rather fortunate with regard to the literature review. She had, after all, completed an initial assignment on equal opportunities and women managers, and had a fair grasp of the book literature in this area. Indeed, at first Grace believed that all she now needed to do was to visit 'home' to gather some data from her contacts to complement her existing knowledge. Her project idea, however, incorporated more than just the glass ceiling. As her work progressed, Grace realised that although she had extensive anecdotal knowledge of the Philippines, it was difficult to evaluate such knowledge in an objective way without access to wider sources of information about its political, economic and social context. In addition, she came to realise that business in the Philippines was another area about which she needed a greater understanding.

Other challenges that faced Grace were:

- Although she had already undertaken some reading about the glass ceiling, new material was being published all the time and it was hard to pick out what was most useful.

- The library of the UK Business School where Grace was based was well resourced with regard to materials related to equal opportunities and women in management. The library resources were more limited with regard to business and management in the Philippines, however.

- Information relevant to her project – about women managers, equal opportunities, the culture and environment of the Philippines, and so on – could be found in a range of different types of writing, from articles in newspapers and trade journals to less reader-friendly and more academic publications such as refereed journal articles, scholarly books and monographs. Grace's challenge was to know what was most relevant and useful.

Many people are worried by the requirement to review the literature. The amount of written material around seems to be limitless, and assessing its relevance for a potential project seems difficult. The range of different types of material is also extensive and many investigative practitioners are unsure about what the 'best' types are. This chapter addresses some of these difficulties.

WHY READ, WHEN TO READ, AND WHAT TO READ
Why read?

A key feature of any project is to demonstrate an awareness of how your project fits into the wider context of theory and practice in HR. The length and extent of the literature review varies depending on the nature of the qualification (undergraduate, postgraduate diploma, master's, etc) as well as the assessment criteria used by different centres of study. However, for all projects an initial evaluation of what is known, and an assessment of how your findings either confirm or vary from the practice and thinking of others, is a vital component.

In fact there are a range of benefits that will occur once you start the reading process.

- getting ideas for your project – By reading around a topic you can see how other people have tackled similar investigations. You can also get a feel for the sort of views that are relevant to your topic, particularly views that might not be expressed in an everyday work or managerial environment. In this way you can generate fresher or more interesting ideas and you should be able to clarify your initial thoughts about the way forward with your enquiry.

- developing a framework for analysis – Later in the project, when you have gathered some data, you will have to interpret and analyse it. In order to do this effectively you will need to know what the key issues and concepts are, and how they relate to each other.

- collecting secondary data – Reading around the subject might also reveal relevant secondary data. This might include examples of other organisations in a similar position to yours or numerical data that is useful for comparative or benchmarking purposes.

When to read

Start reading as soon as you have some ideas about your project topic. This will help you to establish the scope of your topic and decide what particular aspects of it are most relevant for your project. The reading process underpins the planning processes of your project.

Once you have come up with some initial research questions and/or objectives, further reading will help you to clarify the main issues and concepts so that the primary data you gather covers all the important aspects. New sources of information are always becoming available, and research into HR operates in a context of development and change. It is likely, therefore, that your project will be influenced by what you read as an ongoing process. Although you should undertake most of your reading early on, you will not stop reading until the project report is submitted.

What to read

Broadly speaking, you can divide the sources of information about 'what is already known' (the literature) into two types.

- primary literature sources – Most of these come from within the organisation(s) you are studying. They will mostly be 'unpublished' – for example, internal reports and e-mail correspondence. Documents that are more widely available in the public domain but nonetheless are not widely read (such as company reports, etc) may also be considered to be primary literature sources, as would other 'unpublished' items, such as the dissertation or project reports of others who have researched a similar topic.

- secondary literature sources – What is already known at a more general level about your topic will be found in more widely available published sources such as books, newspaper articles or reports, features and articles in journals, or as information contained on Internet sites.

Although the distinction between these two types of source is not always clear-cut, this chapter focuses mostly on the issues involved in making effective use of published, secondary sources. Obtaining and using primary sources are covered in Chapter 5.

DIFFERENT TYPES OF LITERATURE

ACTIVITY – DIFFERENT TYPES OF LITERATURE

Imagine that you have decided to undertake research on the effectiveness of the graduate training and development programme of an organisation. This might be your own organisation, or you might be interested in a study of graduate training and development programmes more generally. You need to read around to inform the enquiry that you will undertake and to provide you with a framework by which to analyse your data.

DISCUSSION QUESTIONS

In addition to the study of documents available within the organisation(s) you are researching, what other sources will be useful to you in establishing what is already known about graduate training and development schemes?

For each of the sources that you identify list **at least** one advantage and one limitation of it as a basis for establishing 'what is already known'.

How can you access the relevant parts of each source without having to read everything?

Feedback notes

You can probably identify a range of different sources that will help you to find out more about graduate training and development schemes. From time to time, particularly in the summer and autumn, newspapers publish articles about features of graduate training schemes. In addition to widely published news articles you are likely to find information and views about graduate development schemes in a range of trade or professional journals. These include publications such as *People Management*, but other specialist areas (by sector and professional role) have their own journals, such as *Hotel and Catering*, *Health Service Management*, *Accounting Weekly*, *Management Today*, and so on.

There is also likely to be some helpful material in a range of books. Some general HR textbooks contain materials on graduate schemes, usually as a part of a wider coverage of management development. Other books that focus more specifically on management development might devote a chapter or so to graduate schemes. Specialist monographs or published reports on graduate schemes are also available from, for example, the Association of Graduate Recruiters.

Another important source of information is relevant articles in academic journals, such as the *Human Resource Management Journal*, the *Journal of Management Studies* and the *Journal of Management Development*. They provide information that is the result of careful research and academic consideration, and usually incorporate a thorough review of the literature. As a result these articles are useful not only for their content but also for the list of references they provide, some of which you may wish to follow up for your project.

Finally, it is possible that another student at your study centre, or at your work-place, has carried out an investigation into broadly the same area as part of a course of study that he or she has undertaken. The dissertation, thesis or project report that he or she has produced may also be a useful source of information about what is already known.

An overview of different types of sources (primary and secondary) is shown in Figure 11.

Assessing the value of different sources

Many of the weaker student projects focus their attention on the literature towards the middle of the circles shown in Figure 11 and would benefit from an assessment of the value of a wider range of types of literature.

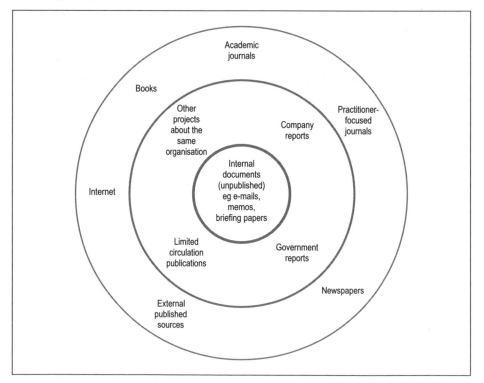

Figure 11 *Different types of literature*

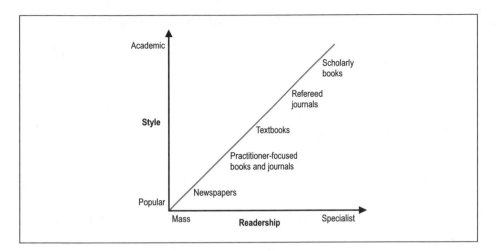

Figure 12 *Different approaches underpinning different types of literature*

When evaluating different sources of information, it is important to identify the main audience that they would have been written for and the style of communication that is appropriate for that readership (see Figure 12). A newspaper article, for example, aims to provide interest for a wide cross-section of the general population and is produced in line with an editorial policy (or position). Issues are thus covered very generally, and the article may not explore all the possible interpretations of what is being described.

Articles in trade or professional journals, although accessible in reading terms, also tend to reflect particular editorial beliefs and priorities and may not consider all possible perspectives. Articles in refereed journal articles, by contrast, while providing a good framework of analysis and critique, may seem more remote from your particular interest, and reading them may be hard work as a result of the careful and evaluative style of writing that is necessary if a full consideration of a range of factors is to be included in the analysis. Although harder work to read, however, they can provide a useful basis for critical and evaluative thinking to enable you to carry out an investigative enquiry that probes and analyses the underlying causes and issues relevant to HR problems or opportunities.

SEARCHING FOR AND FINDING APPROPRIATE LITERATURE SOURCES

The volume of available information made possible with the development of modern IT systems can make the identification of relevant material seem overwhelmingly difficult, and an effective *literature search and selection* process is essential.

Literature searching: starting from textbooks and other projects

ACTIVITY – FIRST STEPS IN FINDING LITERATURE

Imagine that you have decided to undertake research loosely connected with partnership agreements between employers and trade unions. Obtain three to four textbooks that contain chapters with some material relevant to this subject. Study the 'Further reading', 'Bibliography' or 'References' section relating to these relevant chapters and identify articles or books that may be useful for the investigation.

1 Produce a list of five or six possibly relevant sources of information.

2 Explain why it might be necessary to read some of these articles and books, rather than relying on the coverage in the chapters in the textbooks.

Feedback notes

If you have undertaken this Activity (which you could do for any topic) and made a list of possible sources of information, you will find a variety of articles, books and websites that reflect the different preferences of the textbook authors. For this topic these might include:

■ Coupar, W. and Stevens, B. (1998) 'Towards a new model of industrial partnership: beyond the HRM versus industrial relations debate', in P. Sparrow and M. Marchington (eds) *Human Resource Management: The new agenda*. London, *Financial Times*/Pitman.

■ Ewing, K. (2002) 'Industrial relations and labour law', in P. Ackers and A. Wilkinson (eds) *Reworking Industrial Relations*. Oxford, OUP.

■ Guest, D. and Peccei, R. (2001) 'Partnership at work: mutuality and the balance of advantage', *British Journal of Industrial Relations*, 39 (2) 207–36.

■ Haynes, P. and Allen, M. (2001) 'Partnership as union strategy: a preliminary analysis', *Employee Relations*, 23 (2) 164–87.

■ Industrial Relations Services (2002) 'When all else fails', *Employment Review*, No. 719, January, pp.12–16.

■ Institute of Personnel and Development (1998) *Employment Relations into the 21st Century: An IPD position paper*. London, IPD.

■ Millward, N., Bryson, A. and Forth, J. (2002) *All Change at Work?* London, Routledge.

■ Stuart, M. and Martinez-Lucion (eds) (2004) *Partnership and Modernisation in Employment Relations*. London, Routledge.

■ Trades Union Congress, *Partners for Progress: New Unionism in the Workplace*. London, TUC.

This approach can provide you with a list of useful sources that should afford you an initial overview of the main issues in the topic you want to think about. When you are short of time, there is a big temptation not to bother with this process and to 'just' read the information in a few textbooks on the topic you are interested in. However, there are potential dangers with this not-so-short cut. Textbooks are of limited value for an investigative enquiry because the authors have to describe a wide range of material in a generalised way. As a result there is limited scope for a deeper level of examination. An understanding of the main issues relevant to any project topic therefore requires a fuller reading of the texts that the author of the textbook will have briefly summarised. Those who mark your project will be looking to see if you have used sources that are not 'derivative'.

Finding other sources of information: clarifying what resources are available

As you continue with your literature search, find out where information might be most easily available. The main options are:

- university or study centre library – Find out what books and journals are held in the main library that you use, and how to use the library catalogue system. The books and many of the journals will be available in paper format but it is likely that you can access a wide range of other journals and newspapers electronically as a result of arrangements the library already has in place. Make sure you know how to reserve copies of books should they not be immediately available.

- other libraries and inter-library loan facilities – Find out if your study centre has any reciprocal arrangements that enable you to use the resources of libraries of other campuses or institutions. Most libraries operate an inter-library loan (ILL) system for students undertaking projects such that if they do not have a copy of a book or article that is required, they can obtain it for a short period of time (and at a price) from another library. Find out in advance what your entitlement might be to the inter-library loan facility (often students have a fixed allocation of ILLs).

- access to professional libraries – Many HR practitioners, when surveying the literature, will want to make use of a specialised library collection such as that provided for members by the CIPD or the Institute of Management.

- remote access to electronic resources – All libraries now have facilities enabling registered users to gain electronic access to the full text of articles or to abstracts (summaries). Once you know how to do this it is easily achieved from within the library itself. It is also possible to access the resources from a PC outside the institution provided that you can prove you are an academic user from a study centre that is registered with the provider. To do this you need to obtain an ATHENS password, which you cite when accessing material from the relevant databases. You must get this in advance from your study centre library.

Electronic searching

Electronic search engines have become vital ways of finding further sources of information for projects. There are a range of options, from general searches on the Internet as a whole, to more specialised searches utilising academic 'information gateways'. For many, the temptation is to start 'broad' and then narrow down the focus of a search. This can be very time-consuming, however, and if time is precious, it is better to start with the more specialised search processes and then broaden the search only if you feel you need further information.

Academic journal databases

The seven-step model shown in Figure 13 should provide a basis for a reasonable search of literature using academic databases.

1 Identify/generate key words. If you have already done a little reading around (as outlined above), this should not be too difficult. Talk through your ideas with your colleagues, supervisor, adviser, tutor, and so on. Aim for four to six key words or phrases.

2 Define the parameters. A search with the key word 'performance', for example, is likely to bring a multitude of extracts relating to financial performance and

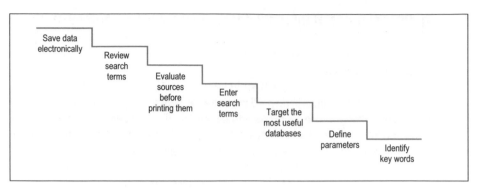

Figure 13 *Seven steps to a literature search*

accountancy rather than anything to do with HR. It is important to include the terms 'personnel' or 'human resources' within your combination of key words. Also establish whether you wish to limit your search to sources that are from the UK and also to sources published in the previous five years.

3   Target the most useful databases. Find out which CD-ROM or online databases and electronic journal collections are available to you. Your library will have information on how to operate these and will also tell you what passwords are required. If possible, persuade a librarian to demonstrate how to do a search with you (you could use your key words).

If you can, start the search process on the library premises. That way, if you have initial problems, you can get help. Also the expense of a trial-and-error process of

Table 4 *Some useful databases for HR research*

Database/electronic journal collection	Comments
ABI/Inform	An index of about 1,000 international business and management journals as well as the full text of some articles. The database also covers non-business publications, however, so be careful with the parameters that you set.
Anbar	Provides abstracts of English-language articles, rated according to their 'contribution to knowledge'.
Emerald	Provides abstracts and/or full text articles (depending on the level of subscription) to a range of MCB publications (that include a range of HR-related journals).
SwetsWise	A search engine for electronic journals (that includes Emerald). It is possible to use key word searches as well as searching for specific journal titles.
Business Source Premier/Business Source Elite	A full text database containing business journals covering management, economics, finance, accounting and international business. The range of publications for which full text access is provided depends on the level of the subscription.

getting used to the different online databases is not yours! Once you know what to do, you may prefer to work 'remotely'. Table 4 shows a selection of useful databases for HR research purposes.

4   Enter search terms. Select 'sort by date' if possible because you need to access literature that is both relevant and up to date. Use link terms such as 'and', 'or' and 'not' to make your search more effective. Also make use of the * truncation term and the ? wild card term to enable the search to include different forms of the same word – eg human resourc* should result in a selection of articles with human resource and human resources in the text, and organi?ation will select organisation and organization.

5   Evaluate sources before printing them. Where possible, establish the usefulness of potential sources before you go to the time, trouble and expense of printing them. Always read the abstract first to identify whether the article is likely to be useful.

6   Review search terms. If your search words are bringing up too many possible hits, change the parameters of the search to select articles with the key words in the abstract, rather than in the article.

7   Save data electronically. If your search generates a number of articles which you wish to print, it might be more effective either to save them to a disk or to e-mail them to a more suitable address, from which you can print them at a more convenient time.

If your search generates articles for which the full text is not available electronically, it is likely that you can obtain a hard copy either through your own library or from another library. Where this is the case, and your library does not have an SFX system, you must note down the exact reference of the article you need (author, title of article, title of journal, issue number, volume, year of publication). This can be time-consuming if done manually, and saving the reference electronically is probably preferable.

Other Internet sources

Having scoured the journals you may feel that there are other resources that could be useful. To find books that are still in print and are relevant to your topic you might search the databases

Table 5 *Some useful HR electronic gateways*

Gateway	URL
Chartered Institute of Personnel and Development	www.cipd.co.uk
Biz – Human Resources Management	www.thebiz.co.uk
HRM Guide Network	www.hrmguide.net
Human resource links to Strathclyde University	www.hrm.strath.ac.uk/links/index.htm
Natlex	http://natlex.ilo.org
Nottingham Trent University	www.nbs.ntu.ac.uk/depts/hrm_link.htm

Sources of information derived from official publications can be found at sites such as those in Table 6, and sources of information about companies are indicated in Table 7.

Table 6 *Some sites for sources of information from official publications*

Name	URL
Ukonline	www.ukonline.gov.uk
Central Office of Information	www.coi.gov.uk
Her Majesty's Stationery Office	www.hmso.gov.uk
Official Documents	www.official-documents.co.uk

Table 7 *Sources of information about companies*

Name	Notes	URL
CAROL	Corporate online service with annual reports covering UK, Europe and Asia	http://www.carol.co.uk
Companies House	Basic information available via Free Company Information link	www.companies-house.gov.uk
Corporate Information	Over 3 million company profiles: searches through search engines	www.corporateinformation.com
Corporate Reports	Company reports and accounts: search by company name or sector; free registration	www.corpreports.co.uk
Financial Times	Key financial data for 20,000 limited companies worldwide	www.ft.com
Fortune 500	Information on companies in the 'Big 500'	www.fortune.com/fortune
FTSE International	Requires registration but then provides free access to detailed information on FTSE indices and member companies	www.ftse.com
Business.com	One of the most substantial and useful resources for business research and information	www.business.com
Scoot	Over 2 million entries	www.scoot.co.uk
UK Company News	Directory of UK listed companies arranged by sector. Annual/interim reports	www.companynews.co.uk

Table 8 *Sites providing international business/HR information*

Name	Notes	URL
CIA World Factbook	Country profiles which provide geographical and government information as well as key economic indicators	www.odci.gov/cia/publications/factbook
Country Commercial Guides	From the US Department of Commerce, this site looks at the commercial environments of countries using economic, political and market analysis	www.export.gov/commercialservices
IMF country reports	Full text access to country reports	www.imf.org/external/pubs/CAT
International Monetary Fund	IMF statistics and articles, including exchange rates and economic indicators for countries of the world	www.imf.org
Mondaq Business Briefing	Access to world business news pages	www.mondaq.com

of the academic book publishers. The latest addresses for these sites are available from bookshops and are usually prominently displayed on the back cover of other books published by the relevant organisation. Other sources of electronically available information can be accessed through specialist HR gateways such as those shown in Table 5.

If your enquiry requires information about more than one country, information by country is available from sites like those in Table 8.

READING THE LITERATURE AND MAKING NOTES

Once you have obtained some literature, it is important that you actually read it! This can seem to be a very time-consuming process that is difficult to fit in with other commitments. For this reason it is important to develop effective reading and note-taking, and it is this aspect that the chapter now considers.

'Just in time' reading and note-taking

Time is the most precious resource, to a student undertaking a project. There is never enough of it, so it is important that the reading and note-taking is carried out speedily, but effectively. Table 9 lists some ideas that may help you to undertake 'just in time' reading. Your aim is to be able to undertake an initial reading of any source in just five to ten minutes, in order to identify areas that demand more careful attention.

Table 9 *Undertaking 'just-in-time' reading*

Strategy	Notes
Decide on your note-taking system and your filing system in advance	Options include (and preferences vary) for systems such as: card-index system word-processed notes A4 paper collection of photocopies
Make an accurate note of the author, title and other details of the source	See Tables 10 and 11 for information on how to reference your work
If the source is a book, 'speed-read' the introduction and concluding chapter and note down the main points	Read from the author's perspective – don't reject it because it is not the approach you instinctively prefer
If the source is an article, look for the abstract or executive summary as well as for the conclusion. Read them quickly and note down the main points	*as above*
If the source is a book or report, look for the contents page and index	Each chapter or section should have an introduction or conclusion, so start there every time and note down the main points made
Speed-read the text, summarising the main text and highlighting any ideas that might be useful to you	Well-written material will highlight key points in the first and/or last paragraphs of each section. The first or last sentences of each paragraph are likely to be the most useful. Use this to speed up your reading
Make notes on the method as well as the subject	As well as the findings from other research, record the methods used (eg interviews, observation, telephone survey)
Make a clear note of useful quotations	Copy out the quote (or highlight if it is a photocopy) but note down the page number it is on. You will need this to reference the quote when you submit your work
Note down any other sources that you need to follow up	Make full notes of the author, title, publisher and date. Also, prioritise follow-up sources – you may not have time to find all of them
Be prepared to read important sources more thoroughly	Make a clear note of the details of all your sources so that you can find and retrieve the ones you need to read more thoroughly without wasting precious time

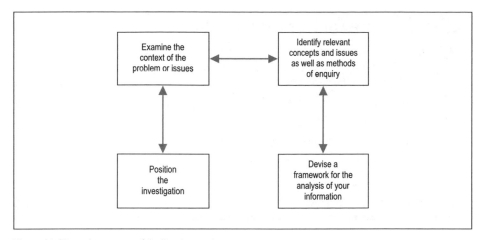

Figure 14 *The main purposes of the literature review*

EVALUATION AND ANALYSIS

As you undertake your reading, it is helpful to keep in mind the main purposes of the literature review (Sharp and Howard, 1996; Gill and Johnson, 2001; Stevens *et al*, 1993; Gall *et al*, 1996), which your notes will help you with. These are shown in Figure 14.

- *Examine the context.* If you are undertaking a project in an organisation that you know well, it is important to understand the influences on the topic you are investigating beyond its immediate priorities. The literature review will help you understand and explain why your project is worthwhile within HR more generally.

- *Identify relevant concepts, issues and methods.* This provides a basis from which to know what data to look for in relation to your investigation.

- *Devise a framework for the analysis of your data.* Obtaining data is the easy part. Knowing how to analyse and interpret it is much harder. Reviewing the literature will help you to devise a framework for the interpretation of the facts that you gather.

- *Position the investigation.* The literature review can demonstrate how your investigative enquiry can add value in a practical way, in terms of the organisation or business sector, as well as in an academic way, through considering important issues in a different way.

Once you start reading and making notes, therefore, you have to consider the information you have found in an analytical way. Merely soaking up and recording facts is not enough; you need also to be an evaluator and a critic. When you are reading, and when you take notes, try to be active in assessing the value of the ideas presented to you, assessing their strengths as well as their weaknesses.

ACTIVITY – READING EVALUATIVELY

Read the following passages, which are extracts from longer articles relating to performance appraisal. For both passages, use some of the tips for 'just in time' reading, but in addition try to answer the following questions:

1   How have key concepts been defined?

2   What variables have the authors identified?

3   What are the limitations of the scope of the enquiries?

4   What assumptions about the issue do the authors seem to work with?

5   What data has been used?

6   How was the data generated?

Extract 1

OUT OF THE TICK BOX

When the former IPM investigated the use of performance management back in 1991, the term was closely associated with performance-related pay (PRP). Ratings were *de rigueur* and appraisal was a top-down process involving unilateral judgements by 'superiors' and their 'subordinates'. Seven years later, the picture is very different.

The latest research from the IPD has found that the process is now much more closely linked to employee development and that many organisations are trying to distance it from pay decisions. . . .

Our findings are based on a survey of more than 550 personnel practitioners, visits to 35 organisations and discussions with 12 focus groups of line managers and staff in six organisations. We also undertook six attitude surveys of employees on the receiving end of performance management, and ran two telephone surveys: one on 360-degree feedback and the other on training in performance management processes and skills. In addition, we interviewed a number of management consultants, union officials and commentators. . . .

Ever since Michael Beer and Robert Ruh coined the term in 1970s, the meaning of 'performance management' has been ambiguous. For the purposes of our study, we developed the following working definition: 'A strategic and integrated approach to increasing the effectiveness of organisations by improving the performance of the people who work in them and by developing the capabilities of teams and individual contributors.'

But this statement is a generalisation. Performance management processes take many different forms. The approach will depend on the context of the organisation: its culture, structure and technology, as well as the views of its stakeholders, the work carried out and the type of people involved. Despite this, we were able to spot some trends among the employers we studied. . . .

In the past appraisal tended to be a bureaucratic system, imposed on line managers by the personnel department. Everyone had to conform to the same procedure and the most important output was a set of ticks on an elaborate form that, once completed, was forgotten about unless it was used to determine the size of someone's pay rise.

Since then, there has been a move to cut the red tape. Performance management is now recognised as a tool for managers to use with their team members, but adapted to fit their own circumstances. The emphasis is placed more on how performance is managed rather than on the outcomes. ...

It is often assumed that most line managers think that performance management is a waste of time, and that if they do it at all, they do it badly. It is also widely held that employees are hostile to the process and feel demotivated by it. Our focus groups and attitude surveys did reveal a dislike for ratings and for linking the process to pay, but most comments were otherwise favourable. ...

These positive responses had caused us to hope that we could establish a link between performance management and organisational effectiveness. The analysis did not detect such a correlation, probably because of the inconsistent application of performance management across organisations and the lack of formal evaluation. Nevertheless, our research has shown that performance management has come a long way, and is now more likely to be part of an integrated approach to people management than it was a few years ago. ...

Extracts from: M. Armstrong and A. Baron, *People Management,* 23 July 1998.
Reproduced by permission of *People Management*

Extract 2

PERFORMANCE APPRAISALS: USAGE, CRITERIA AND OBSERVATIONS

The significance of the performance appraisal has been documented by numerous authors. For example, Larson (1984) states that feedback about performance is an 'integral' component of any organisational control system. This position is supported by other authors (DeCarlo and Leigh, 1996; Morris *et al*, 1991) who contend that performance appraisals may be one of the sales manager's most important job responsibilities.

Perhaps the predominant appeal of the performance appraisal is based on the widely held position that performance appraisals can provide numerous organisational benefits. First, performance appraisals are often credited with increases in salesperson effort, motivation and performance (Churchill *et al*, 1985; Hackman and Oldham, 1975; Mohrman *et al*, 1989; Mount, 1983; Mowen *et al*, 1985; Patton and King, 1985). Correspondingly, many of the benefits of performance appraisals accrue as a result of the appraisal's impact on reducing salesperson role ambiguity. In general, research has shown that performance appraisals reduce role ambiguity (Brown and Peterson, 1993; Dubinsky and Mattson, 1979; Jaworski *et al*, 1993) and these reductions in role ambiguity are commonly associated with increases in effort, performance, satisfaction, commitment and a decrease in turnover (Babakus *et al*, 1996; Behrman and Perreault, 1984; Brown and Peterson, 1994; Cotton and Tuttle, 1986; Dubinsky and Mattson, 1979; Jaworski *et al*, 1993; Michaels *et al*, 1998). ...

The criteria used on assessing performance are typically regarded as being critical because they provide the foundation for a manager's evaluation of a salesperson and thus may influence the degree to which the manager's evaluation is accepted (DeCarlo and Leigh, 1996). While the criteria used in evaluations may be perceived as being important, it has been noted that 'little is known about the bases actually used to evaluate salespeople' (Jackson *et al*, 1995). Thus, there seems to be little agreement regarding the evaluation variables that will provide the maximum benefits to the evaluation efforts.

Researchers have often divided evaluation criteria into two categories. These two categories are frequently given different labels (eg qualitative/quantitative, behaviour/output, subjective/objective), but they are most often labelled input and output criteria (Oliver and Anderson, 1994, 1995; Challagalla and Shervani, 1996; Jaworski and Kohli, 1991; Markowich, 1994; Oliver and Anderson, 1995). Generally, the input criteria are described as including personal qualities, activities or sales strategies (Oliver and Anderson, 1995). The output criteria are described as being related to the results obtained from the individual's job performance (eg sales volume, profits). . . .

The findings in many studies indicate that the input/behavioural criteria are preferred over output criteria (Challagalla and Servani, 1996; Latham *et al*, 1993; Oliver and Anderson, 1995; Pekarne and Von Arnold, 1991). The preference for behavioural criteria is largely predicated on the belief that these criteria are subject to a greater degree of self-control than are output criteria, while the use of output criteria is either outside a salesperson's control or leads to activities which are detrimental to the long-term profitability of the firm (Churchill *et al*, 1985; Challagalla and Shervani, 1996; Oliver and Anderson, 1994).

However, some researchers argue that output criteria should be the preferred criteria. The justification supporting output criteria vis-à-vis input criteria is largely based on the belief that the use of behavioural criteria results in 'less than objective evaluations' (Ilgen and Feldman, 1983; Latham *et al*, 1993; Markowich, 1994).

Still other researchers concede that both criteria should play a significant role in the evaluation process and that no single form of criteria is 'always' preferred (Patton and King, 1985; Oliver and Anderson, 1995; Wanguri, 1995). Research has shown that while positive 'output' feedback is the most effective method of improving performance, positive behavioural feedback tends to have the greatest impact on satisfaction (Jaworski and Kohli, 1991). Correspondingly, other studies have found no differences in the levels of performance that result from either behaviour or outcome controls (Oliver and Anderson, 1994). . . .

The purpose of the study was to assess the characteristics of performance appraisals from the vantage point of the sales person. . . . Thus questions were developed that related to the conducting of performance appraisals, the frequency with which evaluations are conducted, the criteria used in the appraisal process, and the salesperson's opinions of the criteria that should be used in conducting performance appraisals. . . . A total of 250 potential subjects engaged in full-time personal selling activities were identified and their participation solicited. These individuals were then contacted by trained interviewers who obtained answers to the questions through a personal interview process.

A total of 250 potential subjects were identified and their responses solicited. A total of 214 (86 per cent) agreed to participate in the study and provided usable questionnaires. ... The majority of the respondents were male. More than one-half of the respondents were over 34 years old, earned in excess of $37,000, and had at least an undergraduate college degree (63.3 per cent). ...

The results indicated that appraisals are commonly (69 per cent) conducted at least twice annually. This may imply that the firms employing the sales representatives participating in this study feel that the appraisal process yields benefits that make the endeavour a worthy investment.

The results also indicate that not all salespeople felt that they were being evaluated by the 'ideal' set of criteria. ... With regard to the use of criteria, the findings indicate that managers may be well advised to examine the type of employee that they are appraising as they select the criteria used in the evaluation process. The findings indicate that input criteria should be used in situations in which the employees are more likely to be easily observed by their managers and in situations in which salespeople are less educated. Both of these circumstances parallel the situation existing in retail selling, where the findings indicate the greater practice of 'input-based' evaluation criteria. Conversely, managers may opt for the use of output criteria in situations in which their employees are better educated and more experienced.

Extracts from: L. S. Pettijohn, R. S. Parker, C. E. Pettijohn and L. Kent (2001) *Journal of Management Development,* 20 (9) 754–771. Reproduced with permission of Emerald (MCB), Bradford

Feedback notes

These two extracts show how literature sources about similar activities can tackle the issues in different ways and with very different stylistic approaches. Both extracts start from the premise that there are many benefits to be obtained from performance appraisal, although the first extract highlights performance management processes more generally and the second focuses on the appraisal of salespeople. One considers it from an HR perspective, the other from the perspective of salespeople themselves. One considers issues related to the organisational features of appraisal, the other looks at the assessment criteria that may be used within an appraisal process. One study is based on findings from a broad cross-section of those in different organisations, the other is based on structured interviews with salespeople.

Being analytical and critical

Being critical does not (necessarily) mean being negative, but it does involve you in responding to what you have read in a way that examines its component parts and assesses its essential features to determine their value in an objective way. There are a number of ways of doing this.

- Include work that supports your ideas, but also consider approaches that oppose them.
- Make explicit the values and theories that lie beneath what you are reading about, and then consider how successfully the component parts fit together.

■ Make clear distinctions between facts and opinions.

■ Discuss what you are reading in the light of existing critiques of theories and concepts.

■ Relate different readings with each other – look for similarities but also for contradictions or tensions between the opinions and approaches of different authors.

■ Support your arguments and judgements about the value of different approaches with reasoned explanations.

■ Adopt a writing style that is objective and impersonal. Avoid terms like 'should', 'must', 'this is obviously wrong', and so on. Use terms like '[authors] argue that', '[the author] asserts that', 'another perspective is offered by . . .'.

■ Structure your material effectively. Although the reading that underpins any project will involve the collection of facts, the project can only really add value if those facts are organised and classified in an effective way. You will have to reorganise what you have read, therefore, and select what is important in each of the sources before putting it together in a way that is relevant to the concerns of your investigation.

THE STRUCTURE OF THE LITERATURE REVIEW

A key skill in producing an effective review of the literature is to identify what sources to include and to know how to make sure that you achieve all the purposes of the review. It is also important to ensure that the literature review 'feeds into' the subsequent sections of the project report, rather than being a stand-alone exercise done to 'keep the markers happy'.

You must include key academic theories that are relevant to your investigation, and you must also demonstrate that you are up to date in your knowledge of the topic. Another important aspect of any literature review is a critical assessment of previously published work on the topic. This involves identifying its strengths and weaknesses as well as any areas that may have been left out or handled in a biased way.

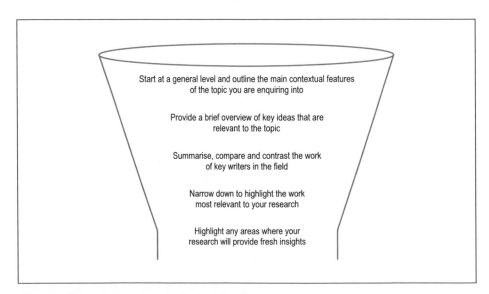

Figure 15 *Indicative structure for a critical review of the literature*

In general the structure indicated in Figure 15 will enable you to write in an effective way to communicate what is already known about the topic.

Case illustration

ACTIVITY – WRITING A LITERATURE REVIEW

The following extract was written by Sarah, a student working for an international telecoms company. The idea of flexible working options had been identified by managers as a way forward for her organisation. When focus groups were carried out, the staff involved also indicated their interest in work-life balance. Sarah's task was to consider possible ways forward to meet the needs of the organisation *and* the employees. The extract reproduces the initial paragraphs of the literature review that Sarah produced, then goes on to list the main subheadings that followed, before reproducing the concluding paragraphs.

Consider this extract and undertake the following review exercises.

1 To what extent does this review of the literature achieve the purposes of a literature review that are shown in Figure 14?
   – examining the context
   – identifying relevant concepts, issues and methods.
   – devising a framework for the analysis of empirical data
   – positioning the investigation

2 How successfully does the review 'funnel' from broad issues to a more focused discussion?

Literature review

This section begins with Atkinson's model and then explores changes in flexibility resultant from changes in the external context organisations operate within; adjustments to the psychological contract; and reconciliation of employers' and employees' needs. Four different types of flexible working time are assessed: part-time hours, job share, variable hours and sabbaticals.

Definitions
'Flexibility' – the ability to bend without breaking. Flexibility makes it possible to adapt or respond to change, to be influenced, to make modification and variations' (Scarnati, 1999; p.194). Organisations need to exhibit the flexibility to adapt rapidly to an ever-changing environment.

Flexible working
What the term 'flexible working' means is not easy to define because the concept is bedevilled with terminological problems (Croucher and Brewster, 1998). The concept's elasticity of meaning is demonstrated by its application to a broad range of organisational issues such as: the ease with which employees can be engaged or dismissed; flexibility of wages; adaptability of workers in the production process; labour mobility between firms and regions; and flexible working time. Broadly the concept represents how well organisations are able to respond to rapidly changing conditions in the absence of constraints and rigidity.

The business case for flexibility tends to emphasise a reorganisation of work to bring about an increase in efficiency and a decrease in costs. Flexibility has varied with employer's interventions – for example, in the 1960s functional flexibility was required to aid economic recovery and appeared to be in the employer's interests.

Working parents are increasingly 'strait-jacketed' by outdated working time patterns and employees are increasingly demanding flexibility, albeit in a different form than employers. Part-time hours, job share, sabbaticals and variable hours can ease the 'juggling' between work and family and also satisfy the need for lifelong learning and other ambitions. 'Flexibility is one aspect of HRM where practice is ahead of theory ... only now is our awareness beginning to catch up with what has happened' (Croucher and Brewster, 1998) Most definitions and studies relate to Atkinson's employer-led model (see below) rather than employee-led flexibility, although 'the mushrooming of definitions for labour flexibility may thus be seen as an attempt to identify the variety of adjustment mechanisms that the real world offers' (Creagh and Brewster, 1998).

Work-life balance
In the equal opportunities context flexibility is concerned with enabling workers with family responsibilities to engage equally in the paid workplace and valuing the diverse work patterns that emerge within organisations. This illustrates Fox's pluralist perspective whereby employees have many different needs and require individualistic support and arrangements (Sheridan and Conway, 2001).

Work-life balance is wider than family-friendly policies in that employers are recognising flexible work options should be available not only to those with childcare or eldercare responsibilities but to all employees (Kodz and Harper, 2002).

There is scope to accommodate the needs of employees alongside those of employers and it is important to change the dominant perspective to make room for employee-driven flexibility. Meanwhile this gap represents a significant HRM problem and until efforts are directed towards achieving mutual flexibility, the effectiveness of such practices will continue to be hampered.

The flexible firm model

....

The driving forces

....

The new psychological contract

....

Reconciling employer's and employees' needs

....

Trends

....

Senior management support

....

Further restraining forces

....

Employees' difficulties

....

Management difficulties

....

The importance of company policies, procedures and legislation

....

Flexible working time

....

Part-time hours

....

Job share

....

Flexitime

....

Sabbaticals

....

Further investigation

The empirical research [covered in the literature review] suggested that employees now have different expectations of work. This project's research therefore aimed to assess the level and strength of demand by employees for a work-life balance and flexible working hours. The empirical research [covered in the literature review] also showed that managerial support is vital to the take-up of initiatives – therefore, the extent of senior and line manager support were also assessed. Policies and procedures are important for fairness and consistency although managers can prefer to retain their prerogative to manage. Line manager's views on the introduction of a formal policy were assessed, along with the barriers and enablers, and pending employment legislation.

From 'The importance of a flexible working policy in helping organisations adapt to changing attitudes regarding work-life balance'.
Reproduced with permission

Feedback notes

Rather than merely describing some theories or initiatives relating to flexibility, Sarah demonstrates her critical thinking abilities by showing the distinction between employer- and employee-led approaches to flexibility, as well as showing how the wider context in which organisations operate has influenced the way that flexibility is now understood. In her review Sarah also probes beneath the surface and identifies some underlying assumptions (eg the pluralist perspective) of some contemporary practices.

A start is made in devising a framework for analysis by indicating the importance of measuring (amongst other things) strength of demand by employees, levels of senior manager support, and the attitudes of line managers towards formal policies relevant to flexible working and work-life balance. Less detail, however, is provided about the methods of enquiry that other researchers have used.

To further enhance this review, it might also have been possible to consider how the investigation Sarah planned might add value to 'what is already known' in the way it builds on other published work.

This extract also shows how it is possible to 'funnel' the direction of attention in the way the review is constructed and written. The approach starts by considering issues at a wide-ranging level, with definitions and the general context. Reference is made to key theories and concepts (for example, the flexible firm model and work-life balance, the psychological contract, etc), and then more detailed attention is paid to work that is most relevant to Sarah's study, particularly related to different forms of flexible working time options.

REFERENCING YOUR WORK

There have been a number of occasions in this chapter already where the importance of appropriate referencing has been highlighted. The tutor's requirements for effective referencing is often seen by students as being unnecessarily 'picky'. However, referencing allows you to get credit for showing what you have read, and how and where you have used what you have read in the preparation of your project.

Three points are important when referencing:

- that you acknowledge the work of other people that has influenced your thinking and activity in the enquiry process
- that there should be enough information to allow readers of your work to follow up your reference, and access it for themselves
- that as consistent an approach as is possible is taken.

Table 10 *Referencing in the text*

Usage	System	Example
For a single author	Family name, year	It has been shown that ... (Jones, 1993); or, Jones (1993) shows that ...
For something written by two people	Family name and family name, year	The main features of ... have been identified as ... (Jones and Brown, 1993)
For something written by more than two authors	First author family name *et al*, year	... is indicated (Smith *et al*, 1993); or, Smith *et al* (1993) indicate that ...
When the author you are referring to is themselves referred to by another author, and you have not read the original work. (This is a secondary reference)	Family name, year, cited in family name, year, page numbers	Another view of the issue is that ... (Smith, 1993; cited in Patel, 2001, pages x–x)
For corporate authors – eg of a consultancy report	Corporate name, year	Key issues for EDC industries are ... (EDC plc, 1993)
For publications with no obvious author, such as ACAS	Most obvious identifier, year	Key stages in the discipline process are ... (ACAS, 1993)

In management and business publications the most commonly-used format for referencing is the Harvard system, which is based on the surname of authors and date of publication, rather than on any system of footnoting or numbering. This system is briefly outlined below.

Referencing in the text itself

You can demonstrate how you have used sources through appropriate referencing in the text itself. The Harvard system uses the author's surname and year of publication as the main way to identify documents within the text. Preferred practice varies in different publications as to how to punctuate references, and the order of various pieces of information, but the practical illustrations of referencing within the text shown in Table 10 may be helpful.

Quotations

When you quote directly from a source, you should place the quotation in inverted commas and the page number should be given in the reference after the year of publication. For example: 'The employment relationship is central to personnel and development, whether in terms of the direct employment of staff by an organisation, or the subcontracting of work to external bodies' (Marchington and Wilkinson, 1996; p.7).

Referencing in the bibliography or references section

Having provided some information about your sources in the text, it is important to provide full details in the section that follows the end of the main text of the report (but comes before the appendices).

Strictly speaking a reference list is a list of all sources that you have cited within your text, whereas a bibliography is a list of everything you have read or drawn upon while researching your piece of work, whether you have actually cited them in your text or not. In reality, the distinction between the two is often not recognised and the terms are used interchangeably. If you have been careful to acknowledge all your sources within the report, then the list of references will differ only slightly, if at all, from the list of sources you have drawn upon in your research. It is worth checking with your study centre whether a bibliography is required or a reference list is what is expected.

Table 11 *Referencing in the bibliography or references section*

Usage	System	Example
Reference to a book	Name, initial(s) [and any other author's name, initial(s)], (year), title. place of publication, publisher	Marchington, M. and Wilkinson, A. (2002) *People Management and Development*. London, CIPD.
Reference to a booklet	Body responsible for leaflet, (year), title. place of publication, publisher	Department for Education and Employment (1999) *Delivering Skills for All: Second report of the Skills Task Force*. London, HMSO.
Reference to the work of someone cited in a different source (such as a textbook)	Family name, (year), cited in family name, initial, (year), title. place of publication, publisher, page numbers of section being referred to	McGregor (1960), cited in Marchington, M. and Wilkinson, A. (1996) *Core Personnel and Development*. London, IPD; 296–7.
Reference to a particular chapter in an edited book	Family name, initial, (year), 'title', in initial, family name (ed.) title, place of publication, publisher	Iles, P. (1996) 'International HRD', in J. Stewart and J. McGoldrick (eds) *Human Resource Development: Perspectives, strategies and practice*. London, Pitman.
Reference to an article in a journal	Family name, initial, (year), 'title of article', journal name, volume number, (part or issue number): page numbers	Masie, E. (1999) 'Joined-up thinking', *People Management*, 25 November; 32–6.
Reference to an item found on the Internet	This may or may not include the fact that the item was accessed online and also the date of access; more important is the website address	IDS (1999) 'Pay and conditions in call centres', [online] (accessed 8 January 2003) <URL: http://www.incomesdata.co.uk /callcent/htm>

Whether you produce a bibliography or a references section, the aim is to list the publications in full and in alphabetical order. The following information should be provided to allow anyone to follow up your reference and access it accurately:

- author's surname and initial(s)
- year of publication
- title of book/article
- publisher of the book/name of journal in which the article was printed
- if a book, the place of publication (eg London, New York, Paris).

Some examples of appropriate referencing in the bibliography/references section are shown in Table 11.

As mentioned above, some publications show their references in different formats. The final format that you decide on is not, in itself, particularly significant (unless your study centre has precise requirements). The main thing is to reference your work in a consistent format and in an accurate way. If you do not reference appropriately and you utilise material originated by someone else without showing a citation, you may be accused of plagiarism – which, for academic purposes, is a form of cheating (passing off the work of someone else as your own) and, when detected, may result in a serious penalty when your work is marked.

SUMMARY

- An evaluation of what is already known is an important feature of any investigative enquiry.
- Reading around a topic can help to suggest ideas for a project, can provide a framework for interpreting data, and can identify worthwhile sources of secondary data.
- A wide range of different types of literature should be included in the literature review, incorporating both practitioner and 'academic' perspectives.
- Effective literature search processes include both 'manual' and electronic methods.
- Finding literature without reading it is a waste of your time. Effective reading and note-taking are key skills for investigative practitioners.
- An effective review of the literature examines the context of the research problem, identifies relevant concepts, issues and methods, develops a framework for the analysis of data, and positions the investigation.
- A literature review that is both analytical and critical includes work that both supports and opposes your ideas, clearly distinguishes between facts and opinions, establishes relationships between different readings, and is explicit about the values and theories that underpin them. It utilises an objective and impersonal writing style and provides reasoned explanations for arguments and judgements.
- In critically reviewing the literature it is best to start by establishing the broad context, issues, theories and concepts before 'funnelling down' to discuss work that is particularly relevant to the investigation.
- Appropriate referencing is one of the assessment criteria for judging the effectiveness of any literature review. Failure to reference properly, in any event, is poor scholarship and could lead to a charge that someone else's work has been passed off as your own. Plagiarism is a serious offence and the penalties can be significant.

Questions for review/reflection

These questions are designed to enable you to identify key areas for development with your project. The answers to them can also form part of a CPD portfolio or log. This is a requirement of the CIPD for those who wish to upgrade your membership status.

Taking stock

1 Find out about the requirements of your study centre with regard to a review of the literature. What sort of wordcount is expected? To what extent are 'academic' articles and books required within the review?

2 What resources are available to you, and how might you obtain access to library materials at:
   – your place of work?
   – your study centre?
   – any professional institutions of which you or your organisation is a member?

3 Are you able to access electronic library sources 'remotely'? What passwords do you need, and where can you get them?

4 How familiar are you with HR-related Internet gateways and other search engines? Who is the best source of help to explore opportunities of finding out 'what is already known' through the Internet?

Strengths and weaknesses

1 Reflect critically on your use of literature in previous assignments. To what extent have you relied on ideas 'derived' from other places (usually textbooks)?

2 Revisit assignments you have produced previously for your course. What feedback have tutors made about your referencing technique? How confident do you feel about referencing?

3 How effective are your reading and note-taking 'habits' and strategies? In previous assignments how easy has it been to write an overview of what you have read about a topic? How organised is your note-taking system? To what extent do you note down readings that you agree with and tend to skip over those that oppose your viewpoint?

4 To what extent do you adopt a questioning and an evaluative approach when you are reading? How successful are you at making explicit the underlying theories and assumptions in what you read?

5 In your writing are you able to distinguish between facts and opinions? To what extent is your writing style 'objective and impersonal'?

Being an investigative practitioner

1 To what extent is your thinking determined by features like the organisational culture of your employing organisation, your national cultural background, your political preferences, etc? What steps do you need to take to ensure that you consider the issues from a range of perspectives when you are reviewing the literature?

2 What strategies might you adopt to manage the time pressures of organisational and academic deadlines in order to have time to produce a literature review of good quality?

FURTHER READING

The best way to learn how to write an effective literature review is to read them in journal articles and scholarly books. Similarly, the best way to learn how to take notes and to read in an evaluative way is by doing it and learning through practice. The following sources also provide useful tips and hints.

BLAXTER, L., HUGHES, C. and TIGHT, M. (2001) *How to Research*. Buckingham, Open University Press.

BRANSCOMB, H. E. (1998) *Casting Your Net: A student's guide to research on the Internet*. Boston, Allyn & Bacon.

COTTRELL, S. (1999) *The Study Skills Handbook*. Basingstoke, Palgrave.

CRESWELL, J. W. (2003) *Research Design: Qualitative, quantitative and mixed methods approaches*. London, Sage.

DOCHARTAIGH, N. O. (2002) *The Internet Research Handbook*. London, Sage.

HART, C. (1998) *Doing a Literature Review: Releasing the social science research imagination*. London, Sage.

HART, C. (2001) *Doing a Literature Search: A comprehensive guide for the social sciences*. London, Sage.

SAUNDERS, M., LEWIS, P. and THORNHILL, A. (2003) *Research Methods for Business Students*. London, *Financial Times*/Prentice Hall.

WOODS, G. (2002) *Research Papers for Dummies*. New York, Wiley.

Approaches to gathering data in HR research

Chapter outline
How to use this chapter
Using theory to make sense of data
Qualitative and quantitative methods
Planning to gather data
Writing up the methodology
Summary
Further reading

LEARNING OUTCOMES

This chapter should help you to:

- **clarify the overall approach for your research**

- **decide what data to gather and how to get it**

- **highlight key differences between qualitative and quantitative data**

- **evaluate the validity and reliability of your data**

- **write the methodology section of your report.**

HOW TO USE THIS CHAPTER

This chapter draws together some of the themes and issues that have been introduced in Chapters 1–3 to help you to clarify the overall approach and the different types of data that will be most appropriate for your investigative enquiry. By the time you read this chapter you should have a fairly firm idea as to your topic and the focus of your enquiry, as well as some thoughts about the overall research strategy that you will pursue (case study, survey, action research, etc). You should also have done some reading so that you are more aware of where your enquiry fits within what is already known about your topic. Now you need to make further decisions about how you will put your ideas into action and take the project forward in a meaningful, coherent and justifiable way.

An explanation and justification of your investigative methods is required for projects at all academic levels as well as those that are not connected with achieving a qualification. This chapter will help you to develop that justification. When people are in a hurry with their project they are tempted to skip this stage and launch straight into some form of data-gathering. However, the investment of a small amount of time and thought at this stage in the project can reap significant rewards in the quality of the investigation that you undertake.

Case illustration

From research focus to research methods:
Profits rise with a written HR strategy

Firms with a written HR strategy generated 35 per cent higher revenues per employee than those without one, according to a survey. The Global Human Capital Survey Report 2002/3 found that 58 per cent of organisations had a documented HR strategy, with 96 per cent of those firms linking it to their business objectives. Those with a written strategy reported higher revenues per employee.

The research, carried out by PricewaterhouseCoopers, surveyed 1,000 employers world-wide.

Kevin Delaney, partner at PwC, said: 'Our research clearly shows that effective people management does add value to organisations by putting the right practices in place to create a good employment environment.'

Angela Baron, CIPD adviser for organisation and resourcing, said the report supported institute findings. 'It reinforces the message from our own research that HR strategy should be linked to business strategy.'

The automotive industry was one of the 37 sectors surveyed. Bruce Warman, HR director for Vauxhall, said that simply having a documented HR strategy was not sufficient. 'It is about HR intervention supporting the business,' he added.

Other benefits included lower absenteeism and more effective performance management and reward systems, the research said.

But the survey highlighted that corporate social responsibility (CSR) was not high on the HR agenda. Sixty per cent of HR directors believed that CSR was largely a public relations issue.

Warman said: 'When people think of CSR, they think of the social and environmental aspect. In HR we do not take the economic component seriously enough.'

K. Higginbottom, *People Management*, 26 December 2002.
Reproduced by permission of *People Management*

DISCUSSION QUESTIONS

Imagine that you are interested in undertaking a project to investigate how HR strategy works in reality. It is early days yet, and you are not clear how you might go about this. You have read this short article and you are wondering if there are any ideas in it that might be helpful.

1   Write a list of the propositions that this short article makes about HR strategy and its effect on organisational performance.

2   Imagine that you are a student undertaking a project on HR strategy in your own organisation (or a placement organisation). Using ideas from the propositions you have listed, identify one or two research questions that you might try to answer as a part of your study.

3   Having formulated one or two research questions, identify what data you might need to answer them.

4   Imagine that instead of conducting research in one organisation only, you plan to research the issues across a range of organisations. Pick out one or two research questions that you might try to answer, and decide what data you need to answer them.

Feedback notes

There are a number of propositions in this article. The overall thrust of the piece is that having an HR strategy that is linked to business objectives improves business performance. There is also the assertion that 58 per cent of organisations have such a strategy, and that most of them link this strategy with business objectives.

Further, it is suggested that having an HR strategy leads to lower absenteeism and to more effective reward management and performance management systems. There is also a suggestion that HR people do not take the economic aspect of organisational life seriously enough.

Plenty of issues here, therefore, might stimulate ideas for a possible topic. If you were undertaking research in one organisation (that has a written HR strategy), you might think about investigating the process by which the HR strategy was formulated and how the links with business objectives are established. You might also be interested in how the strategy was implemented and the extent to which difficulties were encountered. It might be interesting to investigate how the effects of the strategy are measured. You could decide to investigate the extent to which the strategy has influenced reward management or performance management processes, as indicated in this article. Although some numerical data would be relevant to investigations such as these, it is more likely that you would need to gather more data about processes people go through, their opinions about the strategy formulation and implementation processes, and the way they perceive HR to be undertaken in your organisation.

If you were planning to undertake your research by accessing a range of different organisations, you might choose to ask similar or different questions. You might investigate the extent to which absence rates are lower in organisations with an HR strategy than in those without one. Alternatively, you might ask whether corporate social responsibility is less of an issue for those with an HR strategy than for those without one. Whatever you choose, the chances are that the data you gather will be of a different kind. You are likely to focus more on a range of questions asked of a cross-section of different employers. Once these data are collated you can analyse them in order to answer your research questions.

This breakdown suggests that there are potentially many different ways of approaching investigative enquiries. It is important to think through the issues in order to formulate an approach that is appropriate to your situation and will generate conclusions that are meaningful and valuable. To achieve this, whatever activities you use in your investigation, they must be clearly explained and justified. This chapter seeks to enable you to devise a credible rationale for the method or methods of enquiry you decide upon for your study. In many ways this is a focal chapter of the book in that many of the issues over approaches to research that were introduced in earlier chapters are brought together in this one. Many of the issues over types of data that are introduced in this chapter are in turn considered in more detail in the chapters that follow.

USING THEORY TO MAKE SENSE OF DATA

Many people who embark on an investigative enquiry know well enough that they will have to read and include theories as well as to get hold of data. Mostly they do not expect to have to explicitly consider deeper issues like the relationship between theory and data. This consideration is key, however, because a reasoned perspective on the relationship between theory and data will underpin important decisions about:

- what data to gather and where to look for it
- how you will make sense of information once you have got hold of it.

This section of the chapter sets out to explain the issues 'in plain English' so that you can determine the most appropriate approach for your enquiry towards both theory and data-gathering and interpretation.

WEB-BASED ACTIVITY

Go to a general search engine (such as Google.co.uk or Yahoo.co.uk) and type in the search word 'theory'. (Choose to search on UK sites only in order to limit the list.) Glance through the first 10–20 sites that are given as a result of your search. You do not need to open them unless you become intrigued. What impression does the list of sites you have seen give you of 'theory'? What objections might you feel to the requirement of your project to include theory as well as practice?

Feedback notes
Common sites generated on a search such as this include:

- set theory (a branch of mathematics)
- M-theory (the theory formerly known as 'string theory' or simply 'strings')
- number theory
- political theory
- information theory
- marketing theory

- feminist theory
- group theory.

As discussed in Chapter 1, the word 'theory' is associated by many people with things that are complicated, incomprehensible, specialised and divorced from the practical reality of real lives. Many HR practitioners, who may also be part-time students, and many organisational sponsors of projects are wary of theory, anxious instead to undertake study that they feel will be operationally relevant and valuable.

However, such a perception of theory is mistaken. As noted in Chapter 1, we use theories to generate expectations about the world in order to 'make sense of things'. Theories enable us to predict and explain events. We refine our theories by testing them through practice, or by benefiting through the information we are given by others of their experiences. The same process is applicable to our practices as practitioner-researchers. We refine our theories by gathering data to see how well the theories explain the information we have obtained. Equally, we might obtain information first and then develop or build a theory to make sense of the data in a meaningful way.

Theory is therefore both relevant and useful to HR professionals who make use of a range of frameworks. Some will be derived from 'common sense' and some will be the result of more formal research processes published within the social sciences. Maslow's theory of motivation (Maslow, 1943), for example, still provides something of a basis for a range of career or personal development processes undertaken within organisations.

Because theories play an important part of effective HR practice, it is also important that HR professionals are able to evaluate different frameworks to find those that offer the most appropriate basis by which to understand organisational situations and from which to plan and implement HR interventions.

Case illustration

Judging between theories:
Waterproof

'You change the people or you change the people' has been the mantra of management in the 1990s on both sides of the Atlantic. Yesterday's macho manager who forced change by correcting and directing lesser mortals in a top-down fashion is now likely to be an enthusiast for empowerment and self-managed teams.

In the early 1980s, managers could blame the government for excessive state ownership and the unions for restrictive practices – if only these boundaries were removed, then world-wide competitiveness could be achieved. The Thatcher administration changed all that in the UK. The new political and economic regime led to massive reductions in the labour force, particularly in manufacturing and construction.

Towards the end of the decade, a new management philosophy – business process re-engineering – emerged in the USA. Managers were encouraged to ask themselves: 'What resources do I really need for this set of processes?'

This was not dissimilar to the route taken by the Japanese from the early 1950s, later to be termed 'lean production'. But the path followed in Japan had one crucial difference. Employees who became surplus to requirements would be transferred to other potential growth areas in the re-engineered organisation – or its subsidiaries, suppliers or clients – in that incredible network of mutual obligation that is Japanese business.

The West has had no such network, has often not believed that there are growth possibilities out there somewhere, and has rejected any notion of long-term obligations to employees. Hence the surplus really *are* surplus to requirements.

Employee numbers have fallen dramatically. The City of London has looked, and still looks, for year-on-year headcount reductions by companies as an indicator of their ability to control costs. Wall Street gets jittery when unemployment falls. Far from full employment being the goal, we have become conditioned to the idea of a high level of 'natural' unemployment. A fine concept if you are in work, receiving dividends from profitable companies and have no children looking for jobs. But where is the individual in all this?

For the complaining macho manager of the 1980s, all obstacles have been removed. Privatisation has been the most enduring philosophy from this period, and the economy has undoubtedly benefited. The trade unions are more compliant, even initiators of change, while the workforce accepts the need for flexibility. Overstaffing is a thing of the past. Middle management is emasculated, downsized, delayered and the scapegoat, pictured as the 'corporate concrete' in inhibiting, or at least not embracing, change.

The 'born again' manager now tells the workforce that they are empowered. What is left of middle management is bypassed and self-managed teams are created. This leaves top management to pursue strategy rather than firefight, network to their hearts' content and pacify the City with their short-term focus.

Unfortunately, either the corporate engine will not start or it is badly tuned; in any event, it still cannot compete. Quality suffers and top management asks the why, who, where, when, what and how questions, only to find that empowerment means no controls, no system, no support, no ownership, no instruction and no improvement.

It is actually two sides of the same coin: distance management and management by desertion. Earl Haig and his generals epitomised distance management in the First World War. They directed the war effort from the safety of Paris while the lads, managed by the NCOs, slugged it out in the trenches. Management by desertion still means that you leave them to it, but this time without the NCOs.

It is no wonder that many Western employees keep their heads down during initiatives, fully anticipating the next wonder-solution to burst on the company when the chief executive returns from leave, having read up on the latest management fad. . . .

Extracts from: C. Morton, *People Management*, 11 June 1998.
Reproduced by permission of the author

DISCUSSION QUESTIONS

1 Identify some of the different 'generalisations' or theories about effective management that are highlighted in this article.

2 How can managers judge between different theories so that they do not get caught up in the rush to implement 'fads and fashions' that may bring no lasting benefit to their organisations?

Feedback notes

There are a range of different theories alluded to in this extract, including the theories that empowerment and self-managed teams will lead to improved organisational performance; that less state regulation leads to better management; and that business process re-engineering provides business benefits.

Broadly speaking, there are two ways of judging between different theories. The first is to try them out. One way of seeing if something works is to test it. So if you want to evaluate an approach to management (a theory), put it into practice and see what happens. Through this process you will be able to measure the extent to which the outcomes predicted by the latest approach to management you are testing are achieved. Of course it may be that the process of testing leads in part to what you have been led to expect but also produces some unexpected outcomes, and this would provide a basis for further amendment and development of the original theory.

Another, perhaps less risky, way of evaluating different theories is to critically assess the approach that is being advocated. Here there are questions you might ask, like: What are the assumptions that underpin this latest theory? To what extent do the various parts or concepts that make up the approach make sense or have value? To what extent can there be a relationship of cause and effect between the actions being advocated and the outcomes being promised? To what extent might this theory depend on other factors and contexts? In asking these evaluative questions you are able to form a judgement about whether the approach being advocated is appropriate for all or for some contexts, and you can assess its value taken as a whole.

In a management report or research project setting, both approaches to evaluating theory are valuable. It is important to show that you are aware of theories that are relevant to your investigation. Rather than merely accepting them in an unquestioning way, however, it is also important to show that you can ask pertinent questions in order to make an initial judgement of their value. For most projects – particularly those linked with CIPD courses of study – it is also necessary to gather data in order to evaluate the impact or some of the component issues of the topic you are considering, in practice. Having done this you will be in a position to reflect back on the theories and make a judgement on their relevance and value.

Where do theories come from?

Having established that theory is part of everyday life in HR, at both individual and organisational levels, it is interesting to ask where theories come from in the first place. Gill and Johnson (2001) utilise Kolb's learning cycle (Kolb *et al*, 1979) to illustrate the point that theory and practice are 'like two sides of a coin', and that it is possible to understand the relationship between theory and data in terms of how we learn to make sense of the world.

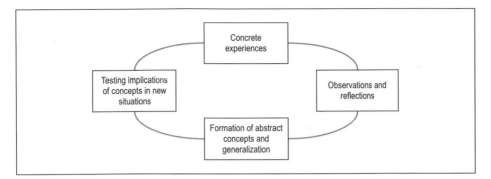

Figure 16 *Kolb's experiential learning cycle*
Source: D. A. Kolb, I. M. Rubin and J. M. McIntyre (1979) *Organisational Psychology: An experiential approach.* Reproduced by permission of Pearson Education Inc., Upper Saddle River, New Jersey.

Kolb suggests that learning involves a number of different stages. Each stage feeds into the others, and Kolb suggests that the learning process can begin at any part of the cycle. This can be illustrated by referring to the learning experience that many HR practitioners go through when they develop their skills in recruitment interviewing. Some HR professionals, in the early stages of their careers, are asked to carry out interviews with no formal training. They undertake their first interviews in a state of nervous tension, armed only with the company's forms and procedures which they have, hopefully, read in advance. They undertake the interview(s), and afterwards they reflect on 'how it went'. There will be some features of their practice that they are pleased with, and some that they will want to improve. They will devise for themselves some general guidelines (the do's and don'ts of interviewing) and they will try them out the next time that they interview. In this way their learning process involves HR practice (doing the interviews), reflection/evaluation (what went well and not so well), generalisation (personal/organisational do's and don'ts) and implementation (applying the do's and don'ts the next time that they interview). This cycle will, of course, repeat itself many times and, over time, the HR practitioner may be able to go on a course or read some books on effective interviewing to enhance the quality of his or her practice. Hopefully, most HR professionals (the more fortunate ones!) may undertake a course *before* first moving round the cycle and putting the generalised guidelines for effective practice into action.

In this way it is possible to see how, at an individual level, generalised concepts and principles (theories) form part of the normal learning process and are interrelated with obtaining information (data) on the basis of our experience and practice. This approach to understanding the relationship between theory and data illustrates how theory formulation can occur in either of two main ways. These are referred to by researchers as the 'deductive' and 'inductive' approaches.

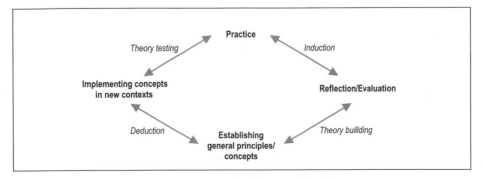

Figure 17 *Inductive and deductive reasoning*

Deduction and induction

Theories can be developed through a process of testing established generalisations. The process involves taking a proposition that is thought to be true and testing it out in different situations. This is referred to as the deductive approach. Here a process of logic is applied to something that is thought to be true, a theory is derived, and then the theory is tested out in an empirical way in different situations, conditions and contexts. On the basis of the evidence that is generated through this process of testing, the theory can be provisionally confirmed, amended, or discarded altogether.

Another way of generating theories is to start at the level of practice. Through a process of observation over a period of time it is possible to establish some general propositions about the nature of what has been observed, and in this way a theory is generated. This is referred to as an inductive approach. The process thus begins with what is effectively a 'clean sheet'. Behaviour or facts are observed, and on the basis of this a generalisation or theory about what is happening (and why) can be developed.

In reality, once a theory has been generated in an inductive way it may be further developed through empirical testing in a deductive way. Both approaches are thus rooted in practical reality. Some research, therefore, operates deductively by gathering data to see if existing theory is confirmed. Other research starts with more of a clean sheet and gathers data in order to develop (or build) a theory to explain the evidence that has been gathered.

Case illustration

Choosing a research approach

Mark was a full-time HR student who was undertaking a work placement at a regional office of a leading banking and financial services organisation. The financial services sector had undergone significant changes during the 1980s and 1990s. Market deregulation had led to increased competition and the need to operate in a more cost-effective way. Technological developments also contributed to a general 're-engineering' within the sector whereby transactional work tended to be centralised and the branch and advisory network was restructured and significantly rationalised. The sector had also been characterised by corporate mergers and massive redundancy programmes. These changes had also required new competencies from staff who remained in the sector as well as the development of a different managerial style and approach.

In the light of these significant changes Mark became interested in theories about the psychological contract (the unwritten expectations that employers and employees have of each other within their employment relationship). The psychological contract is a difficult concept because it is not something that is written down, nor is it directly expressed in any other tangible way. Nonetheless it has been argued that a breakdown of the psychological contract can lead to poor individual and organisational performance. This is caused by reduced levels of organisational commitment, lack of motivation, attendance and absence problems, and high levels of staff turnover.

Mark decided to investigate the state of the psychological contract, as perceived by employees, at his placement organisation.

DISCUSSION QUESTION

What approach (inductive or deductive) would be most appropriate for this enquiry, and why?

Feedback notes

Both the inductive and deductive approach might be utilised in researching this area. A deductive approach is attractive in that there is plenty of literature indicating the main areas of expectations that employees have of the employment relationship. It would therefore be possible to test out whether these are the expectations of employees in this organisation.

Alternatively, you might feel that because the psychological contract is not a written one, existing theories may not reflect the true perceptions and interpretations that people have of work, and so it would be better to work inductively. In this way employees' behaviour could be observed and the enquiry could find out from people (without putting words into their mouths) just how they understand and interpret the work relationship and their expectations of their employer.

Mark considered these issues. He read widely about the psychological contract and increasingly formed the view that because the contract is not spelled out or written down, and because the expectations that people have can change over time in the light of their different contexts, it would be better to observe it at a given moment rather than trying to measure how it has evolved over a period of time. For Mark's project, an inductive approach was chosen.

The main features of the inductive and deductive approaches to research are shown in figure 18. This indicates the different relationship with 'theory' of the two approaches. An inductive

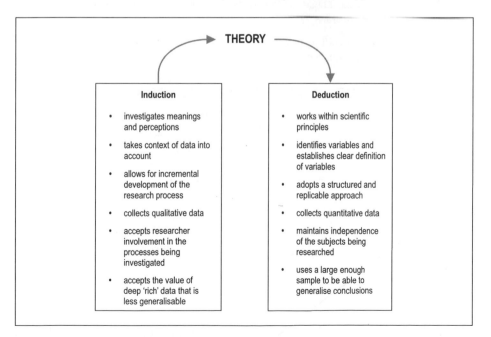

Figure 18 *Inductive and deductive approaches*

approach is often associated with the interpretivist understanding of the research process (examined in Chapters 1 and 2) and the deductive approach can be informed by positivist 'philosophy'. In Chapters 1 and 2 it was noted that both positivist and interpretivist approaches to research can be beneficial, particularly when considering investigative enquiries in the 'real world'. Equally, both deductive and inductive approaches have value in organisational enquiries. The points summarised below (Robson, 2003; Saunders *et al*, 2003) represent ends of a continuum rather than a hard-and-fast distinction, and in organisational studies in particular there can be interaction and overlap between them.

Deduction (theory-testing)

- Deduction involves the formulation of *hypotheses* (statements which the theory suggests are true).

- Hypotheses are then *operationalised* such that the variables involved can be identified and measured in an objective way. Such measurement can be undertaken for this enquiry, but the same approach could be repeated in a different situation.

- Data is then gathered and this information is used to test whether the hypotheses really do describe reality.

- The outcome of the enquiry, as shown against the original hypotheses, is either to modify or to confirm the theory from which the hypotheses were derived.

Induction (theory-building)

- Induction involves observation and investigation into the relationship between *meanings* and *actions* of human subjects.

- Data is collected without prior assumptions about categorisation and measurement.

- The context of the situation is incorporated into the analysis process as the research seeks to understand the internal logic and purposive nature of human actions.

- The outcome of the enquiry is to suggest/build a credible explanation of behaviours that have been observed.

- There is less concern with the need to generalise, although further avenues for research may be identified.

QUALITATIVE AND QUANTITATIVE METHODS

So far this chapter has been concerned with the relationship of theory to the process of gathering and making sense of data. Whichever approach you find most appropriate for your project, it will be necessary to collect data in a systematic way so that meaningful conclusions can be drawn from what you find. Many different methods of gathering data are used in HR research. They tend to be differentiated on the grounds of a distinction between *qualitative* and *quantitative* data.

- Quantitative data is the term given to data that can be quantified (counted).
- Qualitative data is the term given to data based on meanings which are expressed through words and language.

Case illustration

Deutsche Bank detects feelgood factor

Employee commitment at Deutsche Bank has increased significantly over the past year, thanks partly to the successful integration of its recent acquisition, Bankers Trust.

Silvia Steffens-Duch, head of corporate HR, marketing and research at the company, told *People Management* that the bank's annual commitment index score, based on a huge international employee attitude survey, had risen to 72 from last year's score of 67.

Deutsche Bank sets great store by employee commitment, which it includes on the balance sheet in its annual report. It defines commitment as 'identification with the organisation and its objectives and value, willingness to perform and continuance [ie inclination to stay with the organisation]'.

The company uses a 'multi-variant' tool for analysing commitment, which was developed by the Clas Fornell Institute at the University of Michigan. Several thousand of the bank's workforce of 97,466 are sampled annually, and the results can be compared by both business unit and geographical location to identify areas where action is needed. Last year, for instance, commitment scores ranged from 63 in the poorest-performing country where Deutsche Bank operates, up to 77 in Spain.

As result of last year's survey results Deutsche Bank has set up a new HR intranet page which sets out its goals and mission statement. It has also launched a value deployment initiative, called Our Identity, to reinforce identification with the company's objectives and values. It has launched an intranet-based job board, which holds an average of 1,000 vacancies at any one time, to improve retention and mobility within the organisation, and it is about to launch a new competency model for the whole group.

S. Crabb, *People Management,* 8 March 2001.
Reproduced by permission of *People Management*

DISCUSSION QUESTIONS

The attitude survey is a common way of measuring the commitment of employees to their employing organisation.

1 What are the advantages of the survey method for measuring commitment? How has it informed decision-making in Deutsche Bank?

2 What other methods might be used to get information about how people feel towards their work organisation?

3 Which method of gathering data is best, and why?

Feedback notes

There is a range of methods that this organisation could use to find out what people feel about their work organisation. It would be possible to interview people, for example, or engage them in conversation. Alternatively, a series of focus groups could be organised, or perhaps people could be encouraged to keep a diary for a period of time, in which their feelings about work and the organisation could be recorded in their own words.

The attitude survey approach is also a useful way of collecting data. One advantage of it is that because the questionnaire is very structured, it is easily replicable, and so it is possible to compare the results with surveys that have been previously undertaken. Those who are interested in the results are not physically close to those who fill it in, so it also allows for employee anonymity enabling people to respond in a more honest way. As a result of both of these factors (structure and detachment) data generated in this way can be analysed to identify relationships between different variables (such as different countries, or different levels of employee).

On the other hand, it is possible that the questions in the questionnaire might be interpreted differently by people with different backgrounds (cultural and organisational). Such a survey will also be expressed within the language and understandings of HR managers. Although people filling in the survey will tick boxes, then, it may not really reflect what they feel about the organisation. Similarly, surveys can be undertaken by a large number of people, but the depth of their replies is very limited (often to a choice of four options). Where the researcher is more involved, it would be possible to probe for meanings and interpretations and to ask why the respondents feel the way that they do in relation to a question.

Consideration of these issues, therefore, might indicate that a mixture of methods in which both qualitative and quantitative data was used would be helpful. Indeed, it is hard to say what method of gathering data would be 'best' because each has advantages but also limitations. Figure 19 provides an overview of the different methods in relation to the extent to which they are structured or unstructured and the level of involvement that the researcher has with the process of gathering data.

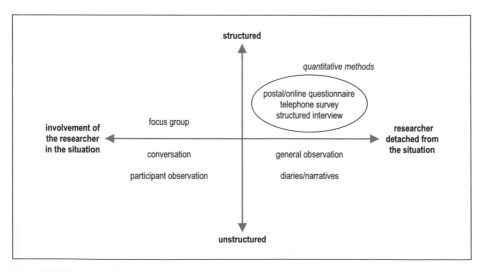

Figure 19 *Different methods of gathering data*

Table 12 *Qualitative and quantitative data*

Quantitative data	Qualitative data
Based in a familiarisation of current research rather than specific situations	Based in a familiarisation with a real-life context or situation
Analysis of a limited number of variables	Analysis of significant themes that are suggested by a range of sources
Concern to establish significant, and separate, relationships between a limited number of variables	Concern to understand the interrelationships between different factors
Variables are expressed in the language of the investigation	The preconceptions of the researcher are suspended and the language of informants is valued and utilised
Seeks to achieve abstraction from repeated observations	Seeks to find out how people understand a situation and how their understanding influences their actions

Sources: Neuman (2003), Jankowicz (2000)

The main differences between qualitative and quantitative methods are shown in Table 12.

Choosing appropriate methods

Case illustration

Local bargaining in the National Health Service: new approaches to employee relations

After decades of industrial relations stability, government pressure in the 1990s led to a series of organisational changes in the National Health Service. The NHS was required to decentralise and establish local bargaining arrangements at NHS Trust level. While this centrally-imposed decision has not succeeded, it provided an opportunity for Trust managers to consider new approaches to employee relations, and to take steps to implement them. This article, in examining these steps, seeks to make a modest contribution of an empirical nature to the debate about the emergence of new approaches to employee relations, and its relations with HRM in general. . . .

The research
The research considered the way the move to local bargaining had taken place in a number of NHS Trusts. Because there was some discretion as to the forms taken by local Trusts, the intention was to look for emerging patterns. Given the importance attached to strategy in recent discussions on HRM (eg Tyson, 1995; Purcell, 1995; Mabey, Salaman and Storey, 1998; Legge, 1995; Lundy and Cowling, 1996), a general hypothesis was put forward: that the requirement to establish local bargaining arrangements would be used by Trusts to develop a more strategic view of employee relations. This would take the form of an attempt to simplify bargaining

---

through the use of single-table bargaining, an attempt to shift discussion of some issues from bargaining to consultation, and the development of new mechanisms for communicating with employees and the encouragement of participation. In addition, a bargaining agenda that focused on simplifying pay rates, introducing performance-related pay and individualised contracts and flexible working would be developed (Marchington, 1995).

The research consisted of the circulation of questionnaires to the senior personnel or HR executive in every NHS Trust in two NHS regions, followed by a small number of telephone and in-depth interviews of personnel/HR managers and directors. One hundred and three NHS Trusts were approached, and completed returns received from 46, a response rate of 44 per cent. Two of the responses came from ambulance trusts, four from mental health care trusts, the rest being either acute hospital or community or combined trusts. Respondents were responsible for approximately 89,000 employees. . . .

The purpose of this article is not to discuss the merits or otherwise of the move to local bargaining, but to see whether Trusts, in changing their local arrangements, acted in a way that reflected HRM values in employee relations. . . .

The evidence suggests that in the establishment of local arrangements a dominant general pattern emerged. NHS Trust managers reported a strong commitment to working with unions in a pluralist framework, an increase in both bargaining and consultation, a continued move to single-table bargaining, a strong trend towards improved communications, modest changes in employee participation plans, and limited interest in individualised pay arrangements. There appeared to be significant variations in the amount of bargaining as distinct from consultation on offer. . . .

Extracts from: F. Carr (1999) *Industrial Relations Journal*, 30 (3) 197–211.
Reproduced by permission of Blackwell Publishing, Oxford.

DISCUSSION QUESTIONS

1 To what extent was the approach taken to this research deductive and/or inductive? Explain your answer.

2 Was qualitative or quantitative data-gathering in this research?

3 How confident are you that similar results would have been achieved if this study had been undertaken using data from NHS Trusts in other parts of the country?

Feedback notes

This research was underpinned by a deductive approach. The 'theory' underpinning it was that the opportunity for local, rather than centralised, bargaining in the NHS would lead to a more strategic approach to employee relations which would be manifested as:

■ the development of single-table bargaining

■ an increase in consultation

- new mechanisms of communication and participation, and
- an employee reward agenda involving simplified pay rates, performance-related pay, individualised contracts and flexible working.

The researchers refer to a hypothesis they generated in the light of the existing understanding of strategic employment relations approaches.

Given that a deductive approach was taken, it might be expected that quantitative data would be utilised to test the hypothesis that was generated. However, although quantitative data was obtained, the investigation also utilised telephone and in-depth interviews. In this way it was possible to include numerical data (such as how many Trusts had introduced new forms of communication in the last year) and data that reflected the opinions and purposes of those managers involved, as expressed in their terms.

In this way the study is characterised by methodological pluralism, the utilisation of more than one type of data in order to answer research questions. Different kinds of complementary data are thus used to research a particular problem, issue or situation with the aim of producing a more rounded interpretation of the evidence. Indeed, the application of different data-collection methods within the same study enables you to check whether the interpretation of the evidence that you have makes sense in the light of other available evidence gathered in a different way. This use of multiple methods to shed light from different perspectives on the same phenomenon is referred to as *triangulation*. Applying different data-collection methods within one study as a way of ensuring that the data really does indicate what you think to be the case (Saunders *et al*, 2003) is an important way of adding credibility to your conclusions.

Saunders *et al* (2003) build on this general point and suggest that a combination of primary and secondary data as well as qualitative and quantitative data can be useful to progress any enquiry at different stages of the project, such as the initial process of defining a topic, in formulating research questions or objectives, and in gathering data in order to answer those questions.

In organisational research, particularly that which is required as part of a taught course of study, there are also other practical issues that influence decisions about methods. Investigative enquiries do not occur in a vacuum. They are influenced by operational issues, time pressures and the preferences and imperatives of others involved in the project, such as the employees, line managers and the project sponsor. Part of the planning process of any project therefore involves discussion and negotiation about the methods to be used, the participants that are available, and the timescale over which the enquiry must be undertaken.

A number of different factors will influence the choice of methods that you make, and these are briefly outlined below.

- the nature of the topic – The nature of your research objectives and questions are a fundamental starting point for deciding on appropriate methods. Key things to ask are: What are my research questions? What data will enable me to answer those questions? What is the most appropriate way to obtain that data?
- the extent of the literature – If you know that there is a lot of literature already about your topic, it is likely that you will choose methods that enable you to build on what is

already known. If, however, your area is relatively new and unexplored, that will also influence your choice of method(s).

■ the timescale – Another issue to take into account is the time available to you. Some methods might be possible to undertake over a shorter timespan than others.

■ resources – Some methods require specialist resources (perhaps facilities to generate transcripts of unstructured interviews) and it is important that you are aware if these are available and if you have time to learn how to use them.

■ issues of access and permission – Some project sponsors in organisational research have clear preferences for different methods, and these must be taken into account in deciding which methods to adopt and whether the nature of the research questions/objectives might have to be reviewed as a result.

Case illustration

Rethinking methods

Shirley was a full-time HR student who was undertaking a work placement in a manufacturing organisation, on which the research for her management report was to be based. In consultation with her manager in the placement organisation, Shirley decided to carry out research on absence in the organisation. Preliminary enquiries had indicated that rates of absence in the organisation were higher than those in other similar companies and this was a matter of some concern to the organisation.

Shirley's initial research objectives were to identify the areas within the organisation where absence rates were highest and to identify the causes of these high levels of absence so that an effective absence management strategy could be put in place. Having undertaken some reading on absence and its causes, she decided that the most appropriate way to gather data to enable her to answer these questions was by a questionnaire to all the staff. However, two weeks before Shirley was about to distribute her questionnaire the company announced a large downsizing project and the likelihood that redundancies would be required. In the climate of uncertainty that resulted, the project sponsor (the HR manager) told Shirley that she was not to approach any of the employees either by questionnaire or in person.

DISCUSSION QUESTIONS

1   What issues should Shirley take into account in this situation?
2   What advice would you give her?

Feedback notes

This situation, which is not uncommon, raises a number of issues and questions such as: Is the project feasible in the light of these developments? Should Shirley change her topic (and perhaps research the redundancy process)? Should she try to arrange an alternative placement? Issues that ought to be taken into account include: Over what timescale must this project be completed (often time is short for full-time students), and how much work has already been undertaken as part of the project?

In the end Shirley decided to continue with a project on absence but to revise the project objectives. Instead of trying to determine the causes of absence, she sought to investigate how managers perceived absence and the different strategies that managers in different parts of the organisation took to encourage attendance. These revised objectives meant that she could focus her data-gathering on managers and utilise a more open-ended interview method, rather than relying on a questionnaire sent to all employees.

In organisational research, therefore, the process of choosing methods by which to gather data is not a static or a linear one. It involves a process of review and revision in consultation with those involved in the project (the subjects) as well as those for whom the final report is intended (the organisation and the project supervisor/tutor/adviser). Nonetheless it is important that the methods that are finally chosen and utilised are appropriate and will enable conclusions to be drawn that are valid and reliable – and it is to these issues that this chapter now turns.

Reliability and validity

A key issue for any investigative enquiry is its credibility – the extent to which the data that have been obtained are both relevant and valuable. To make this assessment it is necessary to consider how reliable and valid the data are. Reliability is the extent to which similar results would be obtained on all similar occasions. Validity is a judgement about whether the data really provides evidence on what it is supposed to be about.

As abstract concepts, both validity and reliability can seem difficult to understand and apply in practice. Nonetheless they are important indicators of the credibility and quality of any investigative enquiry. They can, perhaps, be better considered through answering a range of questions (Easterby-Smith *et al*, 2002; Robson, 2003; Bell, 2001). These questions are listed below.

Questions relevant to assessing reliability

- Would the methods used generate the same results on other similar occasions?
- Would similar observations be reached by different observers?
- Is it easy to understand how raw data has been collated and analysed?

Questions relevant to considering validity

- What difference might the context of the investigation make to the data generated?
- To what extent has the enquiry process itself influenced the possible answers?
- How easy is it to separate cause from effect in the data ('the chicken and the egg' scenario)?
- How sure can you be that other factors (intervening variables) have not affected your data?
- To what extent would your research results be generalisable?

The Activity below provides an opportunity to consider how these questions would apply in a practical situation.

ACTIVITY – VALIDITY AND RELIABILITY

Imagine that you are undertaking a project to investigate the effectiveness of performance-related pay in a given organisation. You will be obtaining information through interviews from a range of people in different departments and at different levels within the organisation. Try to identify the main practical issues with regard to the reliability and validity of the information you can expect to receive in a project such as this.

Feedback notes

Important questions you should consider in a project such as this might include the following:

RELIABILITY

- Would interviews about performance-related pay that took place just prior to an annual pay review process generate different findings if they were undertaken just after the pay awards had been announced?

- Would interviews carried out by someone from the HR function within the organisation generate the same data as interviews that were carried out by an external researcher?

- To what extent might two different people make sense differently of the same raw data that was generated by the interviews?

VALIDITY

- To what extent does data generated in interviews just after the pay review process actually reflect opinion about performance-related pay, or might it really provide opinions about the pay rise achieved (or not) by interviewees?

- To what extent will interviewees give you the answers they think you want?

- If an interviewee who has received a poor appraisal is negative about performance-related pay, can the researcher be sure whether a poor appraisal leads to negative perceptions of PRP or whether negative perceptions about PRP then lead to a poor appraisal?

- How confident can you be that what you have found out about performance-related pay would also be applicable in different types and sizes of organisations?

No one project is going to be able to produce findings that are one-hundred-per-cent reliable and valid. It is, however, necessary that you address these issues so that you are able to determine an approach to data-gathering that indicates you have attempted to take an open-minded approach to gathering data, and that you have taken steps to minimise the limitations of your study and maximise its credibility. This means taking a planned approach to gathering data and being able to justify the decisions that you make. Such justification will be included in the methodology section of the report that you write.

PLANNING TO GATHER DATA

The term methodology means an 'analysis of and rationale for the particular method or methods used' (Jankowicz, 2000; pp.212–13) – ie it represents an answer to the questions: what approach did you adopt to gathering and making sense of data, and why? Key points that are helpful in determining your research process are indicated below, and further illustrated in Figure 20.

■ Clarify the research questions/objectives and research approach first. Planning the methods for any study is a logical sequence of judgements made by the researcher, taking into account what is reasonably possible in the context of the enquiry. The first decisions relate to the research questions or objectives. These decisions will involve discussion with other stakeholders in the project (the organisation(s) and your supervisor, tutor or adviser, etc). It is also necessary to be clear about what approach will be adopted (inductive or deductive, etc) because this will affect the way you organise your reading and the data-gathering methods that you chose.

■ Carefully consider what information you need to find out in order to answer your questions and achieve your objectives. Many students obtain information that is easy

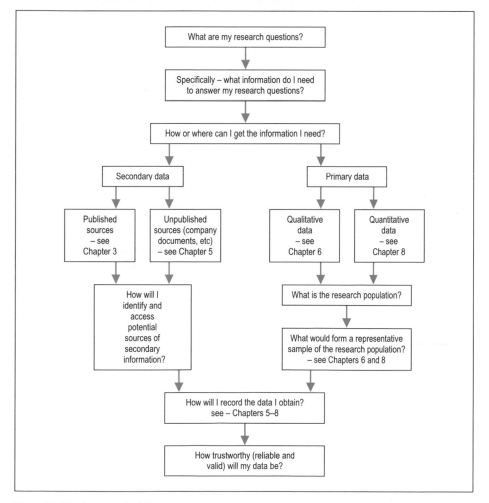

Figure 20 *Planning the methodology*

to find, but it is not always sufficient to answer their research questions. Work out what data you need and where you might be able to get it. Then decide the extent to which this is feasible. Again, discussions with the project sponsor in the organisation(s) and your supervisor/tutor/adviser are likely to be important.

■ Consider what different types of sources of information and data are available to you and make use of as wide a range as possible. Many students rush to collect some form of primary data (eg questionnaire data or focus group data) and they do not utilise other available information such as documentary evidence that already exists within the organisation or secondary data from a range of published sources. Ideas about this are in Chapter 5.

■ Clearly identify and justify the research population and your sample selection. The research population is all the subjects (people) within the scope of your investigation. So, is your study to be concerned with all employees in the organisation, one particular business unit or department, or one specific staff grouping? It is unlikely that you will be able to gather data from the whole population (unless it is very small), so some form of sampling will be required – and you will have to consider, and justify, how you will choose the people who form your sample. This should also be discussed with the project sponsor at organisational level and with your supervisor/tutor/adviser. Issues of sampling are considered in more detail in Chapter 6 (qualitative data) and Chapter 8 (quantitative data).

■ Decide on the type(s) of primary data that you will gather, and allow time to devise and pilot effective data-gathering 'instruments'. Many people choose to use the questionnaire method because they think it will be quick, or the interview method because they think it will be easy. However, many then find that their questionnaire was misinterpreted by a large number of respondents or that their interviews did not provide sufficient information to answer their research questions. All forms of data-gathering require considerable thought in the design process, and it is also important to allow time to pilot the instrument (and then amend it in the light of the pilot) prior to launching into the full-scale data-gathering process. See Chapters 6 and 8 for more on this.

■ Decide in advance how you will record the data that you gather and then how you will go on to analyse it. As part of the planning and design process for any primary data-gathering instrument it is important to be clear about how you will record the data that you get and then how you will go about the analysis. These issues are covered in Chapters 5–8.

■ Consider issues related to reliability and validity. If you can, get someone to act as a 'devil's advocate' and try to expose areas where the validity and reliability of the approach you are planning to adopt could be questioned. As noted already, no organisational study can ever be wholly valid and reliable, but being critically evaluative at this stage will enable you to address any issues that you can resolve. You will also be better placed to discuss the advantages and limitations of your study within the report that you produce.

WRITING UP THE METHODOLOGY

The expectations of the methodology section varies between different study centres, and also depends on the level of the qualification for which the research has been undertaken. It is very important to find out in advance what the requirements of your study centre are, therefore, with regard to the indicative length of the methodology section and also the key areas that must be included within it. All project reports must explain and justify how data (primary and secondary) has been gathered and analysed. The points below indicate the key issues to address, as a minimum, for any investigative enquiry. The threshold of what should be included would be greater for many qualification-related projects – and this is discussed further in Chapter 9.

- appropriateness of the methods – What was the context for the research? For research in one organisation: what was the organisational context? What was the nature of the relationship of the researcher with the organisation(s)? What were the research questions? What approach to data-gathering (qualitative/quantitative or both?) was adopted, and why?

- quality and quantity of data collected and analysed – How were secondary sources identified (literature search as well as any organisational documents, etc)? What primary data was gathered? How was a sample selected? How were data-gathering instruments (questionnaires, interview questions, etc) developed? What were the response rates, and what are the implications of the response rates? How was the data analysed?

- management of access and co-operation – In what way did the context of the study influence the research process as it actually occurred? What ethical issues were raised by the project, and how were they handled? How were non-returned questionnaires or other refusals to provide data taken into account?

- evaluation of methods – What issues of validity and reliability were there? What were the advantages and limitations of the methods and research process used?

SUMMARY

- There are many different ways of tackling research projects in HR, and it is important to formulate an approach that is contextually appropriate and will generate data and conclusions that are meaningful and valuable.

- *Theory* and *practice* are not separate things. People use theories in everyday life to generate expectations about the world and to make sense of things. Theories are refined through practice so that everyday experience informs the generalisation process.

- Theories can be evaluated by testing them empirically (in practice) or by analysing their component parts to establish the extent to which they make sense.

- Theories are developed through the processes of induction and deduction. *Induction* (theory-building) involves observing facts, behaviours and meanings to form a generalised theory about what is occurring and why. *Deduction* (theory-testing) involves identifying propositions from existing theories and testing them in different situations, conditions and contexts in order to refine and amend them where appropriate.

- *Quantitative data* (data that can be quantified) and *qualitative data* (data based on meanings and expressed through language) are both relevant to HR research.

- *Triangulation* is the process of using data from different sources to analyse a phenomenon from different perspectives.

- Organisational research and decisions on methods of gathering data will be influenced by contextual factors such as operational issues, time pressures and the preferences of organisational stakeholders.

- The value and credibility of an investigative enquiry can be assessed by considering the validity and reliability of the data on which the conclusions are based. *Reliability* is the extent to which similar results would be obtained in all similar occasions, and *validity* is a judgement about whether the data really provides evidence of what the researcher claims it is about.

- All project reports require a section that explains and justifies the method or methods that were used. Different study centres have different requirements for this section.

- The methodology section of any report should evaluate the appropriateness of the methodology for the particular enquiry, the quality and quantity of data collected, the appropriateness of the analysis processes, and the management of access and co-operation.

Questions for review/reflection

These questions are designed to enable you to identify key areas for development with your project. The responses to them can also form part of a Continuing Professional Development log or portfolio. This is a requirement of the CIPD for those who wish to upgrade their membership status.

Tacking stock

1 Find out about the requirements of your study centre for the methodology section of your report. What sort of wordcount is expected? What headings or key issues should be discussed?

2 What are the expectations of the organisation(s) with which your research will be concerned? What organisational issues or priorities might affect the methods by which you gather data or the timing of your data-gathering activities?

3 What secondary data sources (organisational documents, etc) are available to you? What level of permission will you need to obtain company information? Who are the 'gatekeepers' of such information?

Strengths and weaknesses

1 How has your review of the literature informed your thinking about methods of data-gathering? How satisfied are you with your review of the existing literature?

2 How clearly articulated are your research questions/objectives? To what extent have your research questions informed your decisions about the methodology?

3 What is your level of expertise in designing instruments of data collection (questionnaire design, interview design, facilitating focus groups, etc)? What development might be helpful in this area, and how might you undertake it?

4 What knowledge and understanding do you have of sample selection processes to enhance reliability and validity? Where might you obtain effective advice about this?

5 What experience and level of expertise do you have in recording and analysing quantitative and/or qualitative data? Where can you learn more about these activities?

Being a practitioner-researcher

1 What skills will you need to enable you to obtain access to organisational information (primary and secondary) and to achieve the co-operation of participants in the enquiry?

2 To what extent have organisational stakeholders got firm ideas about the methods you should use? What skills will you need to manage these expectations and ensure the validity and reliability of the data that you gather?

FURTHER READING

One way of finding out about the advantages and disadvantages of different methods is to read literature sources about your topic for method as well as for content. Every general textbook on research methods covers issues of methodology. The following list represents a selection of them.

COLLIS J. and HUSSEY, R. (2003) *Business Research: A practical guide for undergraduate and postgraduate students.* Basingstoke, Macmillan Business.

CURRAN, J. and BLACKBURN, R. (2001) *Researching the Small Enterprise.* London, Sage.

EASTERBY-SMITH, M., THORPE, R. and LOWE, A. (2002) *Management Research, An Introduction.* London, Sage.

GILL, J. and JOHNSON, P. (2001) *Research Methods for Managers.* London, Paul Chapman.

HAMMERSLEY, M. (1995) *The Politics of Organisational Research.* London, Sage.

JANKOWICZ, A. (2000) *Business Research Projects.* London, Thomson International Business Press.

PUNCH, K. F. (1998) *Introduction to Social Science Research: Quantitative and qualitative approaches.* London, Sage.

ROBSON, C. (2002) *Real World Research.* Oxford, Blackwell.

SAUNDERS, M., LEWIS, P. and THORNHILL, A. (2003) *Research Methods for Business Students.* London, *Financial Times*/Prentice Hall.

SKINNER, D., TAGG, C. and HOLLOWAY, J. (2000) 'Managers and research: the pros and cons of qualitative approaches', *Management Learning*, 31 (2) 163–79.

Acting and observing

Finding and using
organisational evidence

Chapter outline
How to use this chapter
Different forms of documentary evidence
Using data from organisational management information systems
Finding and selecting appropriate documents for analysis
Making sense of organisational information
Summary
Further reading

LEARNING OUTCOMES

This chapter should help you to:

■ identify evidence from within the organisation that will help to answer your research questions

■ determine how to make use of data from management information systems

■ identify the most appropriate and relevant forms of documents for your enquiry

■ consider different ways to make sense of organisational information.

HOW TO USE THIS CHAPTER

This chapter is relevant for all practitioner-researchers who plan to undertake an organisationally-based investigation. There is likely to be a huge range of information that already exists in the organisation that can help you to answer your research questions. Many people invest considerable time generating new data and overlook sources of valuable data that already exist within the organisation(s).

Chapter 3 considered how written and published secondary sources add value to an investigative project. This chapter focuses on the unpublished primary and secondary sources that can be found within organisations.

Case illustration

Investigating the appraisal process

Mark was a full-time student undertaking a work placement with a large organisation. For his research project he undertook an evaluation of the appraisal process currently in use within the company. The aim of the enquiry was to assess whether the appraisal process met the needs of both the organisation and its employees, from the perspectives of both the appraisers and the appraisees. Mark and the manager sponsoring his placement agreed that part of the enquiry would involve the use of questionnaires. In addition, Mark discovered that an organisation-wide staff focus survey had been conducted by an independent organisation during the previous year, in which five questions had been directed at the current performance management system. The organisation agreed that Mark could utilise data from this report relating to these five questions as part of his study.

DISCUSSION QUESTIONS

1 In addition to the data from the survey and the questionnaire data that Mark would generate as part of his research, what other forms of organisational evidence might be relevant for this study? Try to list about four sources of evidence.

2 What difficulties might Mark experience in trying to locate and utilise the information you have identified?

Feedback notes

Internal documents such as staff handbooks, policies and guidelines would be useful in establishing the context of the performance management process. In addition, evidence from proposals relating to the scheme, information indicating how many completed appraisal forms were received on time, and the pay implications of the appraisal process would be relevant. It is likely that completed appraisal forms themselves would form a valuable source of information about the operation of the process in reality.

There is a huge range of potential sources of information that can add value to any investigative enquiry, particularly if it is organisationally-based. Much organisational information is unobtrusive and easy to overlook or neglect. Perhaps this is why many people fail to make use of relevant and worthwhile sources of organisational evidence in their enquiries. Indeed, sometimes students opt for time-consuming data-generation methods that merely serve to duplicate data that are already available within the organisation.

However, there are some difficulties with the effective use of organisational documents. It would be possible, for example, to invest a lot of time in reading many organisational documents and printing off detailed reports from computerised information systems that, in the end, do not add much value to the findings of the project. This chapter therefore seeks to highlight different forms of organisational evidence that are likely to be relevant to any organisationally-based project and to examine different approaches that can be taken to finding it, selecting what is most relevant and useful, and then making sense of it.

DIFFERENT FORMS OF DOCUMENTARY EVIDENCE

ACTIVITY – BRAINSTORMING ACTIVITY

Imagine that you know absolutely nothing about an organisation. It is not possible for you to contact any of the people (either verbally or in writing) who are involved with the organisation, although you *can* access documents within the company. Produce a list of all the sources of information that might help you to know something about the organisation, its purpose, culture, business operations, and so on. Include different kinds of evidence in your list, not just written forms of information.

Feedback notes

There are a wide variety of sources of information that can help you to learn about any organisation (see Table 13). Your list of evidence might include marketing documents, such as company brochures, as well as internal documents such as letters, memos, hard copies of e-mails, agendas, minutes of meetings, reports submitted to working groups, proposals for business projects and also progress reports. In addition, it is possible that there may be information about the organisation to be found in newspaper clippings or articles about the organisation in trade journals or business-related books. It would be possible to get more knowledge of the type of organisation and its type of business if you could access its client or customer database, information about its employees (numbers, skills, length of service, turnover, and so on) and information about the allocation of resources through budgetary records. Organisations also communicate about themselves in non-paper-based forms. Many large organisations have a corporate Internet site, and there may also be a company video as well as copies of radio or TV programmes that have featured the company. Other non-written sources would be valuable in helping you to understand about the organisation. This might include maps showing the sites of different parts of the organisation, architectural plans of some of the buildings, diagrams showing the production or workflow processes, and so on.

ACTIVITY – MAKING USE OF PUBLISHED DIARIES, AUTOBIOGRAPHIES AND MEMOIRS

Imagine that you are undertaking some research into HR issues in professional sport. As part of the background research you are reading diaries and autobiographies of prominent figures in sport. There are a huge range of these and you are not sure how useful such sources will be. If you have the time (and the interest) skim-read one such book.

DISCUSSION QUESTIONS

Why do sporting figures (and others) publish their diaries and autobiographies?
What are the advantages and disadvantages of evidence from sources such as these?

Feedback notes

Sources such as these, produced by people involved, are helpful to researchers in finding out about the context of events that they are enquiring into. An advantage of this sort of accounts is that, like other primary sources, they will have come into existence within a period of time relatively close to the events the researcher is interested in, and have been produced by those who were involved. However, the motives for writing such documents must be taken into account. These will include the commercial incentive for well-known and influential

Table 13 *Different sources of organisational evidence*

Primary sources		Secondary sources
Examples of evidence produced internally for internal use	**Examples of evidence produced internally for external use**	**Examples of evidence produced externally using internal sources of evidence**
Administrative sources ■ personnel records ■ safety records ■ production/service records	Organisational Internet site(s)	Newspaper cuttings
Business records ■ agendas ■ notes from meetings ■ progress reports ■ project proposals	**Corporate brochure(s)** (for clients/potential investors etc)	**TV/radio transcripts/ recordings**
Operational records ■ letters ■ memos ■ e-mails ■ handwritten notes	**Corporate video/DVD** (for PR purposes)	**Books and journal articles featuring the organisation**
Policy documents and procedures ■ HR ■ purchasing and supply ■ finance and accounting ■ marketing	**Marketing information**	
Other internal 'artefacts' ■ briefing notes ■ induction presentations ■ corporate videos (for staff and associates) ■ maps, plans and drawings ■ process diagrams	**Published diaries/ memoirs of key people**	

figures to publish their autobiographies or some form(s) of memoir. Perhaps, also, the compilers are motivated by the desire to ensure that 'their side of the story' is available for posterity. In some ways, therefore, some forms of documentary evidence will have been produced for the attention of future 'researchers', and must be read with this in mind.

Most of the primary sources you may use that have been generated within organisations will not have been produced for the purposes of your research, and so it is important to remember that they are 'inadvertent sources' (Bell, 2001). Other types of evidence (such as an academic book about the company or a TV programme featuring it) are secondary sources, being the result of someone else's interpretation, albeit based on some of the primary sources.

For many researchers, especially those that already work within an organisation on which their research is based, much of the documentary information they may have to hand merely replicates their existing 'tacit' knowledge. However, the people at your study centre who will read (and assess) the findings of any research will be less knowledgeable, and reference to documentary evidence enables you to justify the organisation's context and the particular characteristics that you highlight in your report. In addition, data generated within the organisation may also enable you to challenge taken-for-granted assumptions about 'the way things are around here'.

There are also more reasons for the use of documentary evidence within organisationally-based research (Yin, 2003). Firstly, documentary evidence can provide specific details about particularly relevant events. Research into a culture change process, for example, might indicate that those involved in the change process felt that the need for a major change was triggered by significant factors (such as loss of key accounts, acquisition of a new business, financial and budgetary difficulties within the organisation, and/or similar). However, people make sense of events in different ways, and they may not fully reflect the actual chain of events. Study of relevant documents would enable you to pinpoint whether the factors that are cited by those involved really did occur prior to the change process or whether they have become obscured and repositioned in thinking about the change process for other reasons.

Secondly, documentary evidence can corroborate and augment evidence from other sources. For example, research into appraisal interviews may indicate that appraisees feel their objectives are unachievable and unrealistic. Analysis of a sample of the appraisal forms themselves might yield further evidence about the quality of objective-setting by managers and provide a further justification (or otherwise) for this conclusion.

Thirdly, documentary evidence can provide *inferences*. Research into the management of a redundancy process, for example, would be enhanced by analysis of how the drafts of some statements to staff about the process may have changed as a result of any consultation process that was undertaken. Evidence about who e-mails were sent to (and not sent to) at different stages of any chain of events would also provide useful evidence about the level of involvement of different stakeholders in the process.

What is referred to here as documentary evidence can therefore take many forms, including films, pictures and other artefacts as well as collective, electronic administrative data (such as on a Personnel Information System). This sort of data is often overlooked in investigative enquiries although it should form part of your wider planned data-collection process. In this way the most appropriate sources can be identified and less time will be wasted reading through organisational material that is inappropriate. For most projects documents will be supplementary to other forms of primary and secondary data. For some enquiries, however, organisational documents will be an important part of the data that is analysed, and some research may be based exclusively on primary data in the form of organisational documentary evidence.

This chapter will consider the use of data generated by routine administrative processes first, and will go on to discuss other documents and organisational evidence that can add value to an investigative enquiry.

USING DATA FROM ORGANISATIONAL MANAGEMENT INFORMATION SYSTEMS

All organisations collect information relating to their function and to the people that they employ. These records can form a valuable source of information relevant to your research aims – if you can obtain access to them. Some of this information may exist in the form of card-index systems or collections of paper records in filing cabinets and other forms of archiving. Increasingly, however, administrative records are maintained in an electronic form. It is important at the planning stage to determine how information from this type of source can help you to answer your research questions. Perhaps it will be possible to compare data over different time periods or for different parts of the organisation, as a way of identifying priorities for further probing in your enquiry. But such administrative records are unlikely to provide direct answers to your research questions, and it is important not to waste time with pages of descriptive statistics and cross-tabulations and so on that carry little meaning in their own right.

ACTIVITY – RESEARCH ISSUES WITH MANAGEMENT INFORMATION SYSTEMS

Imagine that you are undertaking research into job evaluation and its impact on pay discrimination. As part of your studies you have become aware that job evaluation has been criticised as perpetuating pay inequality between men and women. A new job evaluation approach was implemented two years ago in the organisation where your enquiry is to take place, and your aim is to evaluate its impact on pay and benefits within the organisation, with particular emphasis on women's pay. The organisation has a computerised Personnel Information System, which contains details of current grades and rates of pay as well as historical data on pay and grading for the last six years. Last year the Personnel Information System was linked with the organisation's payroll system to ensure a consistency of data. Subject to a range of security and confidentiality safeguards, the organisation has agreed that you can have access to the system, but only for the purposes of obtaining quantitative reports and not for the study of the records of any individual employee.

1 What reports from the Personnel Information System would help you to evaluate the impact of the new job evaluation system?

2 What challenges will you face in obtaining this information?

3 What issues should you bear in mind assuming that you are able to generate the reports that you need?

Feedback notes

The development and utilisation of computerised information systems for HR has enabled research enquiries to be undertaken that would have been almost impossible 10 or 20 years ago, and research into pay trends in organisations is one such area. Reports that you might decide to generate (for periods before and after the implementation of the new scheme) could include:

- the number of staff at each grade
- the pay range for each grade
- the proportion of regradings at the time of implementation
- the number of regradings since (and before) implementation
- the proportion of men and women at each grade
- the average pay for women (per year; per month or week; and per hour) in the organisation
- the average pay for men (as above).

One of the challenges you would face in obtaining this sort of data relates to the functionality of the system – ie the extent to which the system itself is capable of generating these reports. Many practitioners have found that information systems are very good at taking in information but that they may not be fully able to generate reports in the form required by those who use them. Establishing whether the system could generate these reports may well, therefore, require liaison with local system experts and/or with the organisation that supplied the system originally.

Assuming that the system is able to generate the reports that you require, a further challenge may be the development of your own skills with the system in order to obtain the reports. Here again it would be necessary to allow sufficient time for you to develop such an expertise.

You may also have highlighted a further range of issues that you need to take into account – and these are outlined below.

- access – Irrespective of whether the information is in paper or electronic form, If It shows people's names or other means of identification, you must find out what level of permission you need to be able to access the data.
- the quality and reliability of the data – How thoroughly and regularly have records been updated? Are there areas of ambiguity in the way the system is set up that might allow for different responses to reflect the same situation? Is the recent data more reliable than the information that is five years old?
- focusing on research questions – Often computerised databases can seem to offer such a range of data that devising and running reports can become rather addictive and valuable time is lost scrutinising information that is nice to have but not really necessary to have.

In spite of these issues, many practitioner-researchers find that data from the Personnel Information System of the organisation in which their research is based can help them to answer (and in some cases to formulate) meaningful research questions. This sort of data can also help you to judge how representative information from survey data you subsequently obtain may be.

FINDING AND SELECTING APPROPRIATE DOCUMENTS FOR ANALYSIS

ACTIVITY – INTERNATIONAL HR

Imagine that you work for a large organisation that has been gradually developing business in other countries over the past 10 years. You have become interested in the extent to which HR practices that are accepted in the UK can be applied in different regions of the world where there are different cultural expectations. You know that your organisation has already established a presence in China and you want to find out how HR has supported that process.

From your reading you have found out that labour costs in China are a fraction of those in other parts of the world, and that the Chinese market, already significant, is expected to account for one quarter of the total world economy by 2025 (Sappal, 2003). However, your study of the literature about culture in different regions of the world has highlighted significant differences between the Chinese and UK ways of doing things. You understand that what equates to the personnel function in China, for example, tends to be focused on administrative and compliance issues. You have also learned of the concern with 'face' in the societal culture of much of the Asia Pacific region of the world such that employees would be likely to be far less comfortable with two-way feedback processes (in appraisals, etc) than is accepted in Europe.

From your initial enquiries within the company you have discovered that competence-based recruitment and selection and a performance management process have been introduced in China, as well as a management development programme that enables a small number of employees from China to visit the UK for a two-week period to learn more about the business.

You have obtained permission to undertake an evaluation of your company's approach to HR in China for your project. You are in the process of arranging contacts with HR people in the UK and in China in order to progress your investigation. In the meantime, the international HR people have provided you with some information so that you can familiarise yourself with the company's approach. They have sent you the following documents:

■ copies of policies relating to personal and career development for expatriate staff

■ a company application form (Chinese labour market)

■ a computer-generated report indicating the numbers of staff employed in China and showing their nationality, rates of pay, and length of service

■ the policy for performance appraisal in China and a copy of the appraisal form that is used

■ a copy of an indicative itinerary for visits of Chinese employees to the UK.

1 Identify the ways in which this sort of information would assist your enquiry.
2 What problems might arise from a study of these documents in isolation? What do these documents *not* tell you?

Feedback notes

There are many ways in which these documents would be helpful to your study. They will provide an overall indication of the policy priorities of the organisation from the perspective of managers in the UK and China. From this basis you can devise a study, utilising data generated from employees in China and the UK that builds on this initial starting point.

Such sources may therefore be very valuable, although a study that was based only on these documents would be very partial. The documents do not tell you, for example, if many applicants in China had ignored the application form and had submitted CVs and accompanying letters that did not easily fit into the competence framework. Also, they do not give any information about the quality of the appraisal discussions or of the perception of career management processes, in reality, of expatriated managers. The documents that you have seen so far represent a UK management perspective, and it would be important to assess the issues from the perspective of others, such as Chinese managers and employees.

It is therefore necessary to take a critically evaluative approach to the use of documentary evidence. It would be naive to believe that something that has been recorded in written form provides evidence that is not biased in any way. Organisational communications are artificial and partial, and they must be critically assessed and compared with other forms of evidence generated in different ways. An overview of the strengths and weaknesses of documentary sources is shown in Table 14.

Table 14 *Advantages and disadvantages of documentary and other organisational evidence*

Advantages	Disadvantages
Not time constrained – repeated study of the documents is possible	Identifying and accessing all relevant documents can be difficult
Unobtrusive – those in the organisation are not inconvenienced and their work is not disrupted.	Partiality – incomplete sets of documents may lead to exaggerated bias in the information the sources provide
Level of detail – sources can provide exact details of names and details of particular events or initiatives as well as quantitative data about organisational processes	The bias or perspective of the author/ producer of the document is not known
Coverage – documents can show trends over time, incorporate many events, and include many locations	Access – the organisation may not be willing to allow access to some forms of documentary or archival records for confidentiality reasons
Time – there are opportunities for an element of longitudinal analysis when the timespan available to undertake other forms of data-gathering is very limited	Analysis – it may be difficult to say whether the documents you are studying caused the phenomenon you are interested in, or resulted from it

Sources: Robson (2002), Yin (2003), Bell (2001)

In order to maximise the advantages of organisational sources of evidence and minimise the difficulties, it is necessary to think systematically about how to locate and select appropriate forms of evidence, and it is also important to take some quality-control issues into account.

The first stage in an effective process to make use of appropriate organisational evidence is to identify and categorise the types of evidence that would be helpful to your enquiry. Having done that it is necessary to locate the sources and then to select the material that will be most relevant to the aims and research questions underpinning your project. In particular it is important not to choose documents that will merely reinforce the conclusions you expect to draw, but to look for evidence that might develop your thinking, and therefore the value of your study.

Once you have obtained the evidence you have selected it is also necessary to evaluate it against the following criteria (Scott, 1990):

- authenticity and credibility – It would be unlikely (but not impossible) that documents from an organisation were not, in reality produced there, but the accuracy of what is described in one source of information must be assessed by comparison with other sources of data about the same issue.

- representativeness – It is also necessary to evaluate the extent to which the views expressed in documents from one part of an organisation (say, the HR department) also reflect the views of other functions (such as marketing or finance). Alternatively, if you are studying documents related to the activities of a trade union, to what extent does the information you are reading about reflect all members of the union, or is it more reflective of the union activists?

- meaning and significance – This may be the most challenging area, particularly if you are unfamiliar with the culture and language (jargon) used within the organisation that you are studying. This difficulty is most apparent where documents may have been generated in a different country with a different cultural context. Words used in HR in the UK, for example, may mean different things when used by the HR department based in Germany. Titles of different jobs are also expressed and understood differently in different countries. Organisational cultures also can lead to different interpretations of the same language. The term 'strategy', for example, is understood in somewhat different ways in different organisations.

So to make best use of documentary and organisational evidence, it is necessary to undertake a deliberate evaluation of it. This involves asking such questions as:

- What kind of document is it?
- What does it actually say?
- Who produced it, and for what purpose?
- What was the context of its production?
- Is it typical or exceptional for its time?
- Is it complete – has it been altered or edited?
- What is known about the author's background and experience?

ACTIVITY – HEALTH AND SAFETY AT WORK POLICY

Department of Health and Safety, Health and Safety Policy

As required by legislation, the organisation has issued a Health and Safety Policy. It is available in all departments, from Health and Safety Co-ordinators and may be viewed in the Personnel Department. Additionally, all staff are issued with an abridged version on appointment.

The Policy is in three parts:

- the health and safety statement
- the organisation for health and safety
- arrangements for carrying out the Policy.

The health and safety statement, which is signed by the CEO, is set out below.

The Board of Directors has ultimate responsibility for health and safety in the organisation. Its duties are discharged through the Personnel Director, taking all reasonable and practicable steps to ensure the health and safety of all those that make use of the organisation's facilities.

Success in health and safety management is dependent upon the integration of health and safety into all management functions within the organisation.

The Personnel Director is responsible for the formulation, implementation and ongoing policy development in the field of health and safety.

The promotion, enhancement and maintenance of a positive health and safety culture within the organisation is achieved by:

- all staff displaying a positive attitude to health and safety
- all staff taking care of their own health and safety and the health and safety of those who may be affected by their acts or omissions
- management at all levels accepting that they are responsible for the staff they supervise and are accountable to those to whom they report for health and safety
- management ensuring that all activities are adequately resourced both financially and physically.

The organisation will maintain proper arrangements with employees' recognised trade union representatives for joint consultation on, and participation in, measures for promoting health and safety at work.

This safety policy will be reviewed at least annually by the Health and Safety Committee and amended as circumstances require.

It is a fundamental belief of the Board of Directors that all injuries can be prevented.

Compliance with the Health and Safety at Work Act 1974 and the relevant statutory provisions is to be regarded by all staff as the base from which to work.

Health and safety issues affect everyone who uses the organisation's facilities. The responsibilities of staff are:

Health and safety responsibilities of all staff
The organisation is committed to creating a working environment which is safe and healthy. All staff have an essential role in the creation of an active and positive health and safety culture.

The organisation requires all staff to take reasonable care of their own safety and of the safety of others.

These responsibilities include:

- using equipment, machinery, substances and safety equipment as instructed and respecting the use of safety equipment
- co-operating with the organisation and informing organisational staff with responsibility for health and safety of any risk or threat to health and safety
- informing the organisation of any areas where health and safety arrangements, including training, may be considered inadequate.

Imagine that you came across this document on the Internet site of a large organisation as part of your enquiry into Health and Safety at Work issues in UK organisations.

Evaluate it in terms of the issues summarised below:

- What kind of document is it? Is it authentic and credible, and what does it actually say?
- Who produced it and for what purpose?
- What was the context of its production?
- Is it typical and representative of such documents or exceptional for its time?
- To what extent is its meaning clear?
- Is it complete – has it been altered or edited?
- What is known about the author's background and experience?

If you were researching into health and safety in this organisation, in what ways is this a useful document, and what other information would you require?

Feedback notes
Your evaluation of this document would probably highlight the following issues. There seems to be very little doubt about the authenticity of the policy statement in that it reads like the policy of a large company and it was accessed on the Internet site of a large, reputable organisation. It has been produced to comply with legal requirements and it is very typical of other Health and Safety at Work policy statements. In this sense its espoused meaning is

clear, but what is not known is the extent to which those in the organisation really do subscribe to its clauses and intentions.

Another unknown area is the extent to which the policy statement has been amended over the years – it was accessed electronically in 2004 but a policy statement has been a legal requirement for nearly 30 years. It is also not clear who authored the statement and the extent to which other stakeholders had an opportunity to contribute to it.

Further information is required, therefore, on these points, and it is also necessary to access other organisational evidence (such as accident statistics and reports by Health and Safety Co-ordinators, etc).

MAKING SENSE OF ORGANISATIONAL INFORMATION

So far this chapter has addressed the identification and selection of relevant organisational and documentary evidence. Having accessed such information, it is also important to consider the most appropriate way to analysis it.

WEB-BASED ACTIVITY – COMPARING DOCUMENTS

Go to a general web-based search engine (such as Google, Alta Vista or Yahoo) and enter the search terms 'harassment' and 'bullying'. From the hits for this sort of search you are likely to be able to access the harassment and bullying policies of a range of different public sector bodies. If you were interested in researching into harassment and bullying as part of your topic, what steps would you take to make use of the information contained within these documents?

Feedback notes
It is likely that in pursuing your interest in harassment and bullying you may wish to make an assessment of the different policies of different organisations, identifying and probing areas of similarity and difference between them. You might also try to find out how harassment is defined in different organisations and the different routes open to a victim of bullying in different situations. In this way, you will need to engage in a process of categorisation and comparison.

Information from policy documents alone, however, represents a very partial and unrepresentative selection of how harassment and bullying is managed in practice in different organisations. Much of the significance of the information is only apparent when considered in relation to other documents and evidence from within the organisation(s). Analysis of documentary evidence therefore tends to be comparative and involve abstracting elements of relevant information, grouping these elements, and comparing them with other relevant evidence.

Induction and deduction

The analysis of organisational evidence can be undertaken in one of two different ways, which are illustrated in Figure 21, and which link to the different approaches of relating theories and evidence that are discussed in Chapter 4.

A deductive approach towards the analysis of documents would make use of a theory or framework of practice that has already been established and consider the extent to which the

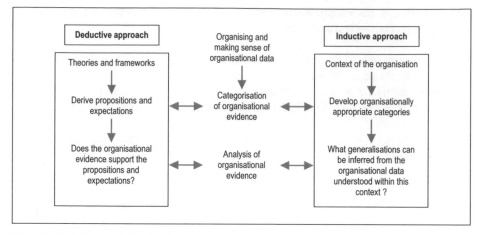

Figure 21 *Analysing organisational evidence*

documentary evidence indicates that this theory is occurring in reality. Thus the basis on which the evidence is analysed (the analytical framework) is derived from the literature.

Alternatively, it is possible to analyse the information from the context of the organisation from which it has been generated. In this way data from the evidence is organised utilising organisationally appropriate categories, and further detailed analysis on the basis of which conclusions are drawn takes place from this more inductive approach to analysis. Yin (2003) argues that researchers should choose one or the other of these analytical strategies. However, because different types of organisational evidence may lend themselves to different analytical approaches, and the boundaries between the inductive and deductive approaches may not be as clear as Yin's argument would suggest, the use of both could be appropriate (Gill and Johnson, 2001; Saunders *et al*, 2003).

Qualitative and quantitative analysis

A key theme of this chapter has been the diversity of organisational evidence and the potential of data available within the organisation to add value to investigative enquiries provided that there is a clear rationale underpinning the data-gathering and evaluation process. In addition it is necessary to ensure that the data is analysed in a systematic and rigorous way, treating it with as much care as would be accorded to other forms of data gathered.

Because organisational evidence is characterised by diversity, there is also a range of different ways in which it can be analysed. Qualitative analysis may be appropriate for some of the organisational data, and quantitative analysis may be required for other forms of information. Some of the evidence you have obtained may be suitable for both qualitative and quantitative analysis processes.

The examination of images from corporate websites, for example, as well as 'messages' from company newspapers or copies of written communications relating to a particular topic, might be qualitatively analysed, establishing and examining themes and categories in chronological order or some other sequence. (Qualitative analysis is examined in Chapter 7.)

Quantitative analysis may be appropriate for other types of organisational data, such as information from the organisation's Personnel Information System. It might also be possible to examine the frequency of different events or categories by examining the texts of organisational documents. (Quantitative techniques are considered in Chapter 8.)

The following activity demonstrates how both qualitative and quantitative analysis may be utilised.

ACTIVITY – CATEGORIES FOR ANALYSIS: ANALYSING HR JOB ADVERTISEMENTS

Obtain a copy of *People Management* (or visit www.peoplemanagement.co.uk) and identify four advertisements for different HR positions. These should be broadly comparable (eg all generalist HR posts or all training and development posts) and should be based within the same UK region (eg London and the South-east) but should be differentiated by the salary being offered. Try to find a job advertisement within each of these annual salary categories:

- £19,995 or less
- £20,000–£29,995
- £30,000–£39,995
- £40,000 or more.

Decide how you would go about analysing the main differences and similarities between what is expected from HR professionals at these different salary levels, utilising the content of the advertisements only.

How might you assess how the expectations of HR professionals has changed over the last ten years?

Feedback notes
Possible categories that you might try to use when undertaking your analysis might include:

- the responsibilities of the job
- length of experience
- range (and type) of work
- level of qualification
- job title.

In addition, it is likely that when you start to compare the texts of the different advertisements you will notice particular expressions that seem to be significant (such as 'strategic', 'results-oriented', 'complex problems', etc). You might find that the size of the advertisements varies, and you might also notice a different approach to graphics and the layout of the advertisements.

In order to make sense of this data, therefore, quantitative methods as well as qualitative methods may be appropriate. In this example it might be interesting to quantify the number of times particular phrases or key words appear in the advertisements. If you were interested in investigating how perceptions of what an HR role involves have changed over time, it would be possible to access copies of advertisements over a period of ten years and analyse trends in what was expected of the post-holders as well as trends in the salaries offered.

SUMMARY

- The range of sources of information about any organisation includes materials produced within the organisation for internal use and for external use, materials produced externally about the organisation, and administrative records and data.

- The term 'documentary evidence' refers to films, pictures and websites and other artefacts as well as to those things more usually referred to as documents.

- These sources of information can add value to any investigative enquiry, particularly if it is organisationally-based. Such information can help you to establish the context of the organisational situation that you are investigating, provide specific details about relevant events, and corroborate and augment evidence from other sources.

- Organisational evidence may be in the form of primary data (produced by those involved) or secondary data (produced by someone else using primary data) and then accessed by the researcher.

- Most, but not all, organisational evidence is inadvertent – it was not originally produced for the purposes of your investigative enquiry. It will contain 'witting' and unwitting evidence that may be useful to you.

- Key issues when evaluating data from administrative records and information systems are: access and confidentiality; data quality and reliability, and relevance of the data to the research questions.

- Key issues when evaluating documentary and organisational evidence are: the authenticity and credibility of the sources, how representative the evidence is, and the meaning and significance of what is contained in the documents.

- Effective utilisation of organisational evidence requires identification and location of evidence that is relevant to the research questions and effective sample selection.

- Organisational evidence can underpin an inductive and/or a deductive approach to analysis.

- Organisational evidence is diverse in its form and nature. To make sense of the information may require qualitative analysis and/or quantitative analysis.

Questions for review/reflection

These questions are designed to enable you to identify key areas for development with your project that you should discuss with your project tutor/supervisor/adviser if possible. The responses to them can also form part of a Continuing Professional Development log or portfolio. This is required by the CIPD for those people who wish to upgrade their membership status.

Taking stock

1   To what extent are you so familiar with the organisation that your knowledge of many of its features is 'tacit'? What sources of evidence would justify your understanding through making your knowledge explicit?

2   What sources of organisational information (primary and secondary) may help you to answer your research questions? What are the views of your project tutor, supervisor or adviser and of any sponsor of your project within the organisation?

3   Are there non-written forms of data that would provide useful evidence for your project?

4   In what ways may data from any Personnel Information System be useful to achieving your research objectives? What would be the most helpful format for the data?

Strengths and weaknesses

1   What level of skills would you need to generate specific queries and reports from information management systems? How might you develop the skills you need? Who would be the best person to help with this?

2   What information search skills do you need to identify and select appropriate documentary sources? How might you develop these?

Being a practitioner-researcher

1   Who might be helpful in arranging access to organisational and documentary forms of evidence? What are the implications for confidentiality and ethics if you make use of internal documents?

2   What level of permission will you require to utilise data from a Personnel Information System (whether paper-based or electronic)?

3   How can you check on the meaning and significance of some of the terms and expressions used within any organisational sources that you study?

4   How might you ensure that you take into account any biases (such as a management perspective) in the documents that you analyse?

FURTHER READING

Issues of documentary evidence are discussed more fully in disciplines such as history, literature and social policy than in many general business research methods books. However, there are useful chapters in the following texts:

BELL, J. (2001) *Doing Your Research Project*. Buckingham, Open University Press.

BLAXTER, L., HUGHES, C. and TIGHT, M. (2001) *How to Research*. Buckingham, Open University Press.

BRYMAN, A. (1989) *Research Methods and Organisation Studies*. London, Unwin Hyman.

COWTON, C. J. (1998) 'The use of secondary data in business ethics research', *Journal of Business Ethics*, 17 (4) 423–34.

NEUMAN, W. (2003) *Social Research Methods: Qualitative and quantitative methods*. New York, Wiley.

ROBSON, C. (2002) *Real World Research: A resource for social scientists and practitioner-researchers*. London, Blackwell.

YIN, R. K. (2003) *Case Study Research: Design and methods*. London, Sage.

More general texts about organisational information systems, with chapters or references to HR or Personnel Information Systems include:

BODY, D. (2002) *Managing Information Systems: An organisational perspective*. Harlow, *Financial Times*/Prentice Hall.

LAUDON, K (1994) *Essentials of Management Information Systems: Organisation and technology*. New Jersey, Prentice Hall.

MARTIN, C. (1992) *Information Systems: A management perspective*. London, McGraw-Hill.

MCNURLIN, B. (2002) *Information Systems Management in Practice*. New Jersey, Prentice Hall.

SCOTT, J. (1990) *A Matter of Record*. Cambridge, Polity Press.

Collecting and recording qualitative data

Chapter outline
How to use this chapter
The use and importance of qualitative data in HR research
Observation and participation
Data from individuals
Focus groups
Sample selection for qualitative research
Making sense of the data
Summary
Further reading

LEARNING OUTCOMES

- **This chapter should help you to:**

- **consider how qualitative data can contribute to your HR research**

- **assess how participation or observation might provide some data for your project**

- **highlight how to collect and record interview- and diary-based data**

- **become familiar with the use of focus group and other group interview techniques in HR research**

- **identify an appropriate sample of respondents to provide trustworthy data.**

HOW TO USE THIS CHAPTER

Nearly all HR investigative enquiries that are organisationally-based make use of qualitative data of some sort, and this chapter sets out the options for gathering it. You may be tempted to go straight to the fourth section of the chapter, on interviews, or the fifth, on focus groups, but if your project is likely to be influenced by your own observations of the work environment, you should make sure you consider the issues in the third section, on observation and participation. The process of gathering qualitative data is far more effective if some thought has also – *before* you launch into action – gone into how it will be analysed. You should therefore read both Chapters 6 and 7 before making decisions about your data-gathering process.

When you come to write the methodology section of your report, you will need to reflect on your data-gathering process as well as on your sampling decisions and analysis processes. These are covered at the beginning and end of this chapter.

Case illustration

Accidental costs

Injuries to UK employees from accidents at work cause more than 7.5 million lost working days each year, statistics released by the Health and Safety Executive (HSE) reveal.

But that figure is a gross underestimate of the true cost to employers: the law requires reporting of only fatal and serious injuries, and the HSE estimates that only 43 per cent of employee injuries are reported.

The HSE's latest statistics, for 2001–2002, reveal that 249 people died in accidents at work, a 15 per cent fall compared with the previous reporting year.

There were 27,477 major injuries (including broken limbs, penetrating eye injuries and amputations) and 127,084 'over-three-day' injuries – a slight reduction on previous years. Slips and trips remain the biggest cause of non-fatal injuries (37 per cent of the total).

While the number of work-related injuries in Britain has gradually declined, this improvement is cold comfort when one considers the true cost of lost working time caused by occupational ill-health – much of it preventable. ...

Extract from: B. Allen, *People Management,* 23 January 2003.
Reproduced by permission of Becky Allen, *Occupational Health Review,*
and John Ballard, The Art Work Partnership

ACTIVITY – HEALTH AND SAFETY AT WORK

Imagine that you have been asked by an organisation to undertake some research into safety in the workplace. The organisation concerned is aware of and complies with the law relating to health and safety, having a Health and Safety at Work Policy and a Health and Safety Committee, as well as publicising procedures to be followed in the event of an accident, and so on. However, there is concern about the lack of a safety culture in the organisation and it is felt that accidents may be occurring at different parts of the workplace which, for some reason or another, have not been reported. The CEO wants to know why the procedures relating to accidents and hazards do not seem to be consistently put into practice, and what can be done to ensure a positive health and safety culture within the organisation.

1 What sort of information would you need to gather to find out whether and why minor accidents are not being reported?

2 How might you gain access to the information you need?

3 What issues might impact on the quality and reliability of the data that you gather?

Feedback notes

In order to find out about accidents and non-reporting it will probably be necessary to explore how different factors at work may contribute to people's reporting behaviour. It will be helpful to find out how different people understand the health and safety issues and the impact this has on their actions in relation to reporting accidents and potential hazards. Your investigation may, therefore, take account of a variety of different perspectives. What difficulties do managers and supervisors experience when trying to implement the procedures? What are the issues from the perspective of employees in different parts of the organisation? How are things understood by the Health and Safety manager and by employee representatives?

This sort of information is not likely to be quantifiable. Although your research might enable you to estimate the extent of under-reporting, most of the information you gather will be in the form of words and language which reflects people's perceptions of safety issues in the workplace. You may decide to interview people, therefore, or hold some focus groups to find out about different opinions. You might also observe people at work to compare the requirements of the health and safety procedures with organisational life in reality.

Accessing such information will not be easy. Watching people at work is not a popular undertaking, and employees are likely to behave in a more safety-conscious way when you are around. Interviewees may also tell you what they think you (or the CEO) want to hear, rather than what they would say to each other.

THE USE AND IMPORTANCE OF QUALITATIVE DATA IN HR RESEARCH

The issues highlighted in the case illustration above are common for many HR enquiries, particularly those that are organisationally-based and form part of a problem diagnosis and problem-solving process. Although quantitative data can identify the extent to which things are, or are not, occurring in organisations, it is less helpful in answering the question *why* things are the way they are. Most organisationally-focused HR projects therefore include the use of some qualitative data. This chapter considers the key issues with gathering and recording qualitative data.

The recording and analysis of qualitative data is an integrated process, so Chapters 6 and 7 are also closely linked. This chapter focuses on gathering and recording the data, and Chapter 7 considers how it can be analysed.

Qualitative data can be broadly categorised as encompassing *information in the form of words and language* from:

- observation and participation
- one-to-one interviews or conversations
- individual accounts or diaries of events and/or activities
- focus groups (or other group interviews).

Because the data generated by such activities is in the form of words, it is not readily quantifiable. It is also generated through a process that is (at most) loosely structured and in which the questions posed are not standardised. For these reasons the preconceptions and standardised categories of the researcher are suspended, as far as is possible, and the language and expressions of the informants is valued and utilised.

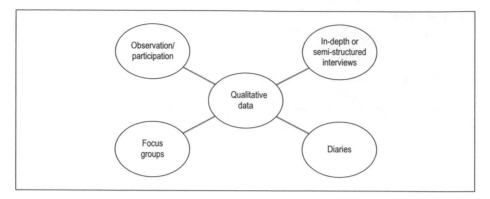

Figure 22 *Different types of qualitative data*

It is important to differentiate between the different types of data in order to record and analyse it appropriately. Many investigative practitioners assume that an interview will automatically generate qualitative data. However, structured interviews – in which the questions (and options for answers) are pre-designated and organised in line with predetermined categories for analysis – produce data that is essentially quantitative. In-depth and unstructured interviews, by contrast – in which the language, expressions and meanings of the informants are recorded and utilised for analysis in their own terms – generate qualitative data. Similarly, structured observations of work activity – in which a very systematic approach to recording the number of incidences of particular behaviours, contributions or interactions is utilised – also generate quantitative, rather than qualitative, data. Such data can be useful, but it is considered in Chapter 8, whereas this chapter focuses on gathering and recording qualitative data.

OBSERVATION AND PARTICIPATION

An obvious way of finding out information about people's behaviours and actions at work is to watch and listen to them. If you are undertaking a project in an organisation in which you already operate – either as an employee or as a work placement student – there are likely to be plenty of opportunities for participation in, or observation of, organisational processes. However, if these practices are to be used in an objective way, as part of a systematically undertaken research enquiry, it is important to distinguish between different types of observation and participation and the uses to which data gathered in this way may be put.

Case illustration

Managers fail to blow whistle on fraud

More than 50 per cent of managers are aware of fraudulent practices at work, yet 40 per cent would not blow the whistle, according to a new report.

The survey of over 800 managers also revealed that a quarter would not rule out giving a clean reference to a dishonest member of staff, and two-thirds agreed that everybody lies to the boss sometimes.

The Business of Ethics, which was co-compiled by KPMG Forensic Accounting, discovered that women had a more liberal attitude towards issues such as personal phone calls in the workplace. The most ethical person was likely to be a male financial director aged over 40 in a medium-sized public sector organisation. . . .

Extract from: *People Management,* 28 December 2000.
Reproduced by permission of *People Management*

The case illustration above provides quantitative information about the extent of unorthodox behaviour in the workplace. Finding out more about such practices through some form of survey, and even through interviews, is very difficult. (Would you admit to telling lies to your boss if you were interviewed?) The extracts of the following article describe how 'participant observation' was used to investigate unorthodox behaviour in the entertainment industry.

Case illustration

Participant observation

Participant observation may be the only practical way to achieve an awareness of common workplace practices, which are nevertheless easily concealed from external observation, including that of the external auditor and management consultant. . . . Another study, which took six years to complete, with 10,000 hours of disguised participant observation, collected 451 cases of unconventional practices at work in the entertainment industry (Analui and Kakabadse, 1992). It found unconventional behaviour to be an undeniable aspect of workplace activities, and this leads to inefficiencies in many organisations. The research led to the suggestion that there may be three dimensions to such activities. These are the forms they may take: pilferage, rule-breaking, non-co-operation, destructive practices, disruptive practices, and misuse of facilities – the overt and covert styles in both individual and collective forms as the expression and the motives for their occurrence, and the meanings attributed to them. This classification formed the basis for an effective development programme that would assist managers to deal with such behaviour. Both motivation and control were found to be of equal importance, and specific recommendations were made. . . .

Extract from: G. Vinten (1994) 'Participant observation: a model for organizational investigation?', *Journal of Managerial Psychology,* 9 (2) 30–8.
Reproduced by permission of Emerald (MCB), Bradford

DISCUSSION QUESTIONS

1 List what you think are the advantages and the disadvantages of using participant observation as part of an HR-based investigative enquiry.

2 What issues must be taken into account if participant observation is to be carried out?

Feedback notes

A major advantage of gathering data by watching people's behaviour is its directness – rather than asking people about their feelings and so on, you can watch (and later record) what they do and say and then use this for your analysis of the situation. If you ask people at work about 'irregular behaviour', for example, they are unlikely to be prepared to declare any pilferage, but by becoming one of 'them' an observer can see at first hand the types of practices that go on in reality. In many ways participant observation is the only way of finding out about 'real life' in 'real organisations' with very little artificiality intervening between the subject and the researcher.

However, since this research was undertaken there have been significant developments in the ethical and legal arenas that would lead to objections to forms of activity that may be interpreted as covert surveillance. In addition, there are more practical disadvantages. One such difficulty is the time commitment. Although valuable findings may have been generated in the study into the entertainment industry by 10,000 hours of participant observation, most student projects can account for no more than 100 hours! In addition, it is possible to argue that the presence of an observer, however covert that presence may be, might influence behaviour one way or another, so that there is still no knowing what would have happened if the observer had not been part of the situation.

Other issues that are important to take into account are:

- bias – Being a participant watching and listening is easy – but because you have been part of the situation, how can you be sure that the data you record is not biased in some way?

- what to record – When you are observing a situation how do you know what to look out for?

- how to record – Another issue is the form in which data may be recorded. Many HR students claim to have undertaken some observation but are less clear about how they recorded and then analysed their data. Relying on your memory is not a good strategy, so effective methods of recording data are essential. Robson (2002) recommends noting down 'memory sparkers' within a few hours of the event that will help the researcher recall and record more details of what happened. Other researchers keep a diary that they update on a daily basis. Records not made within 24 hours of any observation are particularly unreliable.

- ethics – As noted already, covert observation has a number of ethical implications which make it increasingly inappropriate. Being explicit about the purpose of your observation and obtaining informed consent overcomes many of the difficulties, but may also influence the nature of your findings. For these reasons it is important that you discuss any plans to utilise some form of observation with your supervisor, adviser or tutor.

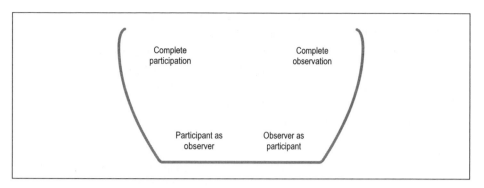

Figure 23 *Participation and observation*

Although there are difficulties, observation and/or participation – in the context of an investigative enquiry – can provide opportunities to record, describe and interpret people's behaviour. It is important, however, to be clear about the purpose of any observation and the way in which it will be carried out. Robson (2002) describes a range of different approaches to participant observation (see Figure 23) which are briefly described below.

- complete participation – The observer becomes as full a member as possible of the group or organisation being studied. Employment within an organisation provides many opportunities to undertake this (Easterby-Smith *et al*, 2002) although the ethical implications of concealing the purpose of your participation need to be clearly thought through.

- the participant as observer – The observer makes clear to those involved that research is his or her explicit role although he or she may also participate in the activity in one way or another. This is not an easy option, and it is important to gain the trust of those involved. It does, however, provide opportunities for you to ask people to explain what is going on and why. Some students use an approach of 'interrupted involvement' (Easterby-Smith *et al*, 2002) and complement it with in-depth interviews of key players after the activities that have been observed.

- the observer as participant – This approach (referred to in Robson, 2002, as the 'marginal participant') occurs when the main role of the observer is merely to observe but, to some degree, participation in the situation is unavoidable by his or her very presence. A researcher who wishes to find out the extent to which new corporate values really have become embedded, for example, may 'loiter' or spend time near a coffee machine or a photocopier to observe what issues people really do discuss when not at their desks. The very fact of his or her presence, however, may mean that the researcher becomes drawn into conversation, or may influence in some way the conversations of those round about.

- the complete observer – This is someone who takes no part in the activity but whose role as an observer and the research purpose is known to the participants. In many ways there is little distinction between this end of the spectrum and being an observer/participant because it is hard to see how the presence of someone there 'to observe' would not affect the behaviour of those being observed.

If you are considering some form of participation or observation, it is important to adopt a systematic and justifiable approach to what you plan to do. Recording data appropriately is one of the key challenges of this approach. Delbridge and Kirkpatrick (1994) suggest that three types of data may be generated:

- primary observations – those things noted at the time, or very near to the time, usually in some form of diary or journal format

- secondary observations – how other people that were there saw things: questioning participants as part of the research process would generate this sort of data

- experiential data – how you felt about what you were observing and experiencing as time passed. Here a diary format is usually used, and it is helpful in enabling the researcher to record how his or her feelings or values have developed or changed as a result of the research process.

Observation and participation are valuable ways of obtaining qualitative data, but it is important to think ahead to ensure that time invested in this approach is productive.

Key issues that underpin the planning process are summarised in Table 15.

Table 15 *Preparing for observation*

Clarifying what you need to know	What are your research questions? What information do you require to answer them?
Is observation the most appropriate way of obtaining the information you need?	Consider alternative ways of gathering these data
What aspects of the situation(s) do you need to find out about?	Are you interested in process or content? Are all subjects equally interesting?
What times are most appropriate to carry out your observations?	Will the timing of your observations affect what you find out?
Getting access and permission	Do you need permission to undertake this observation? If so, what level of authority is required? With whom should you discuss your plans for observation?
Blending in	How 'visible' will you be? Will what you wear, your gender, your age, etc, affect how people behave when you are observing them?
Recording data	How will you record what you observe? Will the data be sufficient to enable you to form conclusions?
Roles and responsibilities	If you are going to participate as well as observe, how will you balance the demands of both activities?
Piloting your methods	Observation is an 'unrepeatable' method, so mistakes cannot be rectified. Pilot your approach first before committing yourself fully to it.

Sources: Blaxter *et al* (2001), Bell (2001)

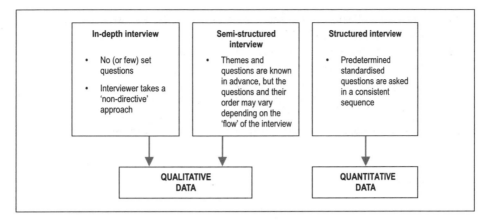

Figure 24 *Types of research interview*

DATA FROM INDIVIDUALS

Interviews

A more common form of qualitative data gathered in the majority of projects by HR practitioner-researchers comes from interviews. Qualitative data is generated by in-depth unstructured interviews and can also be generated from semi-structured interviews. Structured interviews generate quantitative data, and are considered in Chapter 8.

A key issue with interviewing, often overlooked by HR students, is to determine the type of interview that is most suitable to answer their research questions. Each different type of interview has implications for the approach that will be taken to questioning and also to recording data and subsequently to analysis. There are also choices to be made over the medium or method of the interview. Most interviews are undertaken on a face-to-face basis. Increasingly, however, telephone interviews are utilised in HR research, and some researchers also choose to follow-up their data-gathering with some form of electronic conversation, using e-mail with some or all of their respondents.

Case illustration

On higher ground

This article presents some of the preliminary findings from major new research on UK graduate employment, following those who graduated in 1995 from the full spectrum of UK undergraduate degree programmes through the first seven to eight years of their graduate careers.

We first surveyed the graduates in 1998/9 and the findings provided an encouraging picture of graduate labour market integration. Graduate jobs, earnings and career trajectories, however, were very diverse, and there were intriguing gender differences in outcomes and rewards. Would differences and inequalities in the transition from higher education to employment persist, converge or even diverge as the graduates developed their careers?

We went back to this sample in 2002 to conduct a second sweep of the survey and, with a sub-sample of respondents, are carrying out in-depth telephone interviews about their current employment and career development. We were particularly interested in exploring the extent to which members of the 1995 graduate cohort were using their degrees and the areas where changes in the work organisation were creating new opportunities for graduates. . . .

Extract from: K. Purcell and P. Elias, *People Management,* 29 May 2003.
Reproduced by permission of Kate Purcell and Peter Elias

DISCUSSION QUESTIONS

1 In what ways might data generated by in-depth interviews enable these researchers to answer their research questions?

2 What problems might they encounter in collecting data in this way?

3 What challenges would be posed by undertaking in-depth interviews by telephone rather than on a face-to-face basis?

Feedback notes

The interviews envisaged as part of this research should enable the researchers to explore and investigate underlying themes or issues related to the individual career experience and development of those included in the sub-sample. In-depth interviews offer the possibility of modifying lines of enquiry in a way that a questionnaire or structured interview do not. Answers can be probed, enabling interviewees to explain or build on what they have said. In this way data of a 'rich' quality can be gathered that allows for people to provide information about their experiences, feelings and motives. Indeed, the responses of one interviewee might alert the researcher to a line of enquiry that he or she had not previously thought of and so permit some form of incremental development of thinking that would enhance the quality of the research outcomes. It is also possible that the respondents targeted in this survey might be more willing to agree to an interview than to complete a detailed questionnaire because it would help them to reflect on their own career development in a fairly open way.

Yet there are a number of potential problems that may be encountered. Interviewing in an unstructured or semi-structured way is a time-consuming process. Anything under half an hour is unlikely to generate qualitative data of much value, and pressures at work make it unlikely that interviewees could be available for more than an hour. The time-intensive nature of interviewing means that the number of respondents will be lower than would be possible with (say) a postal survey, and the lack of formal structure for in-depth interviews leads to concerns about generalisability.

Another problem area is the issue of recording data. Keeping a record of responses to structured interviews is fairly easy, but interviews where the control, in terms of what is said and how it is expressed, lies with the interviewee are difficult to record with accuracy. Tape-recording the entire interview may inhibit the interviewee. Transcribing a long conversation into (what will be) about 20 pages of closely-typed text is a daunting prospect. However, note-taking during the interview may distract both you and the interviewee. If you choose to make notes about the interview after the event, how can you be sure that you have made the notes in a systematic and full way?

The choice of telephone interviews over face-to-face meetings also raises some interesting issues. On the one hand, conducting such interviews can be easier to arrange where the interviewees are all scattered (as in this case illustration) across a wide geographical area. However, there are also issues about the relationship between the interviewer and interviewee that may detract from the quality of the data that is gathered. A key advantage of a face-to-face interview is the opportunity to develop a positive relationship of trust between interviewer and interviewee, such that the respondent is more prepared to accept probing questions and to 'dig deep' in terms of articulating his or her feelings and experiences. It is also possible that interviewers will realise that a probe is possible as a result of non-verbal cues they notice during the interview conversation. These opportunities are diminished with a telephone interview.

Preparing for the interview

In order to maximise the usefulness of data gathered in unstructured or semi-structured forms of interviewing, therefore, there are some key issues that must be addressed, which are described briefly below.

Interview design

It is very important to allocate time for preparation for all the interviews you propose. Clarify what research objectives or questions your interview data will contribute towards answering, and identify the key themes that you wish to explore with this particular respondent or group of respondents to contribute to your understanding of the issues. The themes you want to explore may have been derived through your review of the literature, by discussions with your tutor, or from other activities such as reviewing company documents. A process for designing interview themes or topics is shown in Figure 25. For each of the themes that you identify, write down a number of questions that you could ask. Be prepared to be flexible, because how you ask your questions will vary depending on how each interview progresses. It is also important to be open to the possibility of new aspects or issues that the conversation within the interviews may bring up. At this stage, therefore, you are clarifying what ground you need to cover and ensuring that you have some way of checking, as the interview progresses, the extent to which you are covering it. It is important also now to ensure that the questions you ask will not cause the interview to be too long. Avoid trying to gather data on too many important issues so that there is no time to explore the themes in a deeper way. It is also vital that you avoid any tendency to ask ambiguous or leading questions. You would be wise to discuss your plan with your supervisor or tutor prior to undertaking the first interview, because mistakes that impact on the data you gather may limit the value of your findings.

Preparation of the interviewee(s)

You are likely to obtain more co-operation from your interviewees if they feel fully briefed and confident of your competence as an interviewer and researcher. It may be appropriate, for example, to provide your interviewees with a list of your themes in advance of the meeting. Many respondents, so briefed, may also be prepared to give you documents that are relevant to the themes, thus providing a useful basis for some later 'triangulation' (see Chapter 4). If you think you would like to ask more sensitive questions, however, it may be better if these are tackled once a rapport between the interviewer and interviewee has been built up.

Preparation of the interviewer

As with all forms of interviewing, first impressions are important. When participating in recruitment interviews it is the candidate who seeks to make a good impression on the HR professional. In a research interview the situation is somewhat reversed. It is the researcher

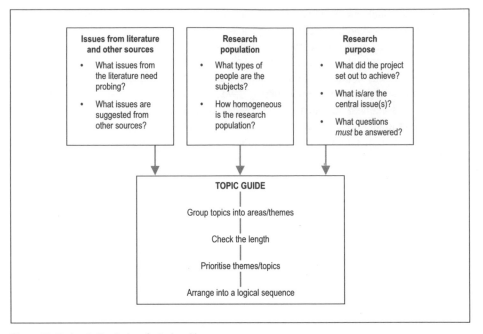

Figure 25 *Factors in the design of a topic guide*

who needs to make an appropriate impression if a rapport is to be developed to allow for a productive interview. This means thinking carefully about what you wear and the language you use. Clothes that are too smart or imposing may inhibit responses from employees who dress differently, and student-quality jeans may be less than appropriate when interviewing the HR director of a work placement organisation. Undertaking some prior research into the key issues for the organisation (key challenges or successes, for example) can be advantageous in two ways. Firstly, by drawing on relevant examples during the interview your credibility may be enhanced. Secondly, your prior research may also allow you to assess the accuracy of some of the information generated by the interview.

ACTIVITY – INTERVIEW SKILLS

Think back to any interview skills training that you have participated in – either as a trainee or as the trainer. If you have never attended an interviewing skills course, think back to recruitment interviews that you have been involved in, either as the candidate or the interviewer.

1   Brainstorm a list of the key skills necessary for effective interviewing.

2   To what extent are the skills needed for recruitment interviewing the same as those needed for undertaking effective qualitative interviews for research purposes?

Feedback notes

An activity such as this, once it gets going, can fill pages of A4 or flipchart paper. The main points that tend to be made (and which all have relevance to conducting in-depth or semi-structured interviews) are:

■   the interview environment

- structuring the interview
- opening the interview
- using appropriate questions
- listening actively
- using silence
- using appropriate language
- observing body language
- probing answers
- moving from one question to the next
- using summaries
- closing the interview
- keeping accurate records.

The effective research interview

Key issues for effective interviews for research purposes are, of course, very similar to the skills developed for recruitment and selection processes. However there are some differences. Most HR practitioners utilise a structured approach to interviewing to allow comparisons to be more easily made between different candidates. With in-depth or semi-structured interviews, however, the aim is to gather data that reflects the unique experiences of individuals. For this reason a less structured approach is used, and this can be a challenge for a practitioner-researcher who is accustomed to a more controlled form of interview with behaviourally structured questions that have been more or less predetermined.

The key skills and issues that underpin successful research interviewing, therefore, are summarised below.

- the interview environment – The environment in which the interview takes place will be very significant in the extent to which the respondent can feel 'safe' in articulating his or her thoughts and experiences. An unfamiliar or noisy environment is likely to inhibit a nervous interviewee. 'Mobiles off' must be a rule for the interviewer. In preparing for the interview it is also important to get across to the interviewee how helpful it will be if he or she can give the interview an agreed spell of time with no disturbances.

- structuring the interview – Although the questions and format of responses are unstructured, it is still necessary to ensure some framework within which the interview can take place. This normally involves:
  - an opening/introduction
  - 'warm-up' questions
  - the main part of the interview, exploring the main themes in a relatively logical way
  - 'cool-off' questions
  - the conclusion/ending: thanking the interviewee, explaining the next steps in the research process, etc.

- questioning and listening – Your job is to get interviewees to speak freely and openly. To achieve this it is important that you listen more than you speak, and that you express your questions in a clear, understandable, and open way. People feel free to expand only if they sense you are interested in what they are saying, and it is also important to ensure that your behaviour and body language does not influence the opinions they offer. Active listening, involving verbal and non-verbal signs of your continued interest in the conversation, are necessary.

Although some research interviews explore general issues about the experience and perspective of the interviewee, it is also possible to focus more on 'critical incidents' or situations that may lead to the identification of behaviours or attitudes relevant to the research questions. This may involve identifying the important aspects of a situation or incident, as perceived by the interviewee, before going on to consider the effect of the situation as experienced by the respondent and others.

Whatever the nature and purpose of the research interview, the most productive types of questions to ask are:

- open questions, in which the interviewee is encouraged to describe or explain an experience. Within an in-depth or a semi-structured interview it is unlikely that specific or closed questions will be appropriate. Multiple questions, long questions, leading questions and also questions involving jargon should be avoided
- probing questions such as 'Tell me more about ...', or 'What factors contributed to ...?', 'How did you feel when ...?', which enable interviewees to reflect on issues in more depth for responses to be further explored.

■ other forms of probes – In addition to the use of specifically probing questions, successful research interviewers use more non-verbal methods of encouraging interviewees to talk further about a topic. Robson (2002) indicates four useful techniques of probing in unstructured interviews:
  - allowing a period of silence
  - offering 'an enquiring glance'
  - using 'verbal' signals such as: 'Mmhmm?'
  - repeating back all or part of what the interviewee has just said.

■ summaries – As with other forms of interviewing, the use of summaries at appropriate times can fulfil a very useful function within the research interview. Sometimes, once started, an interviewee just cannot stop talking in circles about the same thing. Here the use of a summary to check understanding and then build on the contribution by asking a different but related question can allow some 'steering' of the interview. Where complex issues are being discussed it may also be appropriate to offer a summary to check that the interviewer's understanding is complete or to allow the interviewee to clarify where there may be some misunderstanding.

■ keeping accurate records – A key issue with unstructured interviews is the approach that is taken to recording the data that is gathered. This is something that you must explain in the methodology section of your report. There are two options. You can tape-record the interview or make notes during it.

Tape-recording your information

The advantages of tape-recording are that it enables you to concentrate on the process of questioning and listening rather than being distracted by the need to take notes. You can also be confident that responses to your questions have been accurately recorded and can be listened to more than once. However, the interviewee may feel inhibited by the recorder and the relationship between interviewer and interviewee may be affected. You cannot rule out the possibility of a technical hitch, and you must also ensure that the tape in the machine does not run out and so stop recording what is said. In addition, the time necessary to transcribe the entire conversation may be extensive.

If you do decide to use a tape recorder, you should explain why you are doing so and seek the respondent's permission, allowing him or her, if necessary, to turn off the recorder part-way through the interview if he or she feels uncomfortable with it.

Taking notes

There are many different approaches to taking notes. Some people have a sheet with spaces between headings as well as a spare space for unforeseen ideas and responses to be recorded. Others generate something more akin to a mind map as a basis for recording 'trigger words' that represent key pieces of information generated during the interview. One advantage of making some notes, even if you are tape-recording the conversation, is that it encourages you to remain focused on what is being said and not to drift. Whatever approach is taken, it is important to make more detailed notes of the meeting shortly after it has been concluded. Your record of the interview will be based on the short notes that are already made but it is also possible to record features about the environment, the body language of the respondent and the main information that was provided in as much detail as possible. Notes taken in this way (extended summaries) can then be held until you are ready to analyse your qualitative data (see Chapter 7).

Making such notes can also provide the researcher with the opportunity to reflect on what he or she has learned and to incorporate any unexpected directions, indicated by the interview data, into subsequent data-gathering activities.

Table 16 provides a summary of what to do and what not to do in research interviews.

E-mail correspondence

The use of e-mail exchanges rather than a telephone or face-to-face interview has also increased in popularity. It is, perhaps, a further way of gathering data from individuals where physical access to a sample of respondents is very difficult. One advantage is that time-zone

Table 16 Do's and don'ts for qualitative interviews

Do	Don't
Be gently assertive – you want to hear what the interviewee has to say in a sympathetic way, but you also need to guide the discussion through your research topics/themes	Ask more than one question at a time – take great care to avoid multiple questions
Ask both sides of a question – eg if you ask what people like about something, also ask them what they dislike	Get led too far from the point – keep the objectives of the interview clearly in your mind: some diversions lead to areas of interest, but these are very rare!
Tackle difficult or sensitive areas with discretion – when sensitive issues are discussed, make sure you reassure the interviewee of the confidential nature of the process and of your maintaining his or her anonymity	Give your own opinion – if you do, it is likely that you will influence many answers that the interviewee gives

constraints can be minimised and a true conversation between people in different regions of the world is more possible. The technology also makes it possible to undertake 'interviews' on a synchronous basis, thus maintaining the momentum of an interview where necessary.

Case illustration

Research into job evaluation

Patrick was a full-time HR student whose project was undertaken in his work placement organisation, a fast-growth medium-sized specialist clothing company. The organisation, a private firm, was based 80 miles from London, and was experiencing difficulties in attracting sufficient trained specialists such as clothing designers, merchandisers and marketing and promotion experts to sustain its rate of growth. Most of these professionals came from London and attracting them to an out-of-London location had led to individually negotiated salary packages that were often far in excess of local labour market rates. As the organisation matured it recognised the need for greater standardisation in employment rewards. There was a concern that employees were becoming aware that people undertaking like work were not receiving equal benefits. The directors decided to develop a new, more transparent pay structure and to utilise a job evaluation process to align jobs within the pay structure in a more consistent way.

Patrick's project was to evaluate different approaches to job evaluation and to recommend a system that would be beneficial for the organisation. Patrick also sought to investigate the key issues that would affect the successful implementation of such an approach.

Patrick's reading about job evaluation enabled him to amass considerable information about different approaches as well as the difficulties and ambiguities in the process. Patrick asked his placement manager if he could interview managers within the organisation to identify key issues that any evaluation process should take into account. Although his manager still wanted a report about job evaluation, she told Patrick that employees (including managers) were not to be encouraged to discuss such a sensitive topic as pay and job evaluation. Faced with this difficult situation where access to sources of internal data was denied, Patrick had to rethink the research project. There was not sufficient time to start afresh on a different topic, and so the approach to researching into job evaluation required modification.

Instead of interviewing managers within the organisation, Patrick decided to try to access information about the experiences of other organisations regarding the implementation of job evaluation processes. He recognised that the response rate to a postal survey about job evaluation might be limited. Through contacts of part-time students on the same course, however, he approached HR managers in other organisations with a view to obtaining 'rich data' about the approach used and the issues related to operating job evaluation processes.

Patrick was fortunate enough to obtain the co-operation of a small number of HR managers from different organisations in the local area. However, time difficulties prevented him from meeting them all face to face. His main means of communication with the HR managers was through e-mail. Communication through e-mail throughout the data-gathering stage was constant.

Having obtained some initial information about the types of schemes and the context of their introduction, he used the data to devise a series of open-ended questions that were e-mailed to the participants. The questions focused on the systems they used and the reasons why they had been chosen, as well as the difficulties that had been encountered. Further questions tried to gauge the effectiveness of the systems and the reactions of employees towards the system. Patrick was also interested in finding out how frequently the scheme would be reviewed. Through the use of e-mail he also probed the answers to these questions on an individual basis.

DISCUSSION QUESTIONS

What do you see as the advantages and disadvantages of Patrick's approach to obtaining qualitative data to achieve his research aims and objectives?
What further opportunities does the medium of e-mail offer in gathering qualitative data?
To what extent would Patrick's findings enable his placement organisation to move forward with implementing a job evaluation process?

Feedback notes

Patrick's situation is one that is experienced by a small but significant number of practitioner-researchers. For one reason or another, often outside the control of the researcher, organisational factors mean that the initial approach to data-gathering has to be rethought. Although the use of e-mail 'conversations' enabled Patrick to access data in a situation where interviews were not possible, the disadvantage of his choice of method of data-gathering is that it was more the result of circumstance than it was a positive choice springing from the purpose of his investigation. Although e-mail 'conversations' lack an immediacy, they do provide respondents with an opportunity to think and reflect on their response to questions, prior to replying. Once sent, the message(s) can be recorded and analysed repeatedly, so note-taking becomes less of an issue.

However, there are further disadvantages. The concern with data security within the Internet or an organisation's intranet must be taken into account. As with telephone interviewing, of course, it is not possible to make use of non-verbal communication, and reliance on the written word is required. The development of trust and rapport between interviewer and interviewee is also likely to be more difficult and people may be less willing to commit their feelings to the page, even an electronic screen page. Such difficulties do not preclude the use of interactive virtual conversations or correspondences, but it is important to reflect on the implications of this method for the quality of data gathered in the methodology section of your report.

It is also interesting that Patrick's initial plan to interview a representative sample of managers from within the sponsoring organisation had to be reformulated in such a way as to oblige him to arrange contacts with one person (the HR manager) from the small number of participating organisations rather than with a sample of their managers. Patrick's sampling approach, therefore, changed from trying to achieve a representative sample of internal managers to the use of information from more than one organisation, but making use of only one person within each of them.

Diaries

Interviews and other forms of 'conversation' are a powerful way of accessing, to some degree of depth, people's experience and understanding of the work situation they are involved in. Another way of exploring aspects of people's experience in a particular context is through the use of narratives and stories (Coffee and Atkinson, 1996). Some form of diary or journal, written by different participants in events, as a part of a data-gathering strategy may well be worthwhile. In this context a diary is a retrospective record of an individual's or a group's actions over a defined period of time. A detailed record might be kept for just a few days (or even hours) or it might be undertaken less intensively over a period of weeks or months. Diary entries can be written or spoken into a tape recorder.

Case illustration

Organisational Learning in Practice:
How do small businesses learn to operate internationally?

Using a case-study approach to explore the meanings, choices and decisions of those involved in internationalising businesses, the research study reported here sought to identify the process of organisational learning that occurred within internationalising smaller companies. The aim was to identify the relationship between different variables, factors and events, taking into account the social dynamics of smaller organisations as they underwent a process of interaction within an environment which was increasingly international. . . .

The research design incorporated three approaches to data collection. First, in conjunction with a local agency responsible for the provision of advice to small firms which operate internationally, 1,000 UK-based organisations employing fewer than 100 people were invited to a free seminar to consider 'Successful business abroad'. Decision-makers from 17 small businesses, 13 of which were already involved in some form of business overseas, attended. Discussions about their experiences of operating internationally were recorded and initial analysis was undertaken. Following the seminar, organisations which had indicated their willingness to participate more fully in the research project were contacted. . . .

Follow-up visits, including company tours and semi-structured interviews with a senior member of the organisations, were undertaken to explore key issues that had emerged from the original analysis. . . .

In order to highlight routine aspects of the experience within the firm, a member of the company who was involved in the day-to-day operations involving business overseas, but who was not involved in the semi-structured interviews, was also asked to complete a series of diary sheets whereby they reflected upon the critical incidents of the previous few weeks relating to business overseas (Coffee and Atkinson, 1996). These data were incorporated incrementally into the analysis, and

---

used to check for internal consistency within each of the case-study organisations. The provision of a summary report to each company was also used to obtain feedback on the factual accuracy and analysis of each case-study organisation. . . .

V. Anderson and D. Skinner (1999)
Human Resource Development International, 2 (2) 235–58.
Reproduced by permission of Taylor & Francis

DISCUSSION QUESTIONS

1   What advantages are claimed for the use of the 'diary method' within this research? What other benefits might the use of data from some form of diary provide within a research project?

2   What problems might be experienced with the use of diaries as a method of data-gathering?

Feedback notes

The researchers claim, in this extract, that the use of a diary technique allowed for an alternative perspective on events, from that of a 'senior member of the organisation', focusing on the routine as well as the strategic aspects of the situation. This allows for some degree of 'triangulation' (see Chapter 4). Other benefits might also be listed. The use of diaries, for example, might provide information about events that it is not possible to observe, but which can provide for an 'immediacy' that an interview, undertaken some time after the events concerned, would not be able to achieve. In this case illustration diary sheets were used in parallel with interviews with other respondents. It would also be possible to ask an interview respondent to maintain a diary record for a short period and then to follow up the initial analysis of the diary with an interview to explore the issues in more depth.

Like all other methods of data-gathering, of course, there are a number of issues that must be taken into account. Firstly, it is important that the potential diarists are all able to communicate systematically in a written form. Many people are not natural diarists and it is likely that they will give up along the way. Thus it is important to keep in touch and to encourage them – to reinforce how important it is to understand their perceptions of the particular situation or context. Linked with this is the issue that writing a diary is a time-consuming thing for the diarist and he or she should not be pressured into completing one. Bell (2001; p.102) notes that 'reluctant subjects will rarely provide usable data'. Secondly, it is important that those completing a diary are clear about what to record. It may be that you want them to note down any reflections, feelings and motivations in response to what is happening in their lives. However, it is more likely that it is appropriate to provide the diarist with guidance about what should be recorded, stemming from the research questions that are being answered.

A third area of difficulty is the inhibition people may feel about writing down what they *really* think about things or how they *really* spend their time at work. So it is crucial that the confidentiality of this sort of data is assured and that people have confidence in their anonymity within the research process (Riley *et al*, 2000). The final issue to bear in mind is that of representativeness. How can you be sure that the week in which the diary was maintained (say) was a typical week?

FOCUS GROUPS

An increasingly popular way of gathering qualitative data in HR projects is through focus groups. Focus groups are a form of group interview in which a process of dialogue and discussion between a number of participants about a particular topic provides data to help you answer your research questions.

ACTIVITY – OBTAINING DATA ABOUT PARENTAL LEAVE

Imagine that a large organisation in the public sector has asked you to research into the awareness of employees of their parental leave entitlement and their views and opinions about the possibility of more flexible working arrangements for parents in general. The organisation has agreed that focus groups would be an appropriate way of gathering this data.

DISCUSSION QUESTIONS

How many focus groups would you plan to hold, and who should participate in them?
How would you decide what questions/issues to ask about?
What key skills would be required to facilitate the group(s) in an effective way?
How would you record the data that was generated?

Feedback notes

Focus groups provide an opportunity to find out about a range of attitudes and values in relation to a topic such as flexibility and parental leave. You might feel that if your aim is just to familiarise yourself with a range of attitudes towards parental leave and flexibility, two focus groups would be sufficient. However, if it is possible that people's opinions may depend, in part, on their role or position within the organisation, then it will be necessary to organise a larger number of groups, each with between six and 12 participants. One focus group is never sufficient to ensure that valid and reliable data is gathered.

It will also be necessary to make sure that each group consists of similar kinds of people, with enough in common for them not to feel inhibited about contributing their views but with sufficient differences that a range of perspectives may be represented. In this case it would be important to ensure that people with dependent children are included, as well as those with no immediate family responsibilities. You may also want to try to ensure that the perspective of those with elder-care responsibilities are involved. The inclusion of men and women from different age ranges would also ensure an inclusive approach to data collection.

To find out people's views about flexible working arrangements it would be necessary to pose a sequence of questions that stimulate and encourage a flow of discussion. The questions would have to be fairly broad-ranging but also relevant to the particular research purpose. Although you are seeking to explore opinions and feelings, it is also important to remember that participants may have personal sensitivities, and these must be handled carefully. You will also be seeking to obtain data that is specific and detailed, so it is important to encourage people to avoid talking only in generalisations and to explore why they may hold the opinions that they do.

To achieve this you are likely to want to pose about six or seven questions, which move from the more general to the more specific. In a semi-structured interview the flow of conversation may be quite flexible but the group nature of a focus group suggests that the order of your questions is maintained each time. As facilitator you should also be able to probe, steer, and legitimise seemingly unpopular viewpoints. Preventing individuals from dominating the opinions of the group is another key issue.

Recording data from focus groups also needs careful thought and preparation. The energy and concentration required for facilitating the group is likely to mean that you will be unable to take many notes. Some people ask a colleague to join the group in the role of note-taker. Others obtain permission to tape-record the discussion. Another way to ensure some initial record of the data is to utilise flipcharts, whiteboards, etc. The data contained on these can then act as a trigger for a fuller account of the discussion produced by the researcher as soon as possible after the end of the meeting, and certainly within 24 hours of it.

Focus groups are therefore a useful way of obtaining qualitative data. As a method of research within HR they also have the advantage of being quite acceptable to many organisational stakeholders. There are, however, disadvantages as well as advantages of the method, and these are summarised in Table 17.

Table 17 *Advantages and disadvantages of focus groups*

Advantages	Disadvantages
They are cheaper than individual interviews (in terms of the time-cost) and can generate large quantities of data	The large quantity of data may be difficult to summarise and to analyse
Interaction between researcher and participants allows for clarification, probing and follow-up questions	The facilitator may influence the participants too much and so affect the opinions they express
Data can be collected in the participants' own words and take account of deeper meanings and interpretations	There may be undue influence of some participants over others, affecting the quality of the data that is gathered
In some circumstances, more than one topic can be explored in each session	The small number of participants (relative to the size of the research population) leads to concerns about generalisability of the data
Snowballing of ideas can occur as participants respond to the contributions of others in the group	The group dynamics of the session may lead the researcher to attribute more significance to the data than is actually warranted
Participants can feel empowered, especially in action-oriented organisational research	A polarisation effect may occur by which people's attitudes become more extreme after group discussion

Sources: Neuman (2003), Saunders *et al* (2003)

In order to maximise the effectiveness of the focus group approach to data-gathering, therefore, it is important to take some process issues into account (Stewart and Shamdasani, 1990; Riley *et al*, 2000). These include:

■ Carefully work out the boundaries of the topic you wish to be discussed. This must link closely with your research questions/objectives.

■ Think carefully about who should be included (sample selection). Ensure that the sample will be representative.

■ Facilitating focus groups requires a high level of interpersonal skills. If you doubt your abilities here, you could ask someone else to facilitate and you could be the note-taker.

■ Consider how you will ultimately analyse the data. Allow decisions about analysis to influence how you record the data from the focus groups.

■ Generate and pre-test/pilot the questions you propose to ask. As part of this process you can plan how to keep the discussion focused without leading it in an obvious way.

■ Introduce the purpose of the focus group. This should be clear at the beginning, which is also an opportunity to communicate appropriate ground rules and process issues.

■ Build a good rapport with the group. It is important that people think that they can speak freely to each other and in front of you.

■ Ensure that everyone has an equal opportunity to contribute to the discussion. It is important to make clear that all contributions are valued.

■ Clarify feedback arrangements. Be clear about whether you propose to feed back the results of the focus groups to the participants, and communicate this at the time.

SAMPLE SELECTION FOR QUALITATIVE RESEARCH

A key issue that has been raised many times already in this and previous chapters is that of data quality – validity and reliability. This is a particular issue with qualitative data, which is why the choice of participants (the sample selection process) must be clearly thought through and justified within the research report.

Sampling is *the deliberate choice of a number of people to represent a greater population*. In a very small organisation it may be possible to gather data from everyone, but in most cases it is necessary to choose a sample of people from whom information will be obtained.

There are two main ways of determining an appropriate sample. *Probability sampling* involves determining a sample that is statistically representative of the research population as a whole and so should reflect the characteristics of the population. This means that provided you ask exactly the same questions of everyone in the sample, you should be confident that you can generalise the conclusions that you derive from the data to the wider population. Research enquiries that utilise a quantitative approach are likely to adopt probability sampling, and more information about it is contained in Chapter 8.

Most qualitative data-gathering, however, operates from a basis of *non-probability sampling*, which is considered opposite.

Case illustration

Researching into the employment of people with disabilities

Anna was an HR student who wished to investigate the employment experiences of disabled people for her project. She worked for a Housing Association and the organisation was keen to embrace practices of diversity and equal opportunities at all levels. Although they believed their workforce was representative of ethnic diversity and that women and men were treated equally, they were concerned at the low number of disabled people employed in the organisation. Anna's task was to gather data about the experience of working for the organisation from those who were disabled and to investigate how the recruitment process might also affect the employment of people with disabilities. Anna's reading around the subject of disability and employment led her to realise that the stigma of disability leads many people to choose not to reveal their disability to their employer. She wanted to include people with 'hidden' disabilities within her research, to understand the issues from their perspective.

DISCUSSION QUESTIONS

How might you go about gathering data if you were undertaking this project? In your answer decide how you would gather data, and who you would include in your sample in order to investigate:

■ the employment experiences of existing employees with a disability

■ the perspectives of those employees with a 'hidden' disability

■ how the recruitment and selection process might impact on the employment of people with disabilities.

Feedback notes

This situation provides an example of where a probability sample would not provide useful data because the number of people who were registered as disabled within the organisation was very small.

Anna chose two different approaches to gathering her data. In order to investigate the impact of the recruitment and selection process on the employment of people with disabilities she obtained permission to undertake some participant observation by becoming involved in the recruitment process itself, from initial job advertisement to selection interviews. She did this for a period of two months. To find out about the experiences of people once employed, she arranged to conduct semi-structured interviews with those employees who were registered as disabled. Accessing those with 'hidden' disabilities was more difficult, but Anna attempted to use snowball sampling – she asked her interviewees if they would ask other people in the organisation who they knew to have a disability if they would be prepared to be involved in the project.

There are a range of different ways of tackling non-probability sampling, and Anna's approach involved *accidental sampling* by being involved in recruitment processes for a defined period and *purposive sampling* by choosing people to involve whose perspectives might typify important viewpoints pertinent to the research questions. These are described more fully below.

Non-probability sampling

Accidental sampling

This is where the sample is chosen for reasons of convenience or practicability. Many students implicitly operate an accidental sampling approach to any observation that they undertake as part of their data-gathering process. The advantages are that it is convenient and that time and expense trying to undertake a more representative sample selection process is avoided. However, it is possible that the data that is gathered may not be representative of the wider picture.

Purposive sampling

This involves choosing people whose experience and perspectives are deemed to be important to the investigation. There are different ways of choosing a purposive sample. Firstly, you may identify key informants – people who have specialised and unique knowledge and experience of the issue you are trying to find out about (Tremblay, 1982). Many HR projects involve a key informant interview with the HR director, for example, or someone with particular knowledge and expertise in the area of the investigation.

Secondly, it is possible to undertake a *sliced sample* whereby respondents are chosen because they occupy positions at different parts of the organisation (Reeves and Harper, 1981). 'Slicing' is possible horizontally (a selection of middle managers from a range of different functions) and/or vertically (respondents from the top, middle and bottom of the hierarchy). Thirdly, snowball sampling (as we have seen) involves finding new people from which to gather data on the recommendation of those already included within the sample.

Each of these approaches has the advantage that you feel confident that the data gathered will reflect perspectives pertinent to the enquiry being undertaken. However, the people and situations from which you gather data may not be typical – something that is worth exploring during the data-gathering process (by asking people how typical they feel they are) and when formulating your conclusions.

Quota sampling

This involves choosing a sample that reflects as far as possible the diversity of the wider research population in the same proportions. So if you know that the organisation you are researching has a proportion of men to women of 40:60, your sample would seek to ensure that you included four men for every six women. Similarly, if you know that the age distribution of 'under 30s', '30–45s' and '46–60s' is 40:40:20, you would try to choose a sample that reflected this proportionately.

The advantage of this approach is that you can strongly imply that it is broadly representative. However, it still does not mean that every employee had an equal chance of being included because, within the quota, people might have been chosen on the basis of their availability and willingness to participate. Quota sampling can also be applied to observations (Neuman, 2003). For example, if you are observing interactions or other management processes, it may be important to be sure to include all the different times of the day within your schedule of observations. Where different locations are involved (for example, in production, administration, reception areas, etc) it may also be important to observe in a proportionately representative way at the different locations.

Sample size

There are, therefore, a range of processes that can be used to select a sample within a qualitative approach to data-gathering. It is also important to determine how big the sample size should be. With probability sampling there are statistical 'rules' about sample size, but with qualitative enquiries things are less clear and informal considerations are often quite significant. The ideal sample size occurs when new 'cases' (either respondents or observations) cease to add new information or insights, although this is a matter of judgement. It is also important to be able to justify the lower limit to the size of a sample. If the characteristics of the sample are fairly consistent, and the research question is rather a limited one, then a smaller-sized sample may be adequate. Where the research questions are broader and the sample is characterised by greater levels of difference, the sample would have to be larger.

Non-probability approaches to sample selection as a whole have the advantage of flexibility and are often more organisationally acceptable. They also provide opportunities for collaboration within a problem-solving and action-oriented project. The data that they generate provides scope for interpretation and judgement during the process of analysis. However the disadvantages of non-probability sampling must be taken into account when you explain and justify your approach to data-collection.

MAKING SENSE OF THE DATA

With qualitative data, therefore, sample size and sample selection involves a process of judgement and decision on the part of the researcher, rather than the application of specific statistical rules and procedures. The same scope for judgement and reflection is also apparent in the processes of initial analysis processes, and this is worth reflecting on in this chapter although the analysis of qualitative data is considered more fully in Chapter 7.

Unlike quantitative data-gathering, there is a close link between the processes of data-gathering and initial analysis. This is because the process of writing up notes following from qualitative data-gathering processes provides an opportunity to further reflect on and develop the research enquiry. Jankowicz (2000) suggests a series of questions to help with initial evaluation and analysis of qualitative data that can also 'feed in' to further data-gathering on an incremental basis:

- How do the data from this (interview/observation/focus group) compare with the other data already obtained? Are there any apparent trends? What picture seems to be emerging?
- What concepts and research from the literature seem relevant to this data?
- What feelings were engendered by the data-gathering process just undertaken – does the information ring true?
- In what ways might initial impressions formed by this information be checked out?
- How much did the researcher influence what was said? How significant was this influence? Should anything be discounted as a result?
- What unexpected information was gathered? How can its relevance be checked out within the on-going data-gathering process?

SUMMARY

- Qualitative data-gathering forms a part of many organisationally-focused HR research enquiries. It may involve activities such as observation and participation, one-to-one interviews or conversations, individual accounts or diaries of events and/or activities, and focus groups.

- With qualitative data the organisational context can be taken into account and data focused on particular themes and issues can be generated. Data relevant to 'real-time' activity as well as past events can be obtained.

- Qualitative data-gathering processes must endeavour to limit bias on the part of the subjects and the researcher by clarifying what information is to be obtained and how it will be recorded.

- Observation and/or participation in organisational processes provides an opportunity to obtain direct data about organisational realities. A range of options for observation and participation of behaviours and processes in the workplace are possible, from complete participation to complete observation.

- Particular care must be taken to ensure confidentiality and anonymity of participants involved in providing data. The ethical implications of observation must be considered prior to its being undertaken.

- In-depth and semi-structured interviews are common ways of gathering qualitative data. Such interviews require careful preparation and execution. Key skills for research interviews include: asking open questions, active listening, using silence, using appropriate language, utilising non-verbal communication and steering the interview.

- There are advantages and disadvantages to gathering qualitative data electronically or through some form of note-taking. Permission to record activities and conversations should be obtained.

- Where face-to-face interviews are not possible, data may also be obtained through e-mail conversations, telephone interviews and diary entries. These types of data allow people to reflect on their feelings and experiences but lack the one-to-one interaction that is possible in interviews, focus groups and forms of participant observation.

- Focus groups are a form of group interview in which data is generated as a result of a facilitated process of dialogue and discussion about a particular topic. One focus group is never sufficient to generate reliable data.

- Focus groups are often organisationally acceptable ways of gathering data because they are more time-effective than individual interviews and can involve and empower participants within a problem-solving or action-oriented process. However, they can also lead to a polarisation of opinions amongst participants and they can generate a large quantity of data that is hard to analyse in an objective way.

- Most sample selection processes for qualitative research involve non-probability sampling. Approaches to non-probability sampling include: accidental sampling, quota sampling and purposive sampling. Purposive sampling can include the selection of key informants, 'sliced' samples and 'snowball' sampling techniques.

- The nature of the research questions and the homogeneity of the research population will influence decisions about minimum sample size. The upper limit of sample size is a matter of judgement and is reached when it appears that new 'cases' are not generating any new or unexpected insights.

■ The process of initial data-recording and analysis can lead to an incremental development of the research enquiry.

Questions for review/reflection

These questions are designed to enable you to identify key areas for development with your project which you should discuss with your project tutor/supervisor if possible. The responses to them can also form part of a Continuing Professional Development log or portfolio. This is required by the CIPD for those who wish to upgrade their membership status.

Taking stock

1   What opportunities may exist within the organisation(s) in which your research is to be based for the use of some form of participant observation or for some form of diary record to provide qualitative data? To what extent would such approaches to data-gathering help to answer your research questions?

2   How likely is it that some form of semi-structured or in-depth interviews would be an acceptable form of data-gathering within the organisation?

3   Who might be key informants within your investigative enquiry? What access arrangements would be necessary to incorporate them into your sample?

4   What sample selection process is most appropriate for your project? How confident are you (and your tutor/supervisor/adviser) that your sample will be sufficient to provide data of good quality?

Strengths and weaknesses

1   How confident are you of your skills as an in-depth research interviewer, or as a facilitator of focus groups? How might you further develop your skills in these areas?

2   How clear are you about the purpose of the different types of data-gathering you plan to undertake? How clearly developed are the themes to be explored? How clearly are these themes derived from your literature review, other data-gathering activities, your research questions, etc?

3   How well developed are your skills as a note-taker? What system can you develop to ensure that any notes you take while engaged in qualitative data-gathering are formulated accurately and in detail?

4   If you plan to tape-record some of your data, how equipped are you to subsequently transcribe the dialogue into a written form? What arrangements might you make for this?

Being a practitioner-researcher

1 What organisational and ethical issues must be considered if you decide to undertake some form of participant observation? What might be the best way to take this forward?

2 How aware are you of your own personal bias towards anything in the information you expect to gather? What steps can you take to limit the influence of your personal perspective on the data that is generated?

3 What steps will you take to maximise the confidentiality of the data you gather and the anonymity of your subjects?

FURTHER READING

Some very readable accounts of research enquiries that have utilised qualitative data include:

BUONO, A. F. and BOWDITCH, J. L. (1989) *The Human Side of Mergers and Acquisitions. Managing Collisions Between People, Cultures and Organisations.* London, Jossey-Bass.

DITTON, J. (1997) *Part-Time Crime: An ethnography of fiddling and pilferage.* London, Macmillan.

MARS, G. (1982) *Cheats at Work: An anthropology of workplace crime.* London, Allen & Unwin.

The Graduate Labour Market Forum, which co-ordinates the research referred to in Purcell and Elias (2003) has a website with a range of data from and information about the study:

http://www2.warwick.ac.uk/sac/soc/ier/research/glmf

More specialised sources about different techniques of data gathering include:

DELBRIDGE, R. and KIRKPATRICK, I. (1994) 'Theory and practice of participant observation', in V. Wass and P. Wells (eds) *Principles and Practice in Business and Management Research.* Aldershot, Dartmouth.

HEALEY, M. J. and RAWLINSON, M. B. (1993) 'Interviewing business owners and managers: a review of methods and techniques', in V. Wass and P. Wells (eds) *Principles and Practice in Business and Management Research.* Aldershot, Dartmouth.

KRUEGER, R. A. and CASEY, M. A. (2000) *Focus Groups: A practical guide for applied research.* Thousand Oaks, CA, Sage.

MORGAN, D. L. (1988) *Focus Groups as Qualitative Research.* London, Sage.

STEWART, D. W. and SHAMDASANI, P. M. (1990) 'Focus groups: theory and practice', *Applied Social Research Methods Series,* 20. New York, Sage.

TAYLOR, S. and BOGDAN, R. (1984) *Introduction to Qualitative Research Methods: A guidebook and resource.* New York, Wiley.

TREMBLAY, M. A. (1982) 'The key-informant technique: a non-ethnographic technique', in R. Burgess (ed.) *Field Research: A Source Book and Field Manual.* London, Allen & Unwin.

Analysing qualitative data

CHAPTER 7

Chapter outline
How to use this chapter
The process of qualitative analysis
Categorising and coding data
Data display and analysis
Evaluating alternative explanations and formulating conclusions
Writing up the analysis
The use of software for qualitative data analysis
Summary
Further reading

LEARNING OUTCOMES

This chapter should help you to:

- **apply an appropriate process for analysing your qualitative data**

- **identify and categorise themes and issues emerging from the data**

- **group different items or units of data and examine potential relationships between them**

- **evaluate alternative explanations and formulate credible and plausible conclusions**

- **evaluate computer-assisted qualitative data analysis software in relation to your project objectives.**

HOW TO USE THIS CHAPTER

This chapter aims to set out ways of analysing – rather than merely describing – qualitative data. In an ideal world you will read this chapter before beginning the process of data-gathering. The materials and ideas in the chapter will still be useful, however, if you are wondering how to make sense of data that you have already gathered. Many practitioner-researchers, especially those working towards a management report rather than a dissertation, find they do not need to make use of any specialised software to help with recording and analysing their data, so the section that covers some of these issues (*The use of software*) is placed towards the end of the chapter. On the other hand, if you think you will make use of some qualitative data analysis software, it would be worth reading that section before you commence the data-gathering process. Whatever the proposed outcome of your enquiry (qualification-related or not), when you come to write up your project it would be worth re-reading the *Writing up the analysis* section of this chapter.

Case illustration

UK firms need more innovation

The British economy must enter a new and more dynamic phase of development to sustain the relative success of the past 20 years, a government enquiry on competitiveness warned this week.

Commissioned by the DTI and the Economic and Social Research Council, the report states that an emphasis on skills, innovation and enterprise is needed to ensure that the UK makes the transition to a new phase of economic development.

Extract from: C. Mahoney, *People Management*, 15 May 2003.
Reproduced by permission of *People Management*

ACTIVITY – LEARNING TO BE ENTREPRENEURIAL

Imagine that you work in a large organisation that wishes to become less bureaucratic and to foster business growth through the development of skills, innovation and enterprise in key areas where it is felt rapid market growth is possible. The organisation has decided to provide initial funding for a small number of 'spin-off' businesses. The businesses will receive some start-up funding but must establish themselves as viable and profitable in a reasonably short period of time. The organisation recognises that these spin-offs must be led by managers from within the organisation with 'entrepreneurial' qualities which have not, thus far, been particularly encouraged. A careful selection process to identify the most appropriate candidates for these important roles, as well as some development to allow them to enhance their entrepreneurial qualities, will be required. To inform the selection and development process you have been asked to identify what skills and qualities underpin successful entrepreneurship and how people learn how to start up and grow high-performing businesses. You are taking a qualitative approach and you have undertaken semi-structured tape-recorded interviews, each lasting for an hour or more, with ten successful entrepreneurs from a range of different business sectors. You have also been able to visit each of their companies for three days and observe meetings and other day-to-day business activities. (This has taken place over a two-month period.) As a result of this you have amassed ten fat folders full of raw data which includes the tapes for each interview, as well as notes that you made for yourself at the time, notes you have made about what you saw and heard when you were visiting the companies, and a wealth of other company documents that the entrepreneurs were kind enough to give you.

DISCUSSION QUESTIONS

What steps might you take to make sense of this data in order to achieve your objective of identifying key entrepreneurial skills and qualities and ways in which they were learned?
What you will do with the tapes, notes, company documents, and so forth?
List four or five problems you might encounter when formulating objective conclusions on the basis of the data that you have.

Feedback notes

There are many ways in which you might undertake to make sense of the data you have collected. The main challenge, at the start, is its sheer volume. The first objective of qualitative data analysis is one of information management. Some way or other must be found to establish a sense of control over 'what is in there'. Once that has been achieved it will be possible to identify and explore key themes or patterns that the data may suggest. Only then will it be possible to draw conclusions.

Data overload is a common challenge. You may have identified a number of other problems with the analysis of qualitative data. One such anxiety is that data that is analysed early on, when the researcher is relatively fresh, receives more careful attention than information that is considered later in the process. It is also possible that data is incomplete. Perhaps many of the entrepreneurs chose not to talk about difficulties in their experiences, for example, and made sure that some features of their organisations were not 'observed'. In addition, it is possible to ask how an interviewer might discern whether some interviewees were more reliable in what they said than others.

A further problem, although it can also be seen as an opportunity, is that there is no one right way of going about the analysis of qualitative data. Whereas with quantitative data analysis (see Chapter 8) there are procedures and processes that can provide some degree of confidence in the conclusions that are drawn, there is no such consensus with the analysis of qualitative data. There are, however, different approaches that are more or less appropriate for different enquiries undertaken for different purposes – and this chapter will outline some of them.

THE PROCESS OF QUALITATIVE ANALYSIS

What is analysis?

The idea of data analysis can be a difficult one for first-time practitioner-researchers. The process of gathering data often takes longer than expected, and the time available for analysis of the data, particularly with a submission date looming, may be very limited. Yet the analysis of data is fundamental to the quality of the outcomes of any investigative enquiry. Indeed, raw data, on its own, has no meaning and only limited value.

Analysis is a process of thought that enables you to understand the nature of what is being investigated, the relationships between different variables in the situation, and the likely outcomes of particular actions or interventions. Analysis therefore involves finding answers to your research questions using the data that you have gathered by asking questions such as 'what?', 'why?' and 'how?' If the answers to your research questions are to be trustworthy, it is important that you treat the evidence fairly and be careful to include all possible interpretations, rather than the one you (or your project sponsor) would prefer.

In order to achieve this it is necessary to understand and assess the information that you have, reduce it to manageable proportions, abstract information from the different sources of data that you have acquired, explore key themes and patterns suggested by it, and then develop and evaluate a range of alternative explanations from which you can formulate conclusions. This process is illustrated in Figure 26.

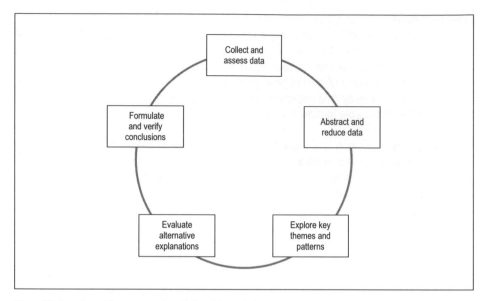

Figure 26 *Overview of the process of qualitative data analysis*

Case illustration

HRD in construction companies

Most large construction companies have undergone a period of significant organisational change over the last 20 years. They have effectively become managers of the construction process rather than direct labour employers (Langford *et al*, 1995; Druker *et al*, 1996). This has left managers and professional staff as their main scarce resource (Kahn, 1995). These staff members have an increasingly demanding role and so require careful management and development if they are to contribute effectively in the long term. Egan (1998) recognised this when he identified the need for a commitment to people as one of the key drivers required to promote change within the industry. He called for a wider commitment to training and development of managers and supervisors as part of his 'Rethinking construction' report (p17). . . .

HRD represents the developmental side of the human resource management (HRM) function in assessing and improving individual performance, managing careers and in providing organisational management development. However, for construction companies, the susceptibility of the industry to economic fluctuations makes the applicability of many of the established aspects of HRM questionable (Bresnan *et al*, 1985; Hendry, 1995; Huang *et al*, 1996). . . .

However, despite the problems that the industry faces in implementing effective HRM policies, if employers are to avoid losing their best staff to their competitors, they must develop more effective ways of rewarding and developing their workforces in the future (Drucker and White, 1996; p.15). This requires employers to meet individual employee career needs and expectations not just in terms of formal employment contracts but also in terms of their employees' informal expectations of the relationship between themselves and their employer. . . .

Accordingly this paper seeks to identify which aspects of organisational HR policy conflict with the individual needs and expectations of those working within the sector, and where psychological contract breaches and/or violations have occurred. . . .

Methodology

The approach adopted was the use of in-depth ethnographic interviews to collect data on the career expectations and levels of fulfilment of a range of informants from different professions, career stages and organisations. A total of 82 construction managers and professionals from a variety of career stages and organisations were interviewed. . . .

Each informant was invited to describe their career history, the influences on their development and their future vocational expectations. A research instrument was developed cumulatively during the interviews, with new questions being added relating to issues emerging from the informants career accounts. This instrument was used to progressively focus data-gathering in subsequent interviews. . . .

Extracts from: A. R. G. Dainty, B. M. Bagilhole and R. H. Neale (2000) 'The compatibility of construction companies' human resource development policies with employee career expectations', *Engineering, Construction and Architectural Management,* 7 (2) 169–78. Reproduced by permission of Blackwell Publishing, Oxford

DISCUSSION QUESTIONS

1 In this study, the research instrument (interview topic guide) was developed cumulatively and new questions were added after some interviews had already taken place. Draw up a list of the main advantages and disadvantages of this practice.

2 How would you go about undertaking some initial analysis of an in-depth interview in order to 'progressively focus data-gathering in subsequent interviews' as in this case illustration?

Feedback notes

The process of incrementally revising the questions that are asked at interviews is a common one within qualitative research, although those who adopt a more quantitative approach are critical of it. The main objection is that it can lead to a situation where different variables are included at different stages in the study. This means that the device for obtaining information is not applied in a consistent way throughout the research process, thus limiting the reliability of the findings (Bryman, 1998; Glassner and Moreno, 1989).

However, given the nature of qualitative data, it is possible to argue that an incremental process of the design of a topic guide or research instrument for data-gathering more adequately reflects the reality of what is being investigated because it 'takes seriously' the meanings and interpretations of situations provided by respondents (Coffee and Atkinson,

1996; Miles and Huberman, 1994). This approach reflects the acceptance by researchers that information in the form of words and language is likely to be imprecise, will be influenced by the context in which it has occurred, and so may be capable of different interpretations.

The role of data analysis in an investigative enquiry

Because analysis is the search for explanation and understanding, it is reasonable to begin this search early on in the research process while data is still being collected. This enables you to seek to establish the extent to which additional data indicates the explanation is plausible or is unlikely. The analysis of qualitative data, therefore, is not a distinct 'last stage' of a project but is something that occurs *throughout* it. There are also no clear rules about how to undertake an initial analysis of qualitative data. One person might produce a summary of the information from an interview in note form. Another might prefer a 'spider diagram' or some other form of chart or table. However it is undertaken, the process of initial analysis involves asking 'What is the essence of what this person is saying?' and 'What seem to be the dimensions of the issues he or she is discussing?' This process of questioning the data leads to some form of categorisation of it (around dimensions or themes). In order to record and make use of these categories as the research process unfolds, you will need to generate some form of label or code for each of them.

Qualitative data analysis is thus different in many ways from the analysis of quantitative data. It is a continuous process, closely linked with on-going data-gathering, and the methods by which it is undertaken are less standardised. The information that is gathered is not tested against theoretical constructs after all the data has been gathered. Instead, evidence and concepts are 'blended' and assessed for plausibility on an on-going basis. The data analysis process involves separating data into different 'pieces' by categorising and coding 'chunks' that reflect themes or dimensions of an issue. Having done this it involves recombining the chunks, looking for possible relationships and patterns within and between different dimensions of the issue you are investigating. This process, which is a cyclical and iterative one, allows the testing of alternative explanations about what is going on. Figure 27 provides diagrammatic detail of the steps in the process of qualitative data analysis.

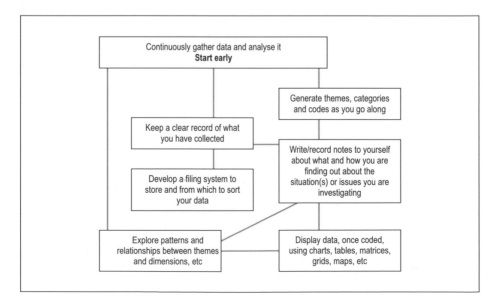

Figure 27 *The qualitative data analysis process*

CATEGORISING AND CODING DATA

Having undertaken some data-gathering, the first step is to assess the information with a view to comparing it with other data and to look for regularities and different characteristics of the situation being investigated. This involves categorising and coding different chunks of the data. The initial categories that you devise are likely to result from a range of different features of your enquiry. Some categories may well be derived from your research aims and objectives; others may be issues you have decided to look out for as a result of a review of the literature. A further source of categories, as noted already, is the analysis of data that you have already collected. You may therefore decide to mark up and code data through grouping features such as 'locations' or 'gender' or 'attitudes', and you may also categorise and label data that is relevant to different features of your research enquiry.

Codes are 'tags or labels for assigning units of meaning' (Miles and Huberman, 1994; p.56). Once you have decided on some categories, you attach category codes to chunks of data – even though those chunks may vary considerably in size. It might be specific words that are coded, it may be a phrase, or it may be a paragraph of your notes. Often chunks are a combination of the three. It is also possible that one chunk of data may be categorised in more than one way and therefore assigned more than one code.

Case illustration

Women and management

A number of articles have appeared in the *Harvard Business Review* (HBR) in recent years in which reference is made to the traditional view that male = manager, and how this has worked against women making inroads into senior management positions. The HBR often intersperses cartoons among the articles – cartoons which appear to perpetuate the male-as-manager norm. The results of a content analysis of the cartoons appearing in the HBR over the five-year period 1988–1992 are presented. The content analysis suggests that women appear as marginal players in the cartoon images of the organisational world. Not only do women appear in substantially fewer cartoons than men, there is also a wide divergence in how men and women are portrayed. ...

The content analysis
Thirty consecutive bi-monthly issues of HBR for the period January/February 1988 to November/December 1992 were surveyed. The cartoons included in the analysis were the 'stand-alone' cartoons – that is, those not associated with an accompanying article. The reason for omitting the cartoons associated with articles was that the content of the article would clearly influence the nature of the cartoon. Two-hundred-and-eighty (280) stand-alone cartoons were collected in total. This represents approximately 42 per cent of the total cartoons contained in HBR over the five-year period. Table A shows the distribution of cartoons across issues and years to be fairly uniform.

As the chief concern of the present study is the manner in which women and men are portrayed in the cartoons, the basis of the content analysis was the occupational representation of women and men.

In the first instance, the cartoons were categorised according to whether women and/or men were in the cartoons. The categorisation was carried out by two independent judges – one female and one male. The agreement rate between the judges on whether the cartoons depicted women only, men only, women and men or neither was 99 per cent. In only three of the 280 cartoons was there disagreement between the raters, and so these three were omitted from the analysis. As Table B indicates, of the 277 remaining, 59 per cent portrayed men only while 2 per cent portrayed women only. Women and men appeared together in 31 per cent of the cartoons, and 8 per cent had neither women nor men.

Not only was there a vast difference in the number of cartoons women and men appeared in, there was also a wide divergence in how men and women were portrayed. As Table C demonstrates, only 13 per cent of the persons portrayed in 'paid' work were women, while the remaining 87 per cent were men. As women now make up over 45 per cent of the paid workforce in the United States (US Bureau of the Census, 1992), there is a significant discrepancy between cartoon imagery and the reality of the workforce.

The next stage of the analysis required the judges to sort the cartoons by who was depicted as the 'boss' – a man, a woman, or neither. The level of agreement between the judges was 92 per cent (257 cartoons). Although this level of agreement was less than that for the first stage of the analysis, it was still very high. Of the 127 instances where both judges determined that a 'boss' was portrayed, Table D shows that men were portrayed in this role 91 per cent of the time, while only 9 per cent portrayed women as the 'boss'. In the remainder of the cartoons (130 cartoons), a 'boss' was not identifiable. As 35 per cent of managers in the United States are women (Hammond, 1992) there is, once again, a major difference between the organisational world depicted by the cartoonists and reality.

Only 11 of the women appearing in the cartoons are depicted as 'bosses' – the remaining women are portrayed in the traditional supportive roles associated with the feminine stereotype. The most common representations are as a secretary or wife, although there is the occasional nurse, air-hostess and fortune-teller! Twenty-five women appeared in the role of spouse, which is more than double the instances in which women are portrayed as the 'boss'. And of the 11 secretaries portrayed, nine are women. The images associated with men, however, are overwhelmingly associated with paid work. For instance, the men are most commonly portrayed wearing suits, carrying a briefcase, sitting at a desk, involved in meetings, pointing at charts or working on a computer. The images in HBR are a constant reminder that management is a man's world.

Of the 93 cartoons in which women appear, only four portray them as decorative/sex objects. This proportion is smaller than is the case for television advertising – where up to nearly 30 per cent of advertisements depict women as decorative/sex objects (Lazler-Smith, 1989). It would seem that HBR cartoonists are not perpetuating the stereotypes of women as decorative objects to the same extent as the images in television advertisements.

It can be seen from the brief review of the cartoons appearing in HBR that women appear as only marginal players in the organisational world depicted by the cartoonists. The images portrayed in the HBR cartoons perpetuate and reinforce our expectations that male = manager. It may be that such cartoons are considered trivial on their own, but cumulatively such messages can play a powerful role in defining the 'appropriate' person for the manager's job. . . .

Table A *Stand-alone cartoons*

	1988	1989	1990	1991	1992	Total
January/February	10	12	10	9	10	51
March/April	13	10	9	10	10	52
May/June	11	10	6	6	9	42
July/August	10	10	8	12	10	50
September/October	10	8	9	8	10	45
November/December	9	8	10	6	7	40
Total	63	58	52	51	56	280

Table B *Cartoons by gender*

	Number of cartoons	Percentage of cartoons
Men only	165	59
Women and men	86	31
None	21	8
Women only	5	2
Total	277	100

Table C *Persons portrayed in 'paid' work*

	Paid workers	Percentage of paid workers
Men	430	87
Women	66	13
Total	496	100

Table D *Cartoons with a 'boss'*

	Number of cartoons	Percentage of cartoons
Men as 'boss'	116	91
Women as 'boss'	11	9
Total	127	100

Extracts from: A. Sheridan (1994)
'Managers in cartoons – they are still men in the *Harvard Business Review*',
Women in Management Review, 9 (4) 20–4.
Reproduced by permission of Emerald (MCB), Bradford

DISCUSSION QUESTIONS

1   What categories have been used in this analysis and why were they chosen?
2   To what extent has this analysis involved quantitative and qualitative data?
3   To what extent, and why, do you think the results of this study demonstrate an implicit bias against women as managers by the publishers of HBR?

Feedback notes

This case illustration shows how both qualitative and quantitative analysis can be utilised in an examination of 'texts'. In this example the texts have been obtained from a published journal and are in pictorial form, but techniques of content analysis can be utilised to examine other data, such as transcripts of interviews. In this example different aspects of the data have been categorised. Some of the conclusions are the result of 'counting' and some result from a qualitative analysis based on inferences about the images (wearing suits, sitting at a desk, etc).

This case illustration shows how qualitative analysis can be very organised and systematic. Indeed, this is vital if the research is to be seen to be 'distanced' from any preconceptions of the researchers. In this case the initial categorisation process was undertaken by independent raters. Care was also taken with the selection of the sample of cartoons that would be analysed, and at least some of the categories for analysis were devised in advance, derived from the purpose and research objectives of the enquiry itself.

The extent to which this analysis proves the existence of some type of hidden discrimination (which would probably now be referred to as institutional discrimination), however, is more problematic. In discussion here you may well have pointed out that these cartoons represented a period that began six years before the research was published (and more than 15 years before this book appeared), and so the evidence is out of date. Whereas analysis of more up-to-date documents is possible, it is true to say that documents, by their very nature, reflect the past and not necessarily the present situation. Additionally, you may have concerns about how representative cartoons are of the wider management and organisational reality. It is also impossible to say whether these cartoons, by their existence, caused or reinforced gender stereotyping, or whether they merely reflect, and were the consequence of the situation as it was 15 years ago.

Considerable reflection about qualitative analysis comes from researchers engaged in case study research and in areas of social sciences research such as in education, health and social policy (see for example, Robson, 2002; Neuman, 2003; Yin, 2003), who suggest that the following elements underpin effective practice.

- *Clarify the research questions and the data sources that are required to answer them.*
  Starting with organisational documents or pages of interview notes and wondering what they may be able to tell you is a recipe for time-wasting. You will achieve a more effective analysis if you are clear about what questions you need to answer and the data that will be relevant.

- *Make use of an appropriate sampling strategy.*
  Sample selection for qualitative data was considered in Chapter 6 with regard to primary data, and the same principles apply if you are undertaking an analysis of other texts. Analysis of qualitative data can be time-consuming. It is detailed work that is difficult to hurry. It may not, therefore, be possible to analyse all the potential sources at your disposal. In this case a justifiable sampling strategy will be required. You may, for example, decide to study half of the 'company newspapers' of the organisation, or interview 20 per cent of the available managers.

- *Decide on the categories for your analysis.*
  It is important to work out how you will deal with and make sense of the information you propose to analyse. This will very much depend on the research questions you are trying to answer. You may establish categories in terms of the *subject matter* (in response to different interview topics). You may be investigating aspects of an organisation's culture and values, so categories that allow you to record and analyse *attitudes* (favourable or not) may be appropriate. Alternatively, you might want to analyse different *methods* of work or activity (eg electronic, paper-based, one-to-one meetings) or different *characteristics* of people (as, for example, depicted by respondents in focus groups).

  In order to work with these different categories you will probably need to assign codes to each category. Neuman (2003) stresses the differences between manifest and latent codes. *Manifest codes* are those that relate to obvious categories (eg the number of times a word appears in a text). *Latent codes*, which are also very relevant in qualitative analysis, are where an underlying or implicit theme is identified and coded (eg whether views expressed in interviews are favourable or hostile towards something). Here the judgement and interpretation of the researcher, when assessing the data, is important.

- *Pilot your analytical method.*
  Before investing too much time in a full-scale analysis of a large volume of data, try out your categories on a small selection. Is what you are counting and how you are categorising things clear and fairly unambiguous? Are there some things for which there do not seem to be any appropriate categories? At this stage it is worth getting someone else to help you with the pilot process. If you both look at the same data, you can assess the extent to which you have both categorised in the same way (particularly where there are latent categories). This provides you with a measure of the reliability of the process (see Chapter 4) and will help you to make revisions to enhance the reliability before going forward with the main analysis.

■ *Proceed with the analysis.*

Once the preparation is complete you can carry out your analysis. This will mean utilising the categories you have devised to make sense of the data. As noted already, this process itself may lead to the identification of further categories which can be incorporated in the analysis of the data that is subsequently gathered.

The coding process itself, therefore, involves the researcher in making judgements about categories within the data. Given the volume of data that can be generated by qualitative research, this can be a daunting process, and Robson (2002) suggests that where data are not immediately available in an easily analysable form, a write-up in summary form should be undertaken. This should occur close to the time that the data-gathering event occurred. It is important to summarise what was said but also to include your own reflections and thoughts – making a clear distinction in the notes, however, between your thoughts and the words that were actually spoken. A template for the production of a summary sheet is included as Table 18.

Having summarised the data it is then possible to read through it carefully with a view to devising or implementing categories and codes for the data. The actual codes that you assign

Table 18 *A template for qualitative data summary sheets*

Data for summary	My reflections
Who was involved? Names Date Time Location	Who else might be a useful source of similar data? How might the date, time and location have influenced the data-gathering process and the information obtained?
What issues were covered?	What issues were omitted, and why? Were any 'unplanned' issues included? What prompted this?
What data of relevance to the research questions was obtained?	What was surprising about the information?
Were new concepts or issues suggested?	What are the implications for subsequent data-collection?

to different chunks of data will vary and may well be influenced by the method you propose to use later in your analysis. Miles and Huberman (1994) suggest the use of codes in the form of abbreviations of words that the researcher is more likely to remember and be able to assign to different parts of data when reading it through. Once the initial coding is complete, of course, it is possible to revisit any original data, such as interview transcripts, and categorise parts of the data according to the codes that have been generated.

ACTIVITY – CATEGORISING AND CODING QUALITATIVE DATA

Amandeep was a part-time student who utilised a qualitative methodology to investigate the challenges faced by small organisations that operate internationally. The following extract is an adapted form of a summary of a research interview he undertook. Read the summary carefully and identify possible categories that he might apply as he commenced his analysis process.

Data for summary	My reflections
Who was involved? Names: *Mr A – Managing Director* Date: *16 June* Time: *2 pm* Location: *His office (close to the factory) –Factory tour also offered and accepted: see notes filed as Company A Factory Tour*	Who else might be a useful source of similar data? *It would be interesting to get the perspective of others at the more operational end of the business – possibly the sales administrator (see notes from interview)* How might the date, time and location have influenced the data-gathering process and the information obtained? *He seemed fairly relaxed and happy to spend an hour at the interview – seemed to think talking through the challenges would help him to deal with them better in future.*
What issues were covered? *Company context – age; number of employees; main business products/services; annual turnover History of business overseas – what types of business, when commenced, why commenced, how significant for the business as a whole; plans to expand international business in the future Challenges of business overseas – what was expected, how did you know what to expect, what actually happened, what problems were experienced, what you had to learn to undertake business overseas, how this was learned.*	What issues were omitted, and why? *Mr A was far more willing to talk about the history of the firm than the specifics of the challenges and what has had to be learned and how.* Were any 'unplanned' issues included? What prompted this? *The historical development of the ownership of the firm was far more complex than I had expected – quite hard to follow but could be something worth exploring in subsequent interviews with other firms, as it seemed to trigger 'bouts' of learning.*

Data for summary	My reflections
What data of relevance to the research questions was obtained? *Company context – company in existence for 45 years. International business has grown in an ad hoc way over last 20 years. Employs 26 people – single-site operation. Business is production of chemical products – turnover approx. £3.5 million. Difficult trading period 3–4 years ago but seem to have turned the corner now and moved to profitability.* *Previously owned by large UK MNC but recently acquired by Swedish organisation. History of business overseas – Exports now account for 60% of turnover. Plan to grow exports as well as domestic markets. Exports worldwide – USA, Iceland, Italy, Cyprus, Turkey, Israel, India and Pakistan, Japan, Thailand, Australia and New Zealand. All export sales managed through distribution agents except New Zealand (they bought out an ex-distributor that was about to go bust). Export production done at same factory as domestic production although the process is a different one. No one person is responsible for the export side of the business – MD does some himself but sales and technical managers also do a lot of travelling. Sales administrator spends about 80% of her time on export-related work.* *Challenges of business overseas – company has made no significant changes to business processes overseas in last 12 months but recent change of ownership has focused interest on export side – new parent company keen to grow this element. Attended a seminar recently and has been implementing the learning points from this. They are OK on technical, export-related side of things but need to reassess their relationship with distribution agents – realised at the seminar that they know too little about their customer needs and expectations. Key things about operating overseas – never do it on a whim –do desk research about target market and then get a list of people to approach about being an agent. Most important thing is establishing two-way trust – are they competent and do they think you are competent? Do you trust them and do they trust you?*	What was surprising about the information? *Mr A seemed very reflective – aware of the need of the whole organisation to learn in order to improve performance re business overseas – also he seemed willing to invest time in this (hence his willingness to talk to me). Most CEOs of small organisations are much more dismissive of organisation development issues.*

Data for summary	My reflections
Were new concepts or issues suggested? *Background of MD – Mr A had previous experience in an international retail firm and is now applying this with Company A. Others in management team have no previous experience of international business.*	What are the implications for subsequent data collection? *Ask about previous work experience of key figures (CEO and other members of management team) and enquire how important that might be.*

DISCUSSION QUESTIONS

1 What categories might be applied to this data?

2 Decide on what codes to assign to the different categories and have a go at coding this data.

3 Compare your categories and codes with someone else who has undertaken the same activity.

4 As the data-gathering and analysis process went on, Amandeep needed to assess the relationships between categories he identified and coded from this interview with the data from other interviews. What advice would you give him for this?

Feedback notes

One of the interesting things about qualitative data analysis is that two analysts may categorise data in different ways. This is because data analysis is affected by the personal assumptions and interests of the analyst – something that must be reduced as far as possible. Your assumptions will be influenced by your interests. If you want a particular outcome, you may also, unconsciously, see things in a way that you feel is expected in the given context. It is important, therefore, to be aware of the difference between 'is' and 'ought to be' and to undertake the categorisation with as open a mind as possible. It is also very important to value (and code) data that does not fit with what you expect.

Some of the categories that you may have come up with might reflect the contextual questions about the organisation at the beginning of the interview – such as the age of the organisation, the number of its employees, its main business products/services, its annual turnover, the proportion of turnover from overseas business, the overseas markets in which it operates, the methods of trading internationally, its international business strategy, who is responsible for international business, and so on. Other categories may include data about the interviewee, such as his or her gender, background, time in this organisation. Categories relating to particular challenges of operating overseas might include 'learning needs', 'preparation for entry to new markets' or 'establishing relationships overseas'.

Having established your categories, you are in a position to develop a list of codes or labels. This will show emerging themes at a glance, and enable you to look for these themes in subsequent data. As the list develops in a cumulative way you are also able to reorganise it, sort it, combine categories where appropriate, and discard or extend categories for further analysis.

Table 19 *An illustrative coding list*

CONT	Company context
CONT/SECT	Business sector
CONT/SECT/PROD	Products/services
CONT/AGE	Age of company
CONT/EMP	Number of employees
CONT/TO	Turnover
INT	International business
INT/TO	International business turnover
INT/MARK	International markets
INT/MARK/METH	International methods of market entry
INT/SRAT	International strategy
INT/RESP	Responsibility for international business
MGR	Senior management
MGR/GDR	Gender of senior manager
MGR/EXP	Past experience of senior manager
MGR/LOS	Length of service of senior manager
CHAL	Challenges
CHAL/LERN	Challenge – learning needs
CHAL/PREP	Challenge – preparation
CHAL/RELN	Challenge – relationships

A possible coding list from this illustration is shown in Table 19.

Categorising and coding data forms the first part of the data analysis process. The purpose of the activity is to make sense of the information from each data-gathering event so that, later on, you will be able to compare the evidence from a number of different sources, identifying similarities, patterns and themes. As part of the process of managing data, by reducing its size and scope, you are also establishing ideas by which you can identify what may be of particular significance or importance.

Maintaining a researcher's diary, in which you can write down ideas that occur to you as you are working with the data, is a good way to make sure that you can follow up on leads and evaluate alternative explanations. To overcome the influence of your prior assumptions on the interpretation of the evidence it is important that you try to distance yourself from it, and to look at it from more than one perspective. It is especially important that you value (rather than ignore) data that does not fit with what you expect to find. Once you have undertaken some initial coding, therefore, it is highly advisable to meet with your project tutor, supervisor or adviser and ask him or her to act as a 'devil's advocate' – looking for interpretations or features of the data that you may have overlooked or overemphasised.

Having categorised and coded your data, you are now in a position to move on to interpretation.

DATA DISPLAY AND ANALYSIS

Deduction or induction?

Having simplified and categorised information, the process of grouping and displaying data forms the next stage of the analysis process (Miles and Huberman, 1994). The aim is to find ways of presenting data to enable relationships to be examined. There are no hard and fast rules on how data must be displayed. The objective is to find a way that can bring different dimensions of relevant data together. Experimentation with different forms of data display, therefore, may well be necessary. A deductive approach uses concepts in the literature within the categorisation and display processes. A 'pure' inductive approach, on the other hand, is associated with 'grounded theory' (Glaser and Strauss, 1967; Strauss and Corbin, 1998). This is where the categorisation and coding of the data is expected to emerge from the data itself and not to be influenced by prior theories or frameworks.

The differences between inductive and deductive approaches to research are highlighted throughout this book (see Chapter 4 in particular). It is suggested that qualitative researchers might prefer to adopt a more inductive approach whereby data is collected without prior assumptions about categories and theories so that the context of the situation can be incorporated into the analysis process. However, the collection of qualitative data is not necessarily divorced from theories and frameworks for analysis that have already been developed (as, for example, in the case illustration with the cartoons above). Concepts from the literature review can guide the initial categorisation and coding processes. This enables a comparison of the evidence with what might have been expected from relevant theories. Thus a deductive approach can also be appropriate. Robson (2002) indicates that the use of a hypothesis, even in qualitative research, can be useful in assessing the extent to which the data compares with what might be expected. Indeed, it would be possible for the analysis of qualitative data to be as useful in a theory modification process as might be expected with a deductive approach to research.

The distinction between deduction and induction within qualitative data analysis is therefore not a firm one, and all the approaches to qualitative data analysis described briefly here can be utilised as part of an inductive, deductive or pluralist approach.

Lists, typologies and grids

One way of making sense of data, particularly in the early stages of analysis, is to use lists and grids to display them and explore possible relationships or patterns within them. It may be possible, for example, to use a grid format to indicate a range of outcomes that the data has suggested have occurred. In this way you can get an idea about the prevalence of different 'types', and it may be possible to interrogate the data further within the types of types (ie the typologies) that have been identified.

A grid is formulated when one dimension (eg the rows) represents some concept/model or framework and the other dimension (eg the columns) represents the evidence from different sources. An example of the use of a grid, formulated as part of an analysis of HRD in three small business case study organisations, is shown in Table 20. This compares the HRD processes taken in the three case study organisations with categories derived from the literature ('planning', 'doing' and 'evaluating').

Table 20 *A comparison of HRD in three case study organisations*

	Case 1: Design and build engineers	Case 2: Security and telecoms	Case 3: Youth and community work
Planning	No formal HRD planning HRD not planned in the context of its plans for growth Tends to employ qualified people who need little or no training Plans to introduce ISO 9001 which does require some formality in T&D	HRD has been considered in the light of recent organisational changes No organisational T&D plan in place Individual training plans in place with direct involvement from the MD Plans for a new staff appraisal system	T&D planning is informally, but regularly, discussed during team and individual performance meetings with the development manager More formal planning will now be put in place as a result of the organisation's becoming a 'supplier' to the government's New Deal initiative Would like to implement IiP and more formalised HRD processes in general
Doing	One traditional apprentice Workforce training ad hoc and dependent upon informal sharing of information and skills with peers No management development Management apparently happy with the level of T&D undertaken, although some managers recognise the need for more diverse management skills	One Modern Apprentice Management team have undertaken formal off-the-job development Workforce training is reactive and sporadic	Has designed and implemented its own behaviourally-based selection process Employee exchange visit to Hong Kong Team-building takes place to examine team roles and responsibilities Individual performance reviews/coaching sessions with development manager take place regularly – output is documented

	Case 1: Design and build engineers	Case 2: Security and telecoms	Case 3: Youth and community work
Evaluating	Evaluation occurs as part of feedback on on-the-job errors	The Modern Apprentice's progress is evaluated under the overall Modern Apprenticeship scheme by the college and on-the-job feedback on errors	Informal evaluation takes place during reviews and team meeting The need for more specific evaluation of learning is appreciated
	No internal HRD expertise	No internal HRD expertise	Development manager is familiar with business planning and HRD processes

Source: R. Hill and J. Stewart (2000) 'Human resource development in small organisations', *Journal of European and Industrial Training,* 24 (2/3/4) 105–7. Reproduced by permission of Emerald (MCB), Bradford.

Matrices

A different approach to data display is to compile a matrix. This differs from a grid in that two dimensions of an issue are represented – one by rows and the other by columns. A fictional example of such a matrix is shown as Table 21, in which fictional data and references have been inserted into some of the cells. Here the rows represent evidence relating to different business strategies, and the columns are Ideal-typical approaches to HR, using a model from Storey (1992). The references in the cells (P3, R4, S5, etc) provide a cross-reference to the sources of data (company P, interview 3; company R, interview 4; etc).

There are different methods by which a grid or matrix can be formulated. Such things can be easily generated using qualitative data analysis software (QDAS: see *The use of software*) although, for small projects, it is possible to undertake it by hand with pen and paper. A large surface, such as a whiteboard, or a generous covering of the floor with coded extracts from the original data are quite common. The choice of dimensions for a matrix is also a matter of judgement, and it is possible for many grids and matrices to be compiled from the data for the same project. An analysis by time-sequence may thus be appropriate, or one representing the perspectives of different people at different levels of the organisation.

Display by mapping

Another useful approach to considering the relationship between different categories of data is that of mapping. This can be as simple as physically drawing the layout of a work situation or a flowchart of a number of processes, perhaps to extract and describe the different actions that led to particular outcomes that you have been investigating. Although this can be a useful way of proceeding in an inductive way, it is also possible to utilise this approach in a more deductive manner by devising an overall flowchart of what you expect a process to involve and then comparing it with the reality, as suggested by your data.

Table 21 *The matrix form of data display*

Business strategy	Approaches to HR (Storey, 1992)			
	Handmaiden	*Regulator*	*Adviser*	*Change-maker*
Predominantly cost-minimisation		P3 – "They are always telling us what we can and can't do – mostly what we can't do!" N5 – many procedures and manuals		
Mixed	R4 – "HR do all the induction and welfare stuff – they are the human face of the organisation" R6 – "They take care of the admin – I haven't got time for that sort of thing"		R6 – "When we had to make redundancies, they were the ones we turned to for advice on the law and what we had to do"	
Predominantly differentiation			S5 – line managers are responsible for their own staff – HR are called in when advice is needed	S3 – HR involved with culture change and team-building throughout the organisation

Case illustration

Time sequencing and mapping

The research methodology

The overall research question was, 'How do people learn to act entrepreneurially?', within which we explored the processes through which people learned, the relationships between the experiences of different people, what was learned from their experiences, and whether a conceptual model of entrepreneurial learning could be developed. The life story or biography approach was adopted. . . .

Thirteen people from a diverse range of business backgrounds took part in the research. They ranged from people in their 30s who had built up a new business to those in their 60s who after taking a business through stock market flotation had moved into non-executive roles. During an in-depth interview of about two hours each person was asked to 'tell their story' of how they had built a successful business, and to describe their learning experiences as they had developed their careers and their business ventures. Each interview was semi-structured, aiming to elicit the teller's narrative process of recollection and sense-making, and prompting the teller to reflect and disclose more about significant periods and events. The interviews were audio-taped and transcribed. . . .

Findings from interpreting the narratives

. . .

Life stages

It became evident from the narratives that there were a series of five broad 'life stages' which people experienced as they developed their careers:
(1) Early life – family background, education, adolescence
(2) Early career – first jobs, vocational or professional learning
Subsequent to these stages, the stages of people's careers seemed to fall into three phases of an entrepreneurial process of being involved with specific enterprises:
(3) Engaging and entering a venture – selecting, starting, acquiring, joining a business
(4) Growing a venture – taking control, driving, leading, developing people in the business
(5) Moving out and on from a venture – selling, leaving, finding new opportunities after the business.
It was also evident that each person's learning was strongly co-ordinated, organised and integrated through the act of 'telling their story' and formed a constructive, sense-making process in which the narrator explored reasons, consequences and meanings. Taking each story as a whole, a number of significant themes emerged which seemed to play a key role in integrating and giving meaning to the learning experiences of each person. . . .

Towards a model of entrepreneurial learning

From the interpretation and analysis of the narratives, there are a number of key themes which the respondents were able to integrate and through which they had developed their entrepreneurial capabilities. These are:

- confidence and self-belief
- self efficacy
- personal values and motivation to achieve
- setting and achieving ambitious goals
- personal theory derived from meanings and learning episodes
- known capabilities – skills and knowledge
- social relationships through which learning takes place
- the ability to learn quickly and actively from a range of sources, and the ability to reflect on that learning process.

Rather than any one theme being of superordinate importance, it is proposed that it is their *interaction* which is especially significant in entrepreneurial learning. Through an individual sense-making process, it seems that people learn entrepreneurial capabilities by drawing on and developing the resources which each of these themes expresses. A conceptual model of entrepreneurial learning can be proposed which maps these themes and their interrelatedness in the context of entrrepreneurial development over time (see Figure A).

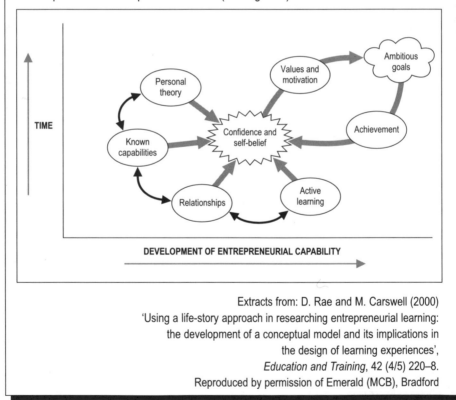

Extracts from: D. Rae and M. Carswell (2000)
'Using a life-story approach in researching entrepreneurial learning:
the development of a conceptual model and its implications in
the design of learning experiences',
Education and Training, 42 (4/5) 220–8.
Reproduced by permission of Emerald (MCB), Bradford

DISCUSSION QUESTIONS

What are the strengths and weaknesses of the conceptual model (the map) that is developed and shown in the article?

Feedback notes

The conceptual 'map' that is generated as a way of bringing together these interrelated features is a helpful visual way of conceptualising patterns of experience, and the relationships between them, as described by the different participants in the research. Often it is developed after other forms of data display and analysis (such as matrices) have been utilised. This form of display takes the different themes and dimensions that have been identified into account as well as retaining a time-series 'momentum'. You might have been critical of this mapping, however – perhaps wondering whether the model that is produced seems rather static, suggesting little scope for the development of progressively ambitious goals over a long timespan for an older respondent. Nonetheless it is helpful to see how the use of data display in different forms can facilitate the process of formulating conclusions and considering the relationships between different dimensions.

These examples of data display, although informed to different extents by an evaluation of relevant literature, attempt to take the data at face value and to develop a conceptual interpretation on the basis of the analysis. Initial coding is undertaken and the data is displayed in different ways in order to make sense of it. Following this it is possible that further 'second-level' categories may be developed. This occurs when the original themes and dimensions are re-examined in an attempt to assess whether there is a structuring of relationships between categories that might indicate causes and consequences, interactions, or some form of grouping. At this point, therefore, an assessment of themes that may require the division of some categories into 'subsets', or where data in some other categories might be combined to offer a more plausible explanation of the issue that is being investigated, can be undertaken (Dey, 1993)

Identifying and exploring key themes and patterns

The process of generating codes and categories, and the organisation (and reorganisation) of your data by means of different display processes, is an iterative and on-going operation as you engage in a search for themes and patterns as part of the analysis process. At this stage it is important that you test ideas and hunches that you may develop as you consider the data. It is important to look for emerging themes that may be scattered throughout different parts of the data relating to one person or group, or that may be apparent in data from different data-gathering episodes.

The process may lead you to further subdivide and recode some of your categories or to integrate one or more categories together. This makes it very important to keep a clear record of what each category means (its definition), particularly if you are undertaking further data-gathering processes and will need to continue with the coding process for the new data (Miles and Huberman, 1994).

Identifying themes is, therefore, an emergent process. Some themes may be generated as a result of the areas you set out to explore when you commenced data-gathering. Others may emerge as a result of initial analysis processes undertaken near to the time that the data was gathered. Yet more themes might be identifiable as a result of subsequent data display processes with which you engage.

Pattern-matching and theory-building

Having engaged in a search for themes and patterns, it is possible to consider the implications of the analysis. Pattern-matching is an analytical process in which you start by predicting a pattern of outcomes, on the basis of existing theory, and assess the extent to which the data matches up to what is expected. There are two approaches to this. One way is to formulate something of a hypothesis about what is expected, and then to consider whether the outcomes are as expected. Alternative outcomes that would be possible if the hypothesis was not plausible are also generated. The data is then compared with the various propositions and outcomes to assess the extent to which the different explanations are plausible. The other approach is to develop a range of alternative outcomes for different (possibly competing) theories and then to identify which of them your data tends to fit.

Theory-building, by contrast, occurs when you assess the themes and issues that have emerged from your data and then develop a conceptual framework as the analysis proceeds. In an incremental way, therefore, you develop propositions and use your data to test them, amending your conceptual thinking on the basis of this process.

EVALUATING EXPLANATIONS AND FORMULATING CONCLUSIONS

The iterative nature of qualitative data analysis also applies to the process of formulating plausible conclusions on the basis of the evidence that has been gathered. With quantitative forms of data-gathering and analysis there are a number of fairly delineated stages, and the drawing of conclusions occurs once all the data has been gathered and analysed (see Chapter 8). With qualitative data, however, the process is less clear-cut. The process of moving from data-gathering to data-reduction and then to analysis and the evaluation of explanations in order to formulate conclusions is an iterative one without a clearly defined end-point. At some moment, however – ideally when new cases shed no new light on the topic of investigation – you should reach a stage at which alternative explanations have been evaluated to the extent that one of them is plausible and the others are very unlikely.

Case illustration

The formation of top managers: A discourse analysis of five managerial autobiographies

What do top managers see as the root of their success? This paper reports on a discourse analysis of five autobiographies from major industrial figures. Those chosen all had some disruption (war, being a refugee, or being an immigrant) between the culture of their childhood and the culture in which they undertook their careers. This makes them more aware than most of their upbringing. Their accounts of their first twenty years are examined, and themes are drawn out for each of them. . . .

Table E: *Emerging themes from the accounts of the first 20 years of the five authors*

	Wang	**Iacocca**	**Edwardes**	**Morita**	**Sieff**
Cultural background	China	Italian immigrant	South Africa	Pre-war Japan	Polish-Jewish immigrant
Career country	USA	USA	UK	Post-war Japan	UK
Themes	Confusion revolution	Bigotry	Emotional distance	Family tradition	Family attitude
	Coping with confusion	Hard times	Self-reliance	Being reared for manage-ment	Race
	Sense of history	Being extra-cautious	Schooling for entre-preneurs	How to manage people	Diplomacy
	Luck	Family closeness		How to manage situations	Philan-thropy
	Balance	Success motivation for immigrants		Being interested or not	Quality

Common themes?

Table E shows the five authors, their country of origin, and the country in which they pursued their main career, and the themes that emerge from their accounts of their early life. A unifying theme to link them all together is conspicuous by its absence.

The difference between them can, I think, be seen on six dimensions:

- easy, as opposed to difficult, to find themes
- personal, as opposed to impersonal
- fortunate, as opposed to master of his own fate
- brought up to manage, as opposed to taught to manage
- certain, as opposed to self-questioning
- orientation toward product, technology, process or opportunity.

Conclusion

Three points need to be kept in mind:

■ Management is not one activity. Different upbringing might lead to equal degrees of success because managers are successful at different tasks in different organisations and cultures. For top managers, however, their task is to a considerable extent what they make it. The common theme is that they all managed to define their jobs in such a way that they were successful at them.

■ These managers are all at the top of very large organisations. They do not typify managerial life. The qualities required to be an excellent middle manager might be quite different. These five might be dangerous role models; the question of how they survived middle management roles and achieved executive status has not been examined in this paper.

■ They all recount childhood experiences as having been important, but none of them suggests that this alone explains his later career. We could no doubt find matched examples of people with similar childhoods who had not gone on to achieve prominence. There are many factors involved in how a career turns out, including an element of chance. However, the five managers whose discourse has been examined in this paper believe that their upbringing was a significant factor in their development as managers, and we should take their views seriously. . . .

Extracts from: B. P. Sims (1993)
British Journal of Management, 4: 57–68, John Wiley & Sons Limited.
Reproduced with permission.

DISCUSSION QUESTIONS

1 What main hypothesis underpins the analysis in this extract?

2 How has the author used the presentation of his analysis to consider alternative propositions following from his research question?

3 In what ways has the evaluation of propositions underpinned the formulation of conclusions?

Feedback notes

This research seems to be underpinned by a hypothesis that successful industrialists experience common factors in their upbringing. In order to examine whether this is the case the author has undertaken a qualitative analysis of autobiographies of five leading industrialists. This analysis has led to the identification of themes for each 'subject', and these have been displayed in a grid format to enable the identification of any common themes or relationships between the different dimensions of the reported upbringing of each of them. It is frustrating that no patterns are discernible – indeed, the analysis indicates that there are more differences than similarities. For that reason, the evaluation leads to the view that common themes are unlikely, and the researcher has reflected on why this may be and what the implications are for the development of managers and for further enquiries in the same area.

In a situation like this it would have been very exciting to identify common factors in the upbringing of the five subjects, and in many qualitative projects there is a strong temptation to 'find' evidence or to 'help' it to fit the explanation that the researcher might prefer. The danger here is the temptation to find evidence to fit prior assumptions (or stereotypes). It is important, therefore, to endeavour to consider the evidence in an impartial way. Indeed, reflection about evidence that supports the opposite of our expectations or assumptions, or about areas where there is no discernible relationship between the data, in relation to the research question that has been asked, is just as valuable as conclusions that were to be expected.

The data analysis process – as illustrated in Figure 28 – involves the generation of a range of possible explanations and/or propositions and the evaluation of these in the light of the evidence that has been gathered. The criteria by which alternatives might be evaluated (see Collis and Hussey, 2003; Lincoln and Guba, 1985; Leininger, 1994; Neuman, 2003) can include asking questions about:

- credibility – To what extent are the different explanations supported by evidence from different sources (triangulation)?

- transferability – To what extent are the explanations context specific? Could they be applied to another situation?

- dependability – How well documented is the research process? Are there things that the people or organisations in the research may have 'hidden' either purposely or inadvertently? To what extent might there have been unconscious non-reporting (on the part of the practitioner-researcher) or have common-place events been overlooked?

- meaning in context – To what extent are the interpretations understandable within their overall context? Has the process of analysis fragmented the evidence such that its analysis is out of context?

- recurrent patterning – To what extent can the explanations be seen to relate to more than one particular time-frame? Is the sequencing within the explanations plausible?

Having evaluated the alternatives, conclusions about which explanations are highly unlikely and which are plausible can be drawn. The content and format of conclusions drawn from qualitative data are also characterised by diversity (Robson, 2002). As the case illustration involving cartoons has shown, qualitative analysis may also involve some forms of quantification which can underpin the process of formulating conclusions.

Different factors that can help with the formulation of conclusions based on the analysis of qualitative data are shown in Table 22.

The nature of the conclusions that are drawn will, of course, depend on the nature of the research questions that underpin the project as a whole as well as the broad (deductive or inductive) approach that has influenced the data analysis process. The drawing of conclusions, however, is something of a point of convergence between these two different approaches (see Figure 28).

A researcher who has adopted a deductive approach and has compared data with theory will consider the evidence and the extent to which it supports propositions or explanations from relevant theories. The conclusions of the analysis will then be able to indicate areas where the propositions are plausible (note: not 'confirmed') and areas where the explanations

Table 22 *Factors in drawing conclusions from qualitative data*

Factor	Example
counting	Fewer than half of the interviewees perceived ...
patterning	Recurrent patterns in the analysis of the organisational documents were ...
clustering	Responses from focus groups in location B reported particular difficulties with ... whereas those closer to ... suggested ...
factoring	Key factors underpinning the perceived effectiveness of the appraisal scheme were ...
variables	The analysis suggests that the practice of ... occurs when ... but it is unlikely to take place when ...
causal networks	The following model indicates the relationships between the six different factors ...
relationship to theory	The incidences of ... that the analysis has identified may best be understood within the ... theory relating to ...

Sources: Robson (2002), Neuman (2003), Yin (2003)

stemming from the propositions are unlikely. As a result, the implications of the analysis for further research as well as for HR practice can be considered.

A researcher adopting a more inductive approach will also be able to draw conclusions and reflect on the implications of his or her analysis for further investigative enquiry and for HR practice. The path to this point will, however, have involved gathering and analysing data without utilising prior theories or frameworks to explore different explanations of 'what is going on'. The output of this iterative process (the conclusions) may be a model or an explanatory

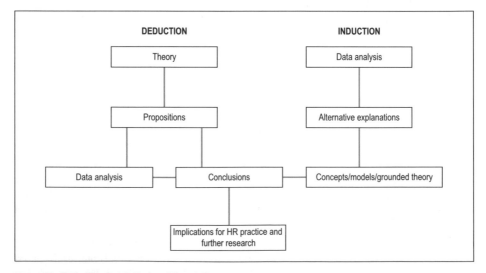

Figure 28 *Evaluating explanations and formulating conclusions*

framework. Reflections about the implications for HR practice and further research to explore the conclusions will also be appropriate.

WRITING UP THE ANALYSIS

The analysis processes outlined in this chapter enable investigative practitioners to identify relationships between different aspects or features of the situation that is being investigated. This enables an evaluation of different explanations in the process of formulating a trustworthy conclusion. If you have undertaken all the data manipulation activities within the process, you will have become very familiar with the different categories and dimensions. However, other people who are to read your work will be much less familiar with it. When the project report is written up, therefore, it is important that readers can know and understand three things:

- how you went about reducing the data and the subsequent grouping and analysis processes – This is usually included within the methodology section.

- the themes and dimensions that you identified from the data – These may well have become very obvious to you as you worked your way carefully through the minutiae of the evidence, but they have to be explained to your readers. The most common way to do this is to offer an overall summary of the main features of the themes and then to illustrate them with a quotation or some other form of example. There are two main implications of this for your practice as a researcher. First, the quotation must be representative (don't squeeze the evidence to fit your preferred explanation). Second, it is important to have a strategy for recording and referencing quotations accurately so that you are able to access them when you need to provide an illustration.

- the justification for the conclusions that you reached – You will demonstrate this in the analysis section by indicating the different explanations that you have evaluated on the basis of the data, and the reasoning behind your conclusion that the selected explanation is the most plausible.

THE USE OF SOFTWARE FOR QUALITATIVE DATA ANALYSIS

Undertaking qualitative data analysis involves the manipulation of vast quantities of data, expressed as words (and potentially in the form of pictures and audio and video files). This is time-consuming and it is difficult to keep track of different items of data. Prior to the development of text-based and database software packages most analysis occurred through 'cut and paste' mechanisms. To operate without qualitative data analysis software (QDAS) required multiple copies of the texts and pictures that formed the data (audio tapes would be transcribed into text). As coding proceeded, different chunks of data could be copied, cut out, clearly marked with appropriate codes and the reference to the original source document, pasted onto card, and then filed in some form of index system. Initial stages of patterning or grouping therefore literally did involve 'laying out' the various relevant items. The main difficulty with this manual approach is the difficulty of keeping track of all the different data. The transcript of a one-hour interview, for example, is likely to take up 20 pages of closely-typed text and the volume of the data can lead to errors in the manipulation process, thus affecting the validity and reliability of the conclusions. But for a project where the quantity of qualitative data is fairly limited, such an approach may well suffice.

A range of software products have now been developed, however, that make the data manipulation process more manageable for research enquiries that have generated a considerable volume of data. Currently, the most frequently used packages are NUD*IST and Ethnograph. Software products are all slightly different and, of course, are being constantly updated. Their common functions include some form of coding and retrieval system and a data-management facility. Some offer a project management function within them, and some also enable some form of hypothesis-building and -testing, incorporating a range of data display tools and options.

Different software packages are appropriate for different types of project. If you are considering using some form of QDAS, it is important to be clear about what the program can offer before you start collecting your data so that it can be built into your data-gathering and analysis process from the beginning. The first step is therefore to find out what data analysis software is supported by your study centre. It is also worth undertaking some initial training on it to acquaint yourself with its functions and evaluate the extent to which it may be helpful in achieving your project objectives. In addition it is important to remember that using software is not a substitute for *thinking*. If you are not at ease with the software, it is possible to lose a lot of time while you try to make the most appropriate use of it.

The main types of QDAS are listed below, and it is possible to find out more about their functions through websites from the software houses, which your study centre will also know of.

- text retrieval packages – These forms of software can search and find individual words and phrases as well as close matches, slight misspellings, similar-sounding words and synonyms. These can then be listed, counted and indexed. The packages also offer a search facility for combinations of words and phrases (and ... or ...) and they display the word or phrase as well as the text surrounding it. Many have a facility for the researcher to write separate notes linked to specific parts of a text.

- text database managers – These software programs differ from text retrieval packages in that they put the data into separate records and as coding occurs, data is held in 'fields'. The search facility can then operate across and within records, allowing for comparisons and contrasts. Records can be sorted and researchers' notes can also be recorded and managed separately. Hypertext links between different topics and themes are possible, enabling cross-tabulation and cross-clarification. It is also possible to organise and display data diagramatically through the coding structure of key concepts to examine possible relationships between different factors and themes.

- visual analysis software – These provide for the visual qualitative (and sometimes quantitative) analysis of graphics, audio and video files, in addition to text-based facilities.

- code-based theory builders – These software programs work from the coded data and provide different opportunities for manipulating and contrasting them. It is thus possible to run queries such as 'if ..., then ...' and display data in time order or on a basis of concurrence. Patterns and relationships between different groups of data that might not be immediately apparent can also be revealed by searching for common and unique characteristics among a set of cases. In the process of generating mapping reports from these software programs, answers to further questions will be needed, which the researcher provides as part of the report-generation process.

Access to specialised software can be problematic for part-time students. Many study centres have a site licence that permits use of the software only within the university or college site.

However, most software providers offer an 'educational' list price for a single-user licence, usually for a defined one-year period, that may be more convenient and appropriate for a part-time student.

The use of software programmes with qualitative data analysis, although making it possible to manage greater volumes of data, does not take away the requirement to think in a logical, evaluative and systematic way as part of the analysis process. Software packages organise data but the initial conceptualisation and the interpretation process still remain the province of the person undertaking the investigative enquiry.

SUMMARY

- Analysis is the thought process that underpins understanding of the relationships between different elements in situations and the likely outcomes of particular actions or interventions. It involves finding answers to your research questions using the data that you have gathered by exploring the relationships between different dimensions and themes.

- Qualitative data relates to the meanings attached to phenomena being investigated. It is not standardised in its format and it is characterised by volume and messiness.

- Qualitative data analysis is an integrated and iterative process. It informs data-gathering and the formulation of conclusions. Data analysis involves data reduction and categorisation; abstraction, grouping and display; and the evaluation of alternative explanations before conclusions are reached.

- Qualitative data analysis involves the categorisation and coding of data. Coding is a means of labelling chunks of data in relation to their meaning. Chunks of data may vary considerably in size, from individual words to a phrase or paragraph. One unit of data may be categorised in more than one way and therefore be assigned more than one code.

- Codes can relate to contextual information or they may be thematic. Categories and codes can emerge from the data; be developed from the aims, objectives and research questions of a study; be derived from concepts in the literature; or follow from the analysis of other sources of data.

- It is important to analyse the data from a range of perspectives and to value data that does not fit with what is expected.

- Maintaining a diary in which notes, ideas, reflections and procedures are noted down assists with the on-going analysis process and can provide a basis for evaluating the degree of detachment that has been achieved.

- Qualitative data analysis can be undertaken utilising an inductive, deductive or mixed approach to the enquiry.

- Data display processes that can underpin analysis include: lists, grids, typologies, matrices, maps and charts. Pattern-matching and explanation-building (theory-building) are also useful approaches to the analysis process.

- The evaluation of alternative explanations is an important part of qualitative data analysis and leads to the formulation of conclusions on the bases of likelihood and plausibility.

- Qualitative data analysis may include some element of counting or quantification as well as the identification of patterns, clusters, factors, variables, causal relationships, and the development of a theory, model or framework.

■ It is important to clarify and justify the analysis process that has been undertaken. Information about the data recording, reduction and coding processes and the overall analytical approach should be included within the methodology section. A description of the main themes that have been identified, illustrated from the data, and an indication of the way the evidence has been used to evaluate alternative explanations should be included in the section(s) devoted to data presentation and analysis.

■ A range of qualitative data analysis software products such as Ethnograph and NUD*IST are available which can enhance data manipulation processes for text-based, visual and audio forms of data. It is important to evaluate available software at an early stage in an investigative enquiry so that the software functions can be utilised throughout the research process.

Questions for review/reflection

These questions are designed to enable you to identify key areas for development with your project which you should discuss with your project tutor, supervisor or adviser if possible. The responses to them can also form part of a Continuing Professional Development log or portfolio. This is required by the CIPD for those who wish to upgrade their membership status.

Taking stock

1 How organised are the data that you have collected so far? What sort of filing process might be applicable?

2 In what format are your data at present? Do they require transcription or summarising in some way?

3 What software options may be available to you through your study centre for the analysis of your qualitative data? What IT development will you need to undertake, regardless of whether you utilise a specific software package?

4 What is your supervisor, tutor or adviser's opinion of the quantity and quality of any data you have collected? Does your supervisor have specific expertise in data analysis that would be helpful to you?

5 How clear are you about your research questions? What are the main themes that you are likely to explore when you analyse your data? What initial categories will you use for the analysis?

Strengths and weaknesses

1 How skilled are you at producing usable summaries of data-gathering events that will remain meaningful in a number of weeks and can underpin an initial categorisation and coding exercise? Is there some way you could practise in advance? Would your supervisor be willing to read through a summary and offer some feedback as a basis for the development of this skill?

2 How successful have your early attempts at coding data been? What have you learned from these early attempts and how might you apply what you have learned to subsequent coding activity? How will emerging categories be identified?

3 How successful have your early attempts at arranging categories and examining links been? How might you find out about, and experiment with, alternative approaches?

4 To what extent will you need to utilise individual quotations as examples of the dimensions you identify? What arrangements will you make for their identification, storage and retrieval?

Being a practitioner-researcher

1 How might you utilise a 'researcher's diary' throughout the duration of your project to inform your thinking while being both a practitioner and a researcher? How might you utilise the diary when writing up the analysis part of your project?

2 What organisational factors might influence the way that you interpret your data? What strategies can you utilise to maintain detachment from the data?

3 What explanations of the data might be 'organisationally preferred'? What alternative explanations might there be? What might enhance your ability to develop and evaluate a range of explanations as part of the analysis process?

4 What actions can you take to maximise the credibility and dependability of the data that you analyse? How can you ensure that the organisational and personal context in which the data has been generated is not lost as a result of the fragmentation involved in the data analysis process?

FURTHER READING

There are a number of useful books devoted to issues associated with research using qualitative data These include:

BRYMAN, A. and BURGESS, R. G. (eds) (1994) *Analysing Qualitative Data*. London, Routledge.

COFFEE, A. and ATKINSON, P. (1996) *Making Sense of Qualitative Data*. London, Sage.

MILES, M. B. and HUBERMAN, A. M. (1994) *Qualitative Data Analysis*. Thousand Oaks, CA, Sage.

SYMON, G. and CASSELL, C. (eds) (1998) *Qualitative Methods and Analysis in Organisational Research*. London, Sage.

YIN, R. K. (2003) *Case Study Research: Design and methods*. London, Sage.

In addition, there are excellent chapters devoted to qualitative data-gathering and analysis which draw on many of the sources listed above in:

DENSCOMBE, M. (1998) *The Good Research Guide for Small-Scale Social Research Projects*. Buckingham, Open University Press.

NEUMAN, W. L. (2003) *Social Research Methods: Qualitative and quantitative approaches*. Boston, MA, Pearson.

ROBSON, C. (2002) *Real World Research: A resource for social scientists and practitioner-researchers*. Oxford, Blackwell.

More specialised texts relating to content analysis include:

HOLSTI, O. R. (1969) *Content Analysis for the Social Sciences and Humanities*. Reading, MA, Addison-Wesley.

KRIPPENDORFF, K. (1980) *Content Analysis: An introduction to its methodology*. London, Sage.

WEBER, R. (1990) *Basic Content Analysis*. London, Sage.

Printed material relating to software and data analysis becomes dated very quickly, and a more up-to-date overview of the types of software products available is likely to be found on the following website:

www.scolari.co.uk

The main principles are outlined in:

FISHER, M. (1997) *Qualitative Computing: Using software for qualitative data analysis*. Aldershot, Ashgate.

LEWINS, A. (2001) *Making Sense of Software in Qualitative Research*. London, Sage.

TESCH, R. (1990) *Qualitative Research: Analysis types and software tools*. New York, Falmer.

Using quantitative data in HR research

LEARNING OUTCOMES

This chapter should help you to:

- consider how quantitative data can contribute to your investigation

- become familiar with different types and purposes of surveys

- design and administer a survey to an appropriate sample of respondents

- collect, organise and present quantitative data effectively

- undertake an initial analysis of quantitative data to answer your research questions.

HOW TO USE THIS CHAPTER

It would be almost impossible to investigate an HR problem or issue without the use of some quantitative data. This chapter aims to identify where to look for appropriate data as well as how to collect it and make sense of it. The chapter does not require you to become an expert in statistical techniques or specialised software programmes. It will, however, help you to identify useful sources of quantitative data both internal and external to your organisation. Any practitioner-researcher who expects to undertake some form of survey should find the fourth and fifth section of the chapter (*Undertaking your own survey* and *Collecting, organising and presenting quantitative data*) particularly helpful. If, in addition to summarising and describing the data you have collected, you propose to analyse it, you should refer to the next section (*Analysing data to answer research questions*), in which initial data analysis processes are explained. There are ideas for further reading at the end of the chapter if you propose to undertake a more sophisticated (multivariate) statistical analysis.

Case illustration

Losing out to inflation

Average pay increases for UK personnel staff are slowing and have fallen well behind the equivalent figure for all workers – as well as price inflation – although they remain slightly ahead of the average rises given to managers as a whole, according to the latest PM/Croner Reward Index.

The average annual rise for HR professionals over the past three months was 2.1 per cent (see Chart A), well below the Average Earnings Index (3.4 per cent) and 3.1 per cent inflation rate recorded by the Retail Prices Index (RPI). Three months ago, in February, personnel earnings were increasing at an average of 2.7 per cent.

As always, the single figure for all personnel professionals masks variations at different levels within the function (see Chart B). For senior personnel managers, earnings have risen at a very comfortable 5.8 per cent over the past 12 months, up from the 5.2 per cent seen in the last review in February. In today's marketplace this is a good performance, especially when compared with that of the next level down, personnel managers. Over the past 12 months the index for this group has fallen by 0.6 per cent. This does not necessarily mean that individual employees have seen their basic pay fall (although this could be the case); it is more likely that the index includes a number of starters who are being paid less than the people that they replaced.

Senior personnel officers have seen their earnings rise by 2.1 per cent over the past 12 months – down on the 3.7 per cent last time. Personnel officers suffered an even greater drop, from 2.7 per cent in February to 0.2 per cent today. The situation is only marginally better for junior personnel officers, who have seen earnings increases of 0.5 per cent in the past 12 months – down from 2.2 per cent in February. . . .

Chart A Average rises in earnings (all employees)

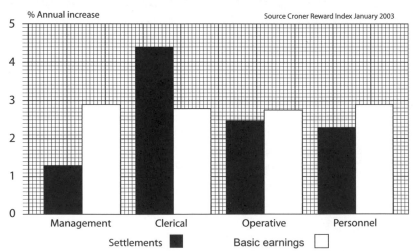

% Annual increase

Source Croner Reward Index January 2003

Settlements ■   Basic earnings □

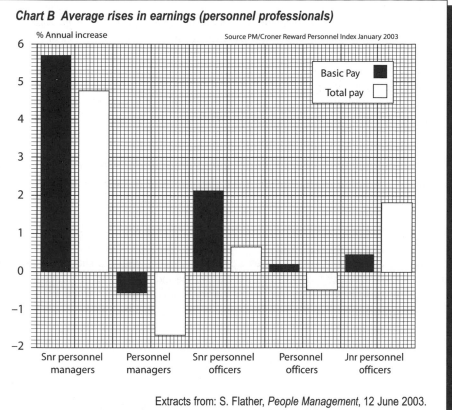

Chart B Average rises in earnings (personnel professionals)

% Annual increase

Source PM/Croner Reward Personnel Index January 2003

Basic Pay

Total pay

Snr personnel managers · Personnel managers · Snr personnel officers · Personnel officers · Jnr personnel officers

Extracts from: S. Flather, *People Management*, 12 June 2003.
Reproduced by permission of Croner Reward Ltd

DISCUSSION QUESTIONS

1   What information does this extract provide? What does it *not* tell you?

2   What additional information would you like to see included in the extract?

3   What information would you need in order to evaluate the trustworthiness of the data that is reported in the extract?

Feedback notes

This short extract provides some interesting information about pay in the HR profession. Pay levels have increased in the profession as a whole, although senior personnel managers have done much better than any other level, and personnel managers seem to have done relatively badly. The information was published in *People Management* in June and refers to a three-monthly survey, following one in February, so it is possible to infer that the data was collected in May and, as such, was fairly up to date when it was published. The article is successful, therefore, in describing trends in overall pay, but the data cannot explain or tell you *why* these trends have occurred.

In addition, further information would enable a reader to make more sense of the data. The main missing element (missing from the extract but not from the article, in fact) is the actual end-point pay rates of the different levels of professional mentioned in the article. It would also be interesting to know the extent to which average pay rates for each level differed in the various regions of the country, and whether the rates of increase were also affected by location.

In order to evaluate the value of this pay survey it is also necessary to know more about it. Questions that might occur to you include: How is the index compiled (what methods are used)? How many jobs are included in the survey? To what extent are the jobs that are sampled representative of all the jobs within the HR profession in the UK?

These issues and others underpin this chapter. Although quantitative data is likely to form a part of any assessment of an HR issue or problem, it is important to be clear about its purpose and to use the data in an appropriate way.

This chapter provides a framework through which to consider the appropriate use of quantitative data in HR studies, but it does not set out to provide a full consideration of quantitative data analysis. Students whose projects are likely to utilise quantitative data analysis in a significant way should consult more specialised texts such as those indicated in the *Further reading* section.

THE USES OF QUANTITATIVE DATA IN HR RESEARCH

As noted earlier in Chapter 4, *quantitative data* is the term given to data that can be quantified (counted). So, whereas the analysis of qualitative data provides opportunities for exploring the dimensions of particular issues, quantitative data allows for the quantification of features of organisational situations. Quantitative data deals in variables that can be counted, measured, described, and compared with other variables.

Quantitative data have an important part to play in answering research questions. Firstly, using quantitative data you can describe a current situation in terms of:

- frequency – How many people over the age of 50? How many times were certain behaviours manifested?
- central tendency – What is the average length of service of employees?
- dispersion – How wide is the difference between the lowest and highest rates of take-home pay in a particular department?

You can compare this data with information from other sources (maybe data from other parts of the organisation) and you can describe trends (spend on training over a four-year period etc).

The uses of quantitative data outlined above are common in most organisations and they underpin decision-making and the evaluation of achievements. However, quantitative data can also be more fully analysed within research enquiries to explore potential relationships between different variables and to assess their significance. It is also possible to investigate possible relationships between two or more different variables. Thus, although much quantitative data in HR is used descriptively, it is also possible to use it to help to explain different phenomena.

Case illustration

Workplace communication and information-sharing

'Information-sharing or employee involvement appears in just about every description of, or prescription for, "best practice" or high-commitment HRM' (Marchington and Wilkinson, 2002; p.184). Pfeffer (1998) argues that information-sharing is important for two reasons: firstly, open communications about workplace issues indicate high levels of trust; and secondly, information about the organisation and its context is essential for effective teamwork and employee participation. It therefore seems reasonable to assume that ensuring employees receive adequate information and maintaining effective workplace communication should be of considerable importance to HR practitioners. ... This paper aims to investigate this issue in more detail and analyse the extent to which the types of communication methods used and the amount and type of information given to employees varies between workplaces with an HR/personnel specialist and those without.

Methodology
. . ..
The analysis undertaken for this paper draws on two key sources. Quantitative analysis is undertaken on raw data from WERS98. The survey provides information on a number of aspects of workplace communication and information-sharing including the use of different methods of downward and upward communication and the range of issues on which information is provided to employees. ...

Additional analysis draws on a study of HR policy and practice among engineering employers in the East Midlands. Findings were obtained via a postal questionnaire directed to the person with senior responsibility for personnel/HR matters at workplace level. Many of the questions are similar to those in the WERS98 study, so the findings provide a useful alternative source of data, albeit on a much smaller scale. ...

Both surveys investigate the communication methods used in workplaces by asking respondents to indicate their use of the following:

Downward communication
Systematic use of the management chain
Team briefing
Company newsletter
Noticeboards

Upward communication
Quality circles
Suggestion schemes
Attitude surveys

The analysis considers the extent to which the number and types of practices used in the workplaces with an HR specialist differs from those without a specialist. It also explores any patterns in the combinations of practices used – ie the balance between downward and upward communication methods.

J. Beardwell and C. Britton, 'Look who's talking':
paper presented to the CIPD Professional Standards Conference, 1 July 2003.
Reproduced by permission of the authors

DISCUSSION QUESTIONS

1   How were the quantitative data for this study obtained?
2   What was the purpose of the study?
3   What variables do you think were utilised within an analysis of the data gathered for this study?

Feedback notes

This study sought to find out about HR and communication in a cross-section of different organisations and made use of data from two sources. Firstly, published data (from WERS98) was used. In addition, the researchers gathered data from an additional one-off survey to help them to answer their research questions.

The purpose of the study was to examine relationships between variables reflecting different approaches to information-sharing and the presence, or otherwise, of an HR function within an organisation. The range of variables that you may have identified might thus be survey responses related to 'systematic use of the management chain', 'attitude surveys', etc. Further variables would include the presence within the organisation of an HR specialist (or not). Other variables that are likely to have been included are: the number of employees, the business sector, the staff turnover of the organisation, the age of the organisation, etc. Having obtained this sort of data, it is then possible to 'interrogate' it in order to try to answer the research questions.

WHERE DOES QUANTITATIVE DATA COME FROM?

The case illustration above indicates that much of the quantitative data used in HR research is likely to come from surveys of one sort of another. It can also, however, be generated from structured observations, through content analysis of texts and other artefacts, etc. In addition, further quantitative data may be derived from organisational Personnel Management Information Systems.

There are three main sources of survey data.

- published surveys, undertaken for purposes other than your research (such as WERS98) – these are useful sources of secondary data
- unpublished surveys, undertaken for purposes other than your research (organisational attitude survey data, for example) – these are further examples of secondary data

- surveys undertaken as a part of your specific research enquiry, including postal or online surveys, telephone interviews and structured face-to-face interviews.

Most of this chapter considers issues relevant to undertaking a survey of your own. First, however, some information about published surveys is provided below.

Data from published surveys

Practitioners undertaking HR research projects, particularly those that are organisationally-based, often make little or no use of published surveys although the data might offer a useful

Table 23 *Examples of regular surveys*

Name	Sample/ frequency	Sponsor	Description
Labour Force Survey	60,000 households/ quarterly	Office for National Statistics	The survey seeks information on personal circumstances and labour market status of respondents during a specific period prior to the survey (1 or 4 weeks, depending on topic). Also undertaken in other EU countries, and ILO comparisons are possible.
Learning and Training at Work	4,000 work establishments/ annual	Department for Education and Skills	The survey collects information on employers' commitment to training and learning opportunities, including provision of job-related training. Also employer involvement with initiatives relevant to training.
Workplace Employee Relations Survey	3,000+ managers, 1,000+ employee reps, 30,000 employees. Undertaken (as WIRS) in 1980, 1984, 1990, 1998	ACAS, DTI, ESRC, PSI	The survey collects information relating to employment relations in workplaces in the UK. Data on issues such as union recognition, negotiating structures, collective bargaining, procedures and agreements, pay systems, consultation and communication, workforce composition, performance measures, etc, included in WERS98.
Reward Management Survey	Reward specialists and people managers in about 500 organisations/ annual	the CIPD	The survey seeks to provide data on current and emerging practice in reward management in the UK. It is sent to respondents in the public, private and voluntary sectors, including small and large organisations.

point of context or comparison. The data from most surveys (often in tabulated form) is available electronically, either through a CD-ROM or the Internet. Useful data sources might include:

- censuses (eg population census of 2001) – National censuses are completed on a mandatory basis utilising a wide range of questions.

- regular surveys – Many regular surveys are likely to be of interest to those working in HR. These include surveys undertaken on behalf of the government, research organisations or professional institutes (such as the CIPD). Some examples are shown in Table 23.

- ad hoc surveys – These are often undertaken for particular purposes. One example of such a survey might be the survey sponsored by the CIPD and a consultancy organisation to investigate the people management issues and reactions to the terrorist events of 11 September 2001, and their likely effect on HR and business generally (see the CIPD website for a copy of this and other survey reports: www.cipd.co.uk).

UNDERTAKING YOUR OWN SURVEY

Surveys are perhaps the most widely-used data-gathering technique in business and management, and HR projects are no exception. Surveys can be used to measure issues that are crucial to the management and development of human resources such as behaviour, attitudes, beliefs, opinions, characteristics, expectations, and so on.

As with any form of data-gathering, surveys can contribute to the achievement of a range of different research objectives. A key issue with any survey design and utilisation is to be clear about its purpose. Some surveys operate from within a *deductive* approach in seeking to analyse the relationships between variables and to establish the existence or otherwise of correlations between them. A hypothesis is formulated and the data is then analysed to confirm (or not) the propositions derived from the hypothesis (see Chapter 4 for a fuller discussion of the deductive and inductive approaches to research). Gill and Johnson (2002), however, point out that some surveys fulfil a more exploratory and *inductive* purpose, by indicating patterns and frequencies that can contribute to theory-building. Other surveys have a principally comparative purpose, seeking to describe data and consider similarities with data from other research populations. The surveys undertaken in many HR projects – particularly for the purposes of CIPD management reports – fulfil a descriptive purpose (those at master's level will probably seek to go further than a descriptive purpose). Attitude surveys are a good example of the descriptive (and sometimes comparative) purpose of some surveys.

Determining a sample

Whatever the purpose of the survey, however, the issue of sample size and selection is crucial to the trustworthiness of the findings. As noted already in Chapter 6, sampling is *the deliberate choice of a number of people to represent a greater population*. There are two main approaches to sampling. *Non-probability sampling* (discussed in Chapter 6) is most often used for qualitative data-gathering. For quantitative data, however, *probability sampling* is more appropriate. This involves determining a sample that is statistically representative of the population as a whole and so should reflect its characteristics in such a way that you may be confident that your conclusions can be generalised to the wider population.

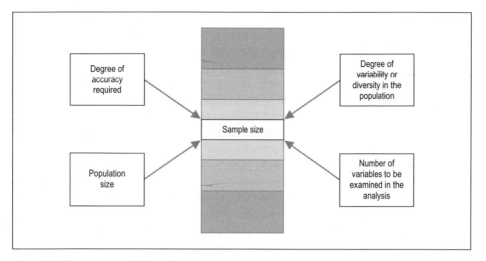

Figure 29 *Influences on sample size*

There are two key decisions with any survey – first, the size of the sample that you select; and second, the way in which you select it so that it is large enough, random, and unbiased.

Sample size

There are no clear answers with regard to how large a sample should be. The following general principles (Neuman, 2003) are helpful:

- the smaller the population, the bigger the ratio of sample size to population size (sampling ratio) should be. Thus:
  - for small populations (under 1,000) a ratio of about 30:100 (30 per cent) is advisable
  - for populations of between 1,000 and 10,000 a ratio of about 10 per cent may be acceptable
  - for populations of over 15,000 a ratio of 1 per cent may suffice.
- the higher your requirement for accuracy (and generalisability), the greater your sampling ratio should be
- the higher the degree of diversity in the population, the higher the sampling ratio should be
- the higher the number of different variables to be examined in the analysis of the data, the higher the sampling ratio should be.

Some of these factors are illustrated in Figure 29.

Case illustration

Determining a sample size and method of sampling

Mike worked in an organisation that wished to achieve the IiP standard. The organisation employed 3,000 people. Two thousand of the employees worked on the main site for the organisation. About half of the staff at the main site were engaged in semi-skilled activities and the other half undertook a range of professional roles (marketing, sales, IT, research and development, etc). There were also ten other sites which employed between 50 and 175 staff each, in different regions of the UK. These had a manager and deputy manager, but the rest of the employees were semi- or unskilled workers. About 75 per cent of staff in the organisation as a whole worked on full-time contracts, but the remainder (including quite a high proportion in the 'outposts') had a range of different part-time working arrangements. About 60 per cent of the employees were male and 40 per cent were female.

Mike was responsible for the IiP project and, with the organisation's personnel director, decided that a staff survey should be conducted in order to assess the extent to which the organisation met the standards required to achieve IiP. Mike had to devise and issue a written questionnaire to be completed by a sample of employees. Mike was particularly anxious about the potential responses of staff at the outposts to any IiP-related questions as he was aware that an assessor could choose to evaluate the extent to which communication, training and development practices in the main site also occurred at the outposts. Concern had already been expressed by some of the managers of the outposts that their staff benefited less from corporate training initiatives, and he was also conscious that their geographical isolation tended to make many of these staff less aware of (and committed to) the organisation's priorities.

Before he set about devising the questionnaire, then, he had to decide what sample size was appropriate and how respondents would be selected to ensure that the data collected was representative of the wider population and did not under-represent any particular group of staff.

DISCUSSION QUESTIONS

1 What process would you advise Mike to use to identify potential respondents to ensure that the sample is representative?

2 What sampling ratio would you recommend, and why?

Feedback notes

Decisions about the sampling ratio must take a number of factors into account. Although the organisation was fairly large, and a sampling ratio of about 10 per cent (300 respondents) could be argued to be sufficient, it is important to feel confident that this does not under-represent the responses of employees at the outposts, particularly the smaller ones. It is also important to ensure that responses represent the range of different professions, levels of management, part-time as well as full-time staff, etc. With this in mind you may recommend a

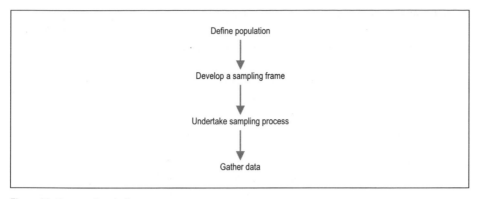

Figure 30 *The sample selection process*

proportionately larger sample from the outposts in addition to the 10 per cent ratio initially identified. Alternatively, you might suggest sampling more intensively from half of the outposts rather than attempting an overall survey of them all.

Having decided on the approach to sample size, however, Mike still needed to work out who would be asked to complete the questionnaire. An accurate listing of all the staff employed by the organisation was obtained from the payroll listing. This list formed the 'sampling frame'. The accuracy of the sampling frame had to be checked (to ensure that all leavers had been excluded from it, and so on). It was also necessary to resolve whether people who were on long-term sick leave should remain in the sampling frame. Mike had to decide whether the sample would be truly random or whether there would be some element of systematic inclusion within the sample.

The case illustration thus demonstrates that there are no hard and fast rules about sample size and selection. Such issues require judgement and justification on the part of the researcher. The process of sample selection is illustrated as Figure 30. When reading the research of others, therefore, it is worth critically evaluating their approach to sample selection and sample size, as well as being prepared to discuss the benefits but also the limitations of the approach that you have taken for any sample you select as part of your project. The main approaches to sample selection are outlined in the section that follows, although fuller accounts can be found in more specialised texts such as Bryman and Cramer (1997), Erickson and Nosanchuk (1992), and Diamantopoulos and Schlegelmilch (1997).

Sample selection methods

Simple random sampling

This approach requires the development of an accurate sampling frame and then the use of a mathematically random procedure (usually the use of published random number tables) to select the elements (the respondents) from the sampling frame. To achieve this you have to give each potential respondent (all the cases in the sampling frame) a number – the first is 0, the next is 1, and so on. You also have to have as many random numbers as there are cases (elements) in your frame. You then go to the random number tables and choose a number at random. This is the first selection for your sample. Then you read off more random numbers in a systematic and regular way (this can be along the rows of the sheet of numbers, every fifth number, or whatever) until you have chosen the number of respondents you require.

The approach does not guarantee a perfect representation of the population, but it does mean that you will be close to it. In addition, it is possible (although not covered in this book) to calculate the level of confidence, or probability, that the sample is (or is not) accurate. However, having used a random approach, it is very important that you actually get your survey data from each respondent represented by his or her number – hence the need for an accurate sampling frame. Every non-respondent diminishes the level of representativeness of the survey data.

Systematic sampling

This approach also requires numbering of all the elements or cases in the sampling frame. At that point, though, you calculate a sampling interval or ratio. Thus, if you want a 10 per cent sampling ratio, you would choose one respondent randomly and then count down one in every ten cases thereafter. Although this might seem easier than the random number approach, it is important to remember that you may not achieve a random sample if the sampling frame (eg the payroll listing from a Personnel Information System) is itself organised in some form of pattern or cycle.

Stratified sampling

With this approach the sampling frame itself is divided into sub-populations (perhaps by department, or by grade, or by age group) and you then draw a random sample from each one. This can be done systematically or using the simple random approach. It is an approach that may be particularly useful when one of the sub-populations is quite small and so could be missed by a simple random approach.

Cluster sampling

Here you identify sample clusters (units) from the overall population and then you draw a second sample from within the clusters. This approach is often cheaper and easier than a simple random approach when the population is very dispersed and difficult to access. However, each stage in the clustering and selection process introduces sampling errors, and so limits the reliability of the data.

Survey design

Surveys are a very popular method within HR investigative enquiries. Sometimes they are adopted because it is felt that a survey will be easier and quicker than undertaking interviews. In reality, though, surveys are equally challenging. They are difficult to design, and if poorly designed, the data they generate is very difficult to analyse. This section offers a brief overview of some of the issues that affect the success or otherwise of a survey, although specialised texts offer a more detailed consideration of the method.

There are two main golden rules for survey design: the first is to maintain clarity, and the second is to keep the respondents' perspective in mind (Neuman, 2003). These rules underpin a number of stages of survey design and distribution, which are represented in Figure 31 (see page 223) and described, stage by stage, in the sections that follow.

Survey strategy

Before launching into the design of the survey it is important to clarify key issues. First, what is the purpose of your survey? What are the important variables that follow from the purposes of your study? Do you intend to compare data you gather with data from other surveys? If so, you must carefully identify the basis on which the data in the other survey(s) was gathered. What form of analysis will you hope to achieve? If you want to test the relationships between different variables, you must ensure that your questions allow you to do this. To what extent are open as well as closed questions appropriate, given the purpose of your survey? How will non-responses to some of your questions impact on the subsequent analysis?

Question structure

This part of the thinking and decision process involves considering a range of issues such as the question format and the method of response. Do you want respondents to tick boxes, circle numbers, or make some other form of response? Will respondents be asked to make one choice from a range of options (multiple choice)? Will they make a choice somewhere between two dichotomous ends of a 'scale'? Is some form of ranking of alternatives going to be appropriate? These are crucial decisions, which will influence the success of your analysis process – and the implications of these are outlined next (Robson, 2002; Collis and Hussey, 2003; Gill and Johnson, 2001; Zikmund, 2000).

- *Open v closed questions*

  The issues around the use of open questions have been considered in the chapters on qualitative research approaches. Although quantitative surveys will mainly make use of different forms of closed questions, a few open questions are often included. This enables respondents to clarify their answers, provide additional detail and show the logic, or thinking process, underpinning different choices. Subsequent analysis is more problematic, however, and comparisons and statistical operations are not possible. Closed questions, by contrast offer a range of advantages. They are easier and quicker for a respondent to tackle – answers will be unambiguous and can be more easily compared. It is also possible to repeat the survey at another time or with another research population. But there are also disadvantages with closed questions. It is possible that by laying a 'menu' of answers in front of respondents you are suggesting things to them that they would not have otherwise have thought of (but may now choose). Also, respondents with no knowledge or opinion may still choose to tick a box. Alternatively, they may be frustrated that their desired answer is not given as one of the choices. There is also no check as to the level of understanding of the question by the respondent, and simplistic choices may be 'forced' which do not really reflect how people feel and act in the real world.

Decisions about the form of questions in a survey are crucial because they impact on what you can do with the data once you have gathered it. The material that follows describes the main options. In order to illustrate the different approaches to formulating questions the scenario of trying to find out about job satisfaction at work is used.

- *Nominal scale data*

  Sometimes called category scales, nominal scale data allows you to classify responses into different groupings. Thus questions that ask respondents whether they are male or female, or which department they work in, allow you to count how many of each there are. However, such categories have no 'arithmetic value' (you cannot calculate the average gender, for example). The data is very useful, all the same. If you were researching into job satisfaction, you could compare the proportion of women recording high or low job satisfaction with the proportion of men. The inclusion of these 'biographical' or 'situational' variables within a survey therefore allows for a range of comparisons to be made.

- *Ordinal scale data*

  This approach to scaling involves categories with some degree of ordering such that different points on the scale show greater or lesser amounts of the phenomenon, relative to other points on it. Thus a question in an attitude survey asking about the level of job satisfaction experienced by the respondent might range from 1 = little satisfaction, 2 = some satisfaction, 3 = generally satisfied, 4 = high level of job satisfaction.

The Likert scale is an example of ordinal scale data whereby individuals indicate their attitudes towards a statement (such as 'I generally experience job satisfaction in my current job role'), usually in five steps, ranging from 'strongly agree' to 'agree', 'uncertain', 'disagree', and finally 'strongly disagree'.

Another approach to ordinal scale data is to ask respondents to rank a set of attributes from the most preferred to their least preferred. For example, ordering the importance of attributes (eg involvement, communication by supervisor, rate of pay, working conditions) that respondents feel contribute to their sense of job satisfaction. Again, however, other than counting the numbers of responses and establishing an order, such questions cannot sustain further statistical interrogation because the distances between the points on the scale are not established. What is the distance between 'generally satisfied' and 'some satisfaction', for example, and would every respondent understand the distance in the same way?

■ *Interval scale data*

Questions utilising interval scales are similar to ordinal scales but the distance between the points is known and the intervals represent equal quantities. Measures of IQ that are calculated from most intelligence tests, for example, work on the basis that '100' corresponds to the norm and that other points indicate the distance of the score from the average. For this reason it is not possible to achieve an IQ of zero but the distance between two people with an IQ of 85 and 100 is known to be the same as the distance between two people with an IQ of 100 and 115.

Some HR surveys include scales divided into, say, seven or eight equidistant points with opposite 'extremes' at each end, and respondents choose the point on the scale that best represents their response. The question about job satisfaction cited above could be phrased as follows to form an interval scale. Yet it remains doubtful that all respondents would understand the difference between a '4' and a '5'.

To what extent do you achieve job satisfaction in your current work role?

Extremely							Extremely
satisfied	7	6	5	4	3	2	1	dissatisfied

This example shows that an interval scale does not have a zero – you cannot go lower than '1'. For this reason some, but not all, statisticians would be uncomfortable with calculations (such as averaging) being performed.

■ *Ratio scale data*

This data represents the highest level of precision. A ratio scale does have a zero (for example, height, weight, time) and so it is possible to say that something lasts for twice as long or costs three times as much. However, the nature of research questions underpinning many HR surveys, particularly in organisational enquiries, tends to mean that ratio scale questions are quite rare.

ACTIVITY – QUESTION DESIGN

Study the extracts from the survey questionnaire reproduced below and identify which of the questions utilise nominal, ordinal, interval or ratio scaling.
Critically evaluate the usefulness of the data that would be gathered.

Section 1 – Your organisation

1 Which of the following best describes your organisation?   Please ✓ one
box only

Sole proprietor .... ☐
A partnership .... ☐
An independent company .... ☐
A subsidiary* .... ☐
*Please state the nationality of the parent company _____

Note for Subsidiary companies ONLY.
Please make all responses in the questionnaire for the activities of the subsidiary, rather than the Group as a whole

2 In which sector does your business principally operate?   Please ✓ one
box only

Industrial Manufactured Products .... ☐
Consumer Manufactured Products .... ☐
Mechanical Engineering .... ☐
Transport (including Aerospace) .... ☐
Services .... ☐
Other (please specify)

_____

3 Where is the principal UK location of your organisation?

_____

4 How long has your organisation been established?   Please ✓ one
box only

Under 1 year .... ☐
1–5 years .... ☐
6–10 years .... ☐
Over 10 years .... ☐

Section 3 – The outcome of international activities

23 Looking back, how difficult was it to achieve the original objectives sought when the organisation moved into international markets?

Please rank ALL of the factors below by placing a ✔ in the appropriate box.

OBJECTIVE (extracts from the options)	Not applicable to this organisation	Relatively straight-forward	Initially difficult	Consistently difficult	Very difficult
Satisfy personal motives within the company					
Utilise excess capacity/reduce production costs					
Expand within the capabilities of the organisation					

24 For ALL the potential problems (listed below) that could have been encountered during the early phase of the international activities, which ones apply to your organisation?

Please ✔ one box for EACH problem which applies to your organisation.

(extracts from a larger series of questions)	Strongly disagree	Disagree	Not sure	Agree	Strongly agree
We inadequately prepared our overseas staff					
Management of agents/ intermediaries was problematic					
Language barriers were a problem					

Other (please specify):

_____

_____

26 To what extent has your organisation's performance been affected because of its involvement with international markets?

Please rank ALL of the factors below, by placing a ✔ in the appropriate box.

(extracts of the options)	Reduced significantly	Reduced slightly	No change	Increased slightly	Increased significantly
Sales turnover (total)					
Number of employees					
Product portfolio					
Competitive standing generally					

Other (please specify):

_____

27 To what extent have other benefits come about because of your organisation's involvement with international markets?

Please rank ALL of the factors below, by placing a ✔ in the appropriate box.

(extracts from the options)	No change	Little change	Some change	Important change	Critical change
Enhanced company reputation					
Greater market awareness					
Professionalism increased					
Organisational/management learning					

Other (please specify):

_____

_____

V. Anderson, G. Boocock, S. Graham and P. Lawrence (1999) *International Business: Experiences and outcomes* (unpublished). Reproduced with permission

Feedback notes

You should have identified the early questions in this questionnaire as nominal scale (or category) questions. Only one response is required, and such questions are unsuitable for mathematical processes other than counting. Most biographical data in HR surveys will be of this type. Although it is not possible to perform 'statistics' on these types of questions, they can be useful in an assessment of whether respondents in one category have responded in greater or lesser way to subsequent questions. The variables in these categories are 'independent' and it may be possible to see if other 'dependent' variables (such as the organisation's performance) vary for these different categories.

In this extract there is only one question that is 'open' in its own right (number 3), although other questions have an 'other' category to supplement their closed, and scaled, approaches. All of the questions in section 3 are ordinal scale questions. There is some degree of ordering but the 'distance' between each of the points within the order is not quantified and is not necessarily regular. To establish interval scales would require a more obvious numbering scale visually representing equivalent distances between each point.

So although these questions have the potential to yield interesting information, the extent to which they can be analysed, beyond descriptions of the frequency with which different categories were chosen, is very limited. Further, although a five-point scale is used in the ordinal scale questions, each point on the scale has a different heading (and therefore a different meaning) and so mathematical comparisons between these different variables is also impossible. This extract demonstrates, therefore, how the question design process has limited the subsequent opportunities for analysis of the data. A more careful planning process, to decide what analysis would be helpful in achieving the research objectives of the project, would have facilitated some revisions in the questions and a more effective questionnaire design process.

Table 24 *Effective survey design*

Initial request/ instructions	Explain the purpose to all participants (a covering letter is often used) Establish the time-scale, processes for return, and confidentiality arrangements
Layout	Ensure that the questionnaire looks neat and attractive and has a reasonable page length It must be easy to read, with clear instructions Provide enough space for respondents to mark their answers Establish a logical order for the questions Use a numbering or sub-lettering system to show groupings of questions
Questions	Begin with 'warm-up' questions Keep the questions as simple as possible Check that all questions are relevant – ask 'need to know' rather than 'nice to know' questions. Be clear about what the objective of each question is in relation to your research Avoid jargon, specialist language, slang or abbreviations Phrase each question so that only one meaning is possible Ensure that the language of your questions is not 'emotionally loaded' Check that there are no multiple or leading questions Edit out any double negatives from the questions Utilise filter questions where some questions may not be relevant for all respondents
Final thanks/ return arrangements	Thank respondents for taking the time to complete your survey Establish the return arrangements clearly Do not commit to more feedback after the research than you are sure you can provide Use the back page for respondents to offer any comments they would like to make

Sources: Collis and Hussey (2003), Neuman (2003), Robson (2002)

Survey design

The next stage in the survey process involves the design of the questionnaire itself. Here, it is important to consider its length, its structure, the order of the questions, the layout, and the method of administration (telephone, post, e-mail, etc) A summary of the main features of appropriate survey design are shown as Table 24.

Survey piloting

Survey design is a complex process and it is easy to become so absorbed in it that potential errors are not picked up. However, if a survey is inappropriately designed, it is likely that the data that it generates will be of very little value. Thus, for all investigative enquiries it is strongly advisable to pilot any survey, prior to its distribution, in order to answer the following questions (Robson, 2002; Saunders *et al*, 2003):

- Is the content of the questions appropriate for the research questions? Have any important variables been omitted? Will the questions that have been asked provide the information that is sought (validity)?

- How long does it take to complete the survey? How acceptable would the length of the survey be to the respondents? Are the instructions clear?
- Are all the questions clear and unambiguous?
- Are any questions likely to be too sensitive for the respondent group?
- How appropriate is the layout of the questionnaire?

It will only be possible to answer all these questions if the pilot incorporates a range of different people. Firstly, it is desirable for a 'subject expert' to offer an opinion on its strengths and weaknesses. Your project tutor, supervisor or adviser, as a minimum, should have the opportunity to offer feedback and suggestions prior to the finalisation of any survey instrument. In addition, useful comments about the length, clarity, and so on, can be obtained from people who are similar to those in the respondent group.

Administering surveys

The final set of decisions regarding the survey relate to the arrangements by which it will reach respondents. It is vital to optimise the response, as far as possible, by ensuring that the survey reaches all those in the sample and by maximising the chance that they will answer your questions and return the completed survey to you. The higher the non-response rate, the less reliable will be your findings. The main options for survey distribution are:

- postal, self-administered questionnaire
- delivered and collected, self-administered questionnaire
- structured telephone interview
- structured face-to-face interview
- e-mail questionnaire
- web-based survey.

Table 25 lists the key factors to be taken into account with each of these, as well as the advantages and disadvantages.

Table 25 *Administering and delivering surveys*

Method of distribution	Key issues	Advantages	Disadvantages
Postal, self-administered	Pre-survey contact will enhance response rate Covering letter Reply-paid envelope Follow-up after one or two weeks to enhance response rate	Cheap Respondents possible across a wide geographical area Respondents can complete when convenient to them Anonymity is possible No interviewer bias	Low response rate Late returns Conditions for completion are not controlled Clarification of questions is not possible Incomplete responses are more likely
Delivery and collection questionnaire	Pre-survey contact and permissions necessary Personal explanation of purpose of survey (replaces covering letter) Respondents can seal their completed survey and place it themselves in a collection box	Good response rate is possible Respondents slightly more involved Anonymity is 'visible' Clarification of a question is possible Controlled conditions for survey completion	Sample restricted to those that can attend at the given time and place 'Unwilling' respondents may make more extreme responses Organisational authorisation may be difficult to achieve
Telephone Interview	Initial contact with respondent may mean calling back at a more convenient time Clear explanation of the purpose of the study is required Decisions about how many calls to each respondent required	Survey can be completed in a shorter time-frame Geographical limitations can be overcome Clarification of questions is possible	Some interviewer bias may occur No scope for recording non-verbal information Higher cost than postal questionnaires
Face-to-face interviews	Competence of interviewer is important Pre-survey contact necessary Possible areas for probes must be clearly specified	Good response rates Surroundings and non-verbal communication can be recorded More probing of issues is possible	Possibility of interviewer bias Expense (time-intensive) Geographical constraints of reaching respondents

Method of distribution	Key issues	Advantages	Disadvantages
E-mail survey	E-mail addresses of sample are required Pre-survey contact enhances response rate Covering message required Attachments can become unattached Arrangements for anonymity required Follow up message to enhance response rate	Speed of transmission No geographical limits No interviewer bias Respondents can complete at a time suitable to themselves	Respondent concerns about anonymity Different software can affect display of images and the format of questionnaire Poor response rate Lost data (particularly attachments) Potential for respondents to alter the questionnaire
Web-based surveys	Establish a website with online questionnaire Explain purpose and provide instructions for completion (replaces covering letter) Hyperlinks need to be operational! Advertise the site widely Ensure that completed returns go straight to the designated e-mail address	Questionnaire cannot be altered Possible to measure 'hit rate' on the site No interviewer bias More control over image and format of questionnaire	Unclear sample – how representative? Those without access to the technology cannot be included Potential for one person to make multiple responses

Sources: Neuman (2003), Robson *et al* (2003)

There are, therefore, many issues that must be taken into account in survey design and distribution. Surveys can provide data from a large sample of respondents that can be counted, described and analysed. If careful thinking and planning underpins survey design and administration, it is possible to gather data of good quality that can be analysed in order to answer research questions.

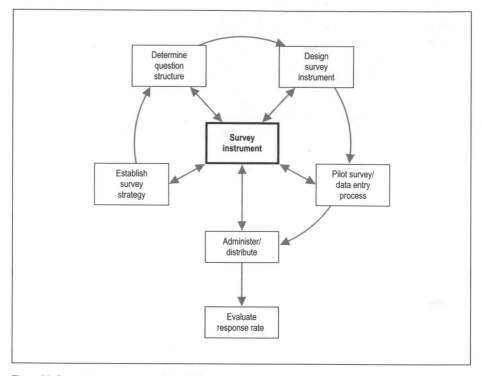

Figure 31 *Stages in survey design and distribution*

COLLECTING, ORGANISING AND PRESENTING QUANTITATIVE DATA

Quantitative data has no value in its raw state. Once collected, it is important to organise and present data – and these issues are considered now. Although this chapter focuses on the organisation and display of data from structured questionnaires, it is important to note that some qualitative data will also be organised and managed in a 'quantitative' way whereby the number of times a theme, phrase or image is recorded forms the basis for some quantitative description and analysis. The collection of quantitative data is quite an uncertain process. As a researcher you can expend time and effort in devising the best survey instrument that you can and then send it to what you consider to be an appropriate sample of respondents. However, at that stage you lose control of the process, because you cannot fully predict how people will respond to the questions you have asked. It is only when you start to get back some data that you can start to make sense of it.

As with all stages of any investigative enquiry, a systematic approach is necessary, and there are a number of steps that you can take to underpin any subsequent analysis you wish to make. The first challenge you face is one of volume. A first-time practitioner-researcher, faced with 100 returned questionnaires and an impending deadline, can feel very daunted about the prospect of manipulating the data in order to answer his or her research questions. Use of a computer will enable you to tackle this process more effectively. If you intend to undertake a description of the frequencies of responses for different variables, a spreadsheet package such as Excel may be sufficient. Most students undertaking a CIPD management report (but not those working at master's level) will find that this will suffice. However, if you wish to analyse the data at a deeper level, the use of software such as SPSS (Statistical Package for Social Sciences) is preferable. Such statistical software is not difficult to master and should

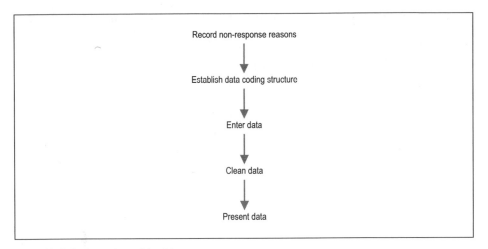

Figure 32 *Collecting and organising data*

be available for student access at your study centre. Your project tutor or supervisor will be able to clarify this for you.

A process to be followed with organising quantitative data is shown in Figure 32 and is explained more fully below.

Record-keeping

In order to evaluate the information provided from your survey it is important that you keep a record of non-responses – ie survey returns that do not find their way to you, and the reasons for this. This should include:

- the number of non-located responses – the number of respondents in the sampling frame who could not be found
- the number of non-contact responses – the number of respondents who were perpetually out (in a telephone survey) or were away during the time of the survey (postal, e-mail or interview)
- the number of ineligible responses – those respondents who, as a result of errors in your sampling frame, turn out not to fulfil the requirements of your sample (joined the organisation too recently, work in a non-sampled department, etc)
- the number of 'refusals' – those who were reached but would not participate in the survey
- the number of incomplete responses – those who got part way through your survey but did not complete it fully.

Such data does not really require a spreadsheet package, and a simple 'tally sheet' – which you can update as the questionnaires are returned – usually suffices.

Establishing a coding structure

This stage is where you work out how you will organise the software to record the different responses. Most software packages are organised in the same initial format as a simple spreadsheet, whereby the variables within your questionnaire are recorded in columns, and each respondent's responses are contained within one row. For each reply option on your survey instrument there must be a discrete code. This will take a numerical form. The first item to code is the identity of the questionnaire. This is your 'audit trail' and ensures that you can identify each questionnaire in the future and, if necessary, return to check the data it contains. To illustrate this process, the coding structure for the questions shown below (copied from the lengthy Activity questionnaire extracts) are illustrated in Table 26.

1 Which of the following best describes your organisation?   Please ✓ one
                                                               box only

    Sole proprietor .... ☐
    A partnership .... ☐
    An independent company .... ☐
    A subsidiary* .... ☐
    *Please state the nationality of the parent company _____

Note for Subsidiary companies ONLY.
Please make all responses in the questionnaire for the activities of the subsidiary, rather than the Group as a whole

2 In which sector does your business principally operate?   Please ✓ one
                                                               box only

    Industrial Manufactured Products .... ☐
    Consumer Manufactured Products .... ☐
    Mechanical Engineering .... ☐
    Transport (including Aerospace) .... ☐
    Services .... ☐
    Other (please specify)

_____

3 Where is the principal UK location of your organisation?

_____

4 How long has your organisation been established?   Please ✓ one
                                                               box only

    Under 1 year .... ☐
    1–5 years .... ☐
    6–10 years .... ☐
    Over 10 years .... ☐

Table 26 *Illustrative coding structure*

Column	Variable name	Description
1	Questionnaire ID	Questionnaire ID number (sequence begins 001)
2	Type of organisation (q1)	1 = sole proprietor 2 = partnership 3 = independent company 4 = subsidiary 9 = non-response
3	Nationality of parent company (q1)	1 = nationality of parent company is provided
4	Principal business sector (q2)	1 = industrial manufactured products 2 = consumer manufactured products 3 = mechanical engineering 4 = transport (including aerospace) 5 = services 6 = other 9 = non-response
5	Organisational age (q4)	1 = under 1 year 2 = 1–5 years 3 = 6–10 years 4 = over 10 years 9 = non-response

You will notice that question 3 has not been included in the coding structure. Such an open question does not allow for the responses to be coded in a simple way. To establish the frequencies of responses to this question would require the researcher to make a judgement about how to divide up the UK and allocate codes manually. If this were to be done, an additional column would be required within the coding structure. A similar system would be required for questionnaires with an entry in the 'other' category for question 2.

Entering the data

Although rather laborious, once the coding structure is established the process of data entry is relatively quick, if somewhat tedious. Indeed, it is a good idea to establish the coding structure for your questionnaire before you pilot it because the very act of coding can highlight potential problems (such as the difficulty with question 3 in this example) that you can tackle prior to survey distribution. You can also pilot the actual data entry with the responses from your pilot, to establish any potential problems.

There are a variety of methods of data entry. The most common for student projects is for a manual process, undertaken by the researcher, although there are software packages available that allow for structured interview data to be entered on a direct basis, and some organisations have facilities for optical mark reading of questionnaire responses.

Cleaning up the data set

When your data has been entered it is important to evaluate how accurately the process has been undertaken. It is extremely rare for no errors to have occurred, and it is important to identify them and correct them, prior to moving on to data presentation. There are two main stages to this process. First, a visual check of the data can be made to look for 'impossible' codes. A coding of '6' when there are only four attributes, for example, is an indicator that the responses for that questionnaire need to be checked again. Second, it is worthwhile choosing a random sample of questionnaires and checking the entries for them. If there are errors in your sample, then the whole data set should be checked again.

Presenting the data

Having entered and cleaned the data, the final stage in this part of the process is to describe and summarise the information using tables and/or charts. This process of descriptive analysis transforms raw data into a form that makes it possible to understand and interpret it. The first stage of this is to describe the frequency of all the different attributes within the survey. The most common approach to this presentation is indicated in the example below, generated from data entered onto SPSS, although it would be possible to present data derived from a standard spreadsheet package in a similar format.

		Frequency	Per cent	Valid per cent (excluding missing responses)	Cumulative per cent
Valid	Sole proprietor	8	3.2	3.2	3.2
	Partnership	8	3.2	3.2	6.4
	Independent company	171	67.9	68.4	74.8
	Subsidiary	63	25.0	25.2	100.0
	Total	250	99.2	100.0	
Missing	(coded as 9)	2	0.8		
Total		252	100.0		

A common mistake made by many students is to neglect to note down the patterns of non-response to a particular question, but this becomes important for subsequent analysis because it is necessary to indicate if the pool of respondents is of a different size for the answers to each of the questions that are being compared.

Having established the 'frequencies', it is also possible to present some of the data in the form of charts. The most common forms, which can be generated by spreadsheet software as well as the statistical packages are:

- pie charts, on which percentage data is represented as a series of categories which are compared within a circle, which represents 100 per cent of all cases (see Figure 33)

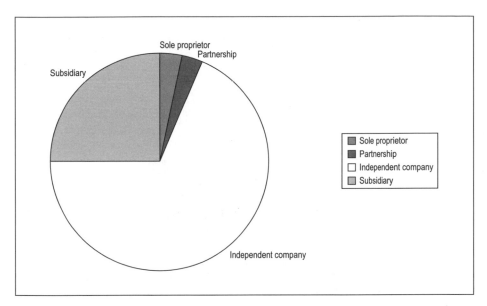

Figure 33 *Sample pie chart: types of organisation*

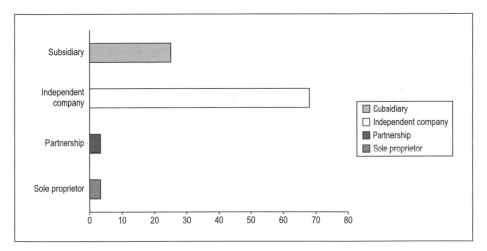

Figure 34 *Sample bar chart: types of organisation*

■ bar charts, on which the length or height of the bars (depending on whether they are presented on the horizontal or vertical axis) represents an appropriate number or percentage (see Figure 34).

These methods of presentation are particularly appropriate for presenting nominal scale (category) data. Other forms of graph can demonstrate the relationship between two variables. Thus a line graph can represent the relationship of one variable with time (the trend in pay rates for different types of staff is often represented in this way, for example). For interval scale data, a histogram is also an appropriate way of representing the data you have collected. Thus a frequency of employee age bands might be represented as in Figure 35.

Although a histogram looks similar to a bar chart, the regularity of the intervals means that the distribution of cases within the organisation can also be evaluated graphically and, where

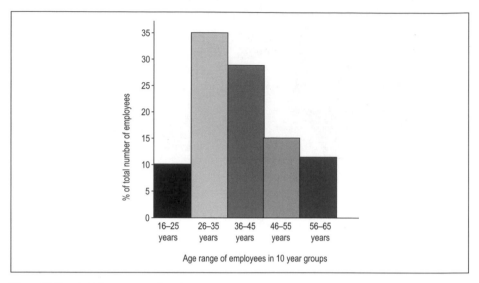

Figure 35 *Sample histogram: ages of employees*

the intervals are the same, can be compared with the distribution in another sample group. Where the intervals are not equal, however, such a representation might confuse rather than clarify understanding, unless the width of the categories on the *x* axis and the height of the columns on the *y* axis were adjusted to compensate. (See the *Further reading* section at the end of this chapter to identify more specialised texts for greater detail on the uses and abuses of histograms.)

For most HR student projects, the use of summary tables and charts, rather than histograms, is likely to form the main approach to presenting data. It is important not to get too carried away with the charting potential of software packages. There are occasions on which charts can promote understanding and comparison, but used too frequently, and with little more than a decorative purpose, they diminish rather than advance the persuasiveness of the research report.

There are, therefore, a range of ways in which data can be summarised and presented. In addition to these quantitative summaries, to assist with an evaluation of the findings that are being presented, your report should include information about the following (Neuman, 2003):

- the sampling frame
- the dates between which the survey was completed
- the research population
- the sample size/ratio
- the sampling method (simple random, systematic, etc)
- the exact wording of the questions asked (a copy of your questionnaire as an appendix)
- the survey method (telephone, postal, or whatever)

- information about any sponsoring organisation
- the response rate (the percentage of contacts who completed the questionnaire)
- for each question, the number of responses (this may vary question by question).

ANALYSING DATA TO ANSWER RESEARCH QUESTIONS

In addition to describing frequencies it is also possible to analyse data further as a means of answering research questions. Statistical techniques allow for a range of analytical processes. Analysis which forms a basis for comparison of single variables is referred to as *univariate* data analysis. That which assesses the relationship between two variables is *bivariate* data analysis, and *multivariate* analysis is carried out where more than two variables are included. These analytical processes enable data to be 'explored'. It is also possible to assess the extent to which your results are due to a real relationship – rather than the effect of random factors – through the operation of *inferential statistics*. This chapter covers univariate and bivariate analysis but not multivariate analysis processes or inferential statistics because these two latter applications are less commonly used in HR student projects. (See the *Further reading* section for texts that offer details of these statistical processes.)

Univariate data analysis

The univariate data analysis that you can legitimately undertake depends on the type of data you have gathered. As noted already, with nominal or ordinal data there is no defined 'distance' between the attributes of the variable. Mathematical operations are therefore not viable, although counting the frequencies and describing them as proportions, percentages or ratios is possible and provides a means of comparison.

For ratio and interval scale data it is possible to calculate 'measures of central tendency' (the mean, the mode and the median) to assist comparisons between different variables. The *mode* is the most frequently occurring value; the *median* is the middle point of the range; and the *mean* is the average value (calculated by adding all the values together and then dividing by the number of cases).

Another worthwhile characteristic to explore for single variables may be the 'spread' or *dispersion* of the variables. The calculation of an average length of service of 5.3 years for those who left an organisation during 2003 may mask the fact that one or two leavers had very long lengths of service and many others left with only a few months of employment with the organisation.

There are two main measures of dispersion. The *range* is the distance between the lowest value and the highest. This is the simplest measure of 'spread', but as noted above it can be misleading. A more informative way of assessing dispersion is to identify the point at which 25 per cent of the respondents (the distribution) have that 'score' or less and the point at which 75 per cent of the sample have that 'score' or less. These are referred to as the 25th and 75th percentiles. The 50th percentile is the median (the middle point of the range). It would also be possible to divide your sample up into ten percentile 'chunks'. A calculation of the 25th and 75th percentile, therefore, (or the 10th and 90th) may be more informative about the dispersion of the values than a simple calculation of the range.

The most popular measure of dispersion that is derived from a calculation of percentiles within any sample is *standard deviation*. This is a measure of the average distance between all the values and the mean. The smaller the standard deviation, the more similar are the values within the distribution. Standard deviation is complex to calculate manually (and not covered here) but is a common function of software and calculator programmes and so can be undertaken easily enough. It is, however, not an appropriate function when applied to nominal or ordinal scale data.

Assuming that you have some interval or ratio scale data, therefore, it is possible to calculate measures of central tendency and measures of dispersion as part of the analysis of your data. But it would also be interesting to assess the relationship between different variables, and this is where bivariate statistics are useful.

Bivariate data analysis

Bivariate data analysis involves considering two variables together in order to describe any (statistical) relationship between them. The term used when there is some degree of association between two variables is *co-variation*. Where there is no association or relationship between two variables, they are referred to as being *independent*.

Bivariate analysis is not difficult to undertake, although it takes patience when there are many variables to consider. There are three major options for bivariate analysis, two of which are described in full here (with examples) and are accessible to those without much understanding of mathematical operations. The third approach (the calculation of measures of association) is described briefly below too, but is otherwise beyond the scope of this chapter.

Scattergram

This approach is the most visually accessible form of analysis. It is appropriate for interval or ratio scale data, and never appropriate if either variable is nominal. It involves plotting a graph (using software, or manually) on which each axis represents the value of one of the variables. If the scatter pattern that emerges looks random, the relationship is one of independence. Where a tendency to a straight line is discernible, a linear relationship is suggested. A U-curve represents a relationship that is described as 'curvilinear' or non-linear.

ACTIVITY – PLOTTING A SCATTERGRAM

Utilise the data given below and plot a scattergram on the empty chart.
What does the scattergram suggest about the relationship between length of service and the number of days of sickness absence during 2003?

Employee ref. Number	Days sick during 2003	Length of service (years)
01	6	1
02	4	1
03	5	2
04	6	2.5
05	2	2.5
06	5	3
07	4	3
08	4	3
09	3	3
10	4	3.5
11	3	3.5
12	3	4
13	3	4
14	2	4
15	3	4.5
16	2	4.5
17	3	5
18	2	5
19	2	5
20	1	5
21	2	5.5
22	1	5.5
23	2	6
24	1	6
25	1	6
26	2	6.5
27	1	6.5
28	2	7
29	1	7
30	0	7
31	1	7.5
32	0	7.5
33	0	8
34	6	7
35	1	2

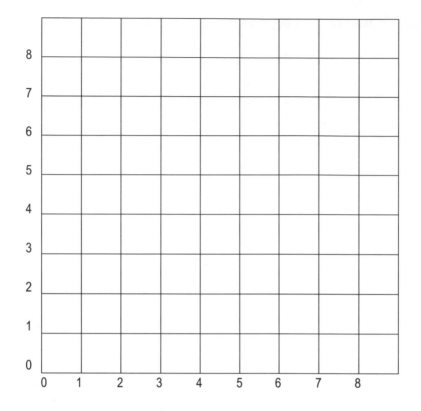

Feedback notes

Before plotting this fictional data you have to decide and clearly label which axis represents the days' sickness and which represents length of service. If you have plotted the co-ordinates effectively, you should be able to see an overall declining trend (you could almost draw a straightish line through the general direction of most of the points on the chart). This suggests a negative relationship between length of service and days of sickness absence during 2003.

However, the presence of data that does not conform with this general trend also indicates that this is not a precise relationship and that there are exceptions. A relationship with a high level of precision would therefore be characterised by points that 'hugged' the line.

Cross-tabulation

You can construct tables for any type of data, and they are particularly useful for analysing nominal (category) data. Their construction involves assessing how the cases in each category of one variable are distributed among the categories of a second variable. They require patience to construct manually but are easily produced using statistical packages. An example is shown as Table 27.

Table 27 *An example of cross-tabulation*

Industrial sector of respondent organisation : Quality of advice from the
Chamber of Commerce

Industry sector	Quality of advice from the Chamber of Commerce					
	Poor	Average	Good	Very good	Not used	Total
Industrial manufactured products	14	33	12	2	22	83
Consumer manufactured products	7	9	8	1	18	43
Mechanical engineering	2	3	6		4	15
Transport	1	3			2	6
Services	4	4	2		12	22
Other	31	61	30	3	68	193

Table 27 is an example of a cross-tabulation in which raw data has been used. To consider the relationships between the variables it is necessary to work out the percentages. In Table 27 percentages calculated by row indicate the proportion of each sector that considers the quality of advice to be 'poor', 'average', etc. Percentages calculated by column indicate the proportion of different organisations within a particular category (such as those that did not make use of advice from chambers of commerce) in terms of their industry sector. The calculation that you make will thus depend on the research questions you are seeking to answer. To 'read' a percentaged table you look for the direction (if there is one) that the percentages indicate. Where there is no relationship in a table, the percentages will look roughly equal. Although percentages provide a useful mechanism for comparison, remember that where the numbers in the overall group are small (less than 50) it is probably more realistic to represent the data in its raw state.

Measures of association
The use of scattergrams and cross-tabulations in bivariate analysis are visually accessible but do not give precise measures of the strength of any relationship that you may spot. Measures of association are statistical tools that enable you to measure both the strength and the direction of any association. There are many such measures, which are appropriate for different types of data. They are beyond the scope of this chapter but a useful summary of their main features can be found in Neuman (2003), Robson (2002) and Saunders *et al* (2003).

When undertaking bivariate analysis it is important to remember that association (co-variation) is not the same as *causation*. If you wish to assess whether one variable *causes* another, you must first eliminate alternative explanations by introducing a consideration of further variables. This is the purpose of multivariate analysis. If your research objectives involve assessing causation, you should consult more specialised texts (see *Further reading*). If you feel this is beyond you – revisit your research objectives!

SUMMARY

- Quantitative data involves the measurement of variables that can be counted, described and compared.

- Quantitative data can be used as part of an inductive or deductive approach to research.

- In addition to surveys undertaken for a particular research purpose, quantitative data can be obtained from secondary sources, such as published surveys, that may be undertaken on a regular or an ad hoc basis.

- Effective sampling techniques are important if the data that is obtained is to be representative of the population being studied.

- The planning process for any survey must take into account the purpose of the research, the research questions, the advantages and disadvantages of different types of questions, and the format in which responses are sought. Question format and structure will affect the forms of analysis that are possible.

- A range of issues are relevant to the questionnaire design process. They include: the initial contact/request/instructions to respondents, the layout of the survey, the language of the questions, and the arrangements for return.

- Piloting the survey and the process of recording and organising the data (data entry) will enhance the quality of the questionnaire and the usefulness of the data it generates.

- Surveys can be undertaken in a range of ways. The main options are: postal, self-administered, delivered and collected, structured telephone interviews, structured face-to-face interviews, e-mail questionnaires, and web-based surveys.

- A coding structure, established in advance, enables data to be electronically organised and summarised.

- Following the initial data entry process it is important to 'clean' the data of any inputting errors.

- Data can be presented in the form of summary tables and charts. These include pie-charts, bar charts, line graphs and histograms.

- Quantitative data can be analysed in a range of different ways. Univariate analysis is undertaken on single variables; bivariate analysis assesses the relationships between two variables; and multivariate analysis involves more than two variables.

- Analytical processes for single variables include the consideration of frequencies, proportions, percentages and ratios. For some types of data it is also possible to calculate measures of central tendency, such as the mean, the median and the mode, as well as the dispersion (range or standard deviation).

- Cross-tabulation allows for an assessment of the relationship between any two variables. For some types of data it is possible to consider such relationships by plotting a scattergram. Statistical measures of association may also be possible to offer a more precise measurement of the strength and direction of any association between two variables.

Questions for review/reflection

These questions are designed to enable you to identify key areas for development with your project that you should discuss with your project tutor, supervisor or adviser if possible. The responses to them can also form part of a Continuing Professional Development log or portfolio. This is required by CIPD for those who wish to upgrade their membership status.

Taking stock

1   How clear are you about your research questions? How significant a part is quantitative data likely to be in answering them? Will this involve describing frequencies or undertaking a deeper level of analysis?

2   What sources of quantitative data may already be available that might be relevant to your research questions? How can you go about accessing and evaluating them?

3   What depth of data analysis is required within the assessment criteria of your study centre for the qualification you are working towards? What are the implications of this for your personal development?

4   Who might you approach for help with the piloting of your questionnaire, and how might you make use of their feedback?

5   What software for data entry and analysis is available to you? What might you do to enhance your competence and confidence in using it?

Strengths and weaknesses

1   What experience do you have of survey design? What personal development areas are you aware of, and how might you meet them?

2   How well do you understand the advantages and limitations of different sampling techniques in relation to your project? What information or support might help you to develop your understanding and apply an appropriate sampling process for your enquiry?

3   How well do you understand the implications of different question structures for subsequent analysis of the data? Who can help you with this decision-making process?

4   How confident are you about the level of your numerical/statistical competence? What development activities would help enhance it?

Being a practitioner-researcher

1   Is there anyone in the organisation (often there is someone in the market research department) that would be able to offer advice and guidance on the survey design, administration and analysis processes? How might you find out about them?

2   How might you go about developing a sampling frame of good quality from which to select a sample? Who may be able to offer support with this process?

3   What organisational factors may influence decisions about sample size and selection? In what way might that affect the quality of the data that you obtain?

4   What permissions do you need to undertake a survey within the organisation? Who might be able to influence these decisions? What actions can you take to influence the response rate for your survey?

5   What level of feedback from the data is required by the organisation? How will this impact on the way you collect, organise and present the data?

FURTHER READING

The following books offer specialist advice on undertaking quantitative data-collection and analysis.

BRYMAN, A. and CRAMER, D. (1997) *Quantitative Data Analysis for Social Scientists*. London, Routledge.

DEVAUS, D. A. (2002) *Surveys in Social Research*. London, Routledge.

DILLMAN, D. A. (2000) *Mail and Internet Surveys: The tailored design method*. New York, Wiley.

OPPENHEIM, A. N. (2000) *Questionnaire Design, Interviewing and Attitude Measurement*. London, Continuum International.

Books that focus on data manipulation and analysis generally include:

CLARKE, G. M. and COOKE, D. (1992) *A Basic Course in Statistics*. London, Arnold.

CLEGG, F. G. (1992) *Simple Statistics*. Cambridge, Cambridge University Press.

COHEN, L. and HOLLIDAY, M. (1996) *Practical Statistics for Students*. London, Paul Chapman.

DIAMANTOPOULOS, A. and SCHLEGELMILCH, B. (1997) *Taking the Fear out of Data Analysis*. London, Dryden.

ERICKSON, B. H. and NOSANCHUK, T. A. (1992) *Understanding Data*. Buckingham, Open University Press.

ROSE, D. and SULLIVAN, O. (1996) *Introducing Data Analysis for Social Scientists*. Buckingham, Open University Press.

In addition, some general business research methods textbooks contain some good chapters on quantitative data-gathering and analysis. They include:

COLLIS, J. and HUSSEY, R. (2003) *Business Research: A practical guide for undergraduate and postgraduate students*. Basingstoke, Palgrave.

DENSCOMBE, M. (1998) *The Good Research Guide for Small-Scale Social Science Projects*. Buckingham, Open University Press.

DIXON, B. R., BOUMA, G. D. and ATKINSON, G. B. J. (1987) *A Handbook of Social Science Research: A comprehensive and practical guide for students*. Oxford, Oxford University Press.

NEUMAN, W. (2003) *Social Research Methods: Qualitative and quantitative methods*. Boston, Wiley.

ROBSON, C. (2002) *Real World Research: A resource for social scientists and practitioner-researchers*. Oxford, Blackwell.

SAUNDERS, M., LEWIS, P. and THORNHILL, A. (2003) *Research Methods for Business Students*. London, Prentice Hall.

You may also wish to consult books related to different software packages, such as:

FIELD, A. (2000) *Discovering Statistics Using SPSS for Windows*. London, Sage.

PALLANT, J. (2001) *SPSS Survival Manual*. Buckingham, Open University Press.

Useful websites from which published surveys can be obtained include:

www.statistics.co.uk – data sets and information on data sources from the Office of National Statistics

www.niesr.ac.uk/niesr/wers98 – data dissemination service for WERS98

www.cipd.co.uk/research – survey information sponsored by the CIPD

www2.warwick/sac/soc/ier/research/glmf – data from ESRC-funded research into the graduate labour market.

Reflection

Communicating your research

Chapter outline
How to use this chapter
Why, what, when and for whom to write.
Structuring and organising your writing
Approaching the submission date
Communicating what you have learned
Summary
Further reading

LEARNING OUTCOMES

This chapter should help you to:

- **clarify what is required by different readers of your research**

- **draft an initial research report**

- **enhance what you have written by revising and redrafting it**

- **reflect on opportunities to share what you have learned.**

HOW TO USE THIS CHAPTER

This chapter will help you to present, write and talk about your enquiry in an appropriate way. Although all of this chapter is relevant to anyone who has to communicate their project, if you are writing up your project for an academic reader you will find that the next three sections of the chapter are the most relevant. If you are thinking about sharing what you have learned in a non-academic environment, either in the form of a presentation or something in written form, then the section before the Summary (*Communicating what you have learned*) is a good place to start.

It would be nice to think that readers will complete this chapter well before they start writing – but it is likely that this chapter will be referred to mostly by people who are acutely aware of a rapidly approaching deadline and need to write fast. All the activities in this chapter are therefore focused on helping you to develop the skills you need to write effectively and submit on time.

Case illustration

Finding the right style

Ray was a Training and Development executive in a large retail organisation. He had developed a very successful career without having studied for any formal qualifications beyond his schooldays and now wished to achieve professional recognition as part of his continuing professional development. He decided to register with a CIPD Professional Assessment of Competence (PAC) Centre in order to upgrade his membership status.

Ray was able to contribute a depth of management and HR experience to his portfolio. He enjoyed the PAC process. Although there was a lot of work to do, his experience had enabled him to develop the skills of producing evidence and narratives for assessment purposes. He was also able to dictate written work to his secretary to be word-processed.

Ray was looking forward to undertaking a work-based investigation for his management report. He planned to investigate how management development in his organisation could benefit from the latest thinking in strategic HRD. He had secured the organisation's agreement to invest in a senior management development programme for the company's executives, and he planned to gather data from them for his management report at the various residential courses that they would be attending. He felt quietly confident that he should be able to achieve the required standard for his report.

The adviser had encouraged Ray to consider the subject for his management report and draft the proposal form. He was also offered the opportunity to attend a workshop where further guidance would be provided. However, Ray had many commitments and could not attend. His adviser sent him the handouts. Ray also deferred the next two scheduled meetings with his adviser, and consequently did not finally agree the subject matter at the proposal stage. He did assure his adviser that he would read the handouts and some books on strategic HR while he was attending the residential sessions that formed part of the senior management development programme he had organised for his organisation. He also felt confident about gathering primary data while he was away. His adviser indicated that he must clarify his project objectives at an early stage, but Ray felt that he was probably clearer than his supervisor realised. Ray suggested that by the time of the next scheduled meeting he could attend he would have written the introduction and the literature review and would have gathered his data.

The following three months were very busy for Ray. He was away from home a lot (attending all the courses) and found he was not able to read as much as he had hoped. Yet he had been able to undertake 15 semi-structured interviews with senior managers. He had recorded the interviews on tape and his secretary had transcribed them for him. Working with his secretary he also dictated some bullet points summarising the main points from the books he had read about strategic HR, as well as an introduction to the organisation and the expected benefits of the management development process being undertaken. In dictating these he was able to draw on the organisation's marketing literature and the proposal submitted by the consultancy he had hired to run the management development programme. His secretary worked hard on the document, making sure to present it attractively, and Ray then e-mailed it to his adviser.

Ray approached the meeting with his adviser in a confident mood. But the meeting was more difficult than Ray had anticipated. His adviser indicated that although it was clear that Ray had done a lot of work thus far, significant improvements would be required in writing up the project.

DISCUSSION QUESTION

What potential areas of improvement do you think Ray's adviser might have had in mind?

Feedback notes

Without having read what Ray wrote it is difficult to work out the observations of his adviser. However, in your discussions you may have picked out the possibility that although Ray had produced some writing that was appropriate for 'business readers' who prefer brief descriptions and lists of key points, this was less suitable for an 'academic reader'. Moreover, being able to use the services of a secretary when producing written work is also attractive to those without such a opportunity – but it can also be a disadvantage because the ability to think and reason things out is often enhanced through the very activity of writing and word-processing for yourself.

When writing for an academic reader Ray needed to be able to stand back from his position within the organisation and undertake a critical analysis of the organisation, rather than reproduce the promotional style of its marketing literature. He also needed to discuss the context of the management development programme from a range of perspectives and in the light of the organisational analysis, rather than repeat its intended benefits as articulated by its providers. Bullet lists summarising points made about strategic HR may be stylistically acceptable for an organisational briefing paper, but such a description is less helpful for a literature review in which academic readers would expect analysis, comparison and evaluation of the themes raised in the literature. It would also be important to understand how themes from the literature informed the questioning during the interviews and the way in which the literature review would also influence the analysis of the data that was gathered.

The above case illustration, although somewhat extreme, highlights a number of challenges that many students experience when faced with the requirement to write up their research or management report. This chapter explores ways in which the process can be managed effectively and, hopefully, can become a rewarding part of the overall research process.

WHY, WHAT, WHEN AND FOR WHOM TO WRITE

Why and when to write

HR practitioners sometimes regard academic writing as dry and uninteresting, lacking in practically-focused recommendations. The requirement to write a lengthy project report in an academic style can seem daunting and time-consuming. Some students find the writing process makes them feel clumsy and inarticulate. They find they have plenty of vague ideas in their head but that translating them into words on paper (or a screen) is nearly impossible. For other people, however, the opportunity to create a piece of writing can be a rewarding opportunity for reflection and 'sense-making' within the enquiry process.

Whether you hate or love writing, there are a number of reasons for doing it. First, by writing up your project you can finish it, submit it and reclaim a significant part of your life with which to engage in activities of your choice! Second, by writing your research report you are able to reflect on and communicate what you have found out. In the context of a qualification-related course of study, this enables your institution, study centre or professional body to award you credit for your achievement.

These are powerful motivators – but there are other, more profound reasons why the writing process is a beneficial one and why researchers engage in it, even without the incentive of a qualification. Saunders et al (2003) point out that by engaging in the writing process researchers are forced to clarify their thinking. Although it is difficult to commit vague ideas to paper, the more times you do it, the clearer your thinking becomes. Within this process some ideas will be discarded, others may be reformulated. In this way, on an incremental basis, what you are trying to explain becomes clearer to you and to those with whom you have to communicate.

Writing is therefore part of the 'reflective' stage of the learning process. Writing is also a learning process of itself – the way to learn to write is by writing (Neuman, 2003). And because that is so, writing is a useful activity to practise throughout the period in which you are undertaking your investigative enquiry. The more you write at all stages of the project, the more you will reflect on what you are doing, and the more guidance you will be able to receive from your tutor, supervisor or adviser. Through the practice of writing you will become better equipped to communicate your research when the time comes to submit the report.

Who are your readers, and what are they looking for?

There are many people who will be interested in the results of your investigative enquiry. As noted earlier, in Chapter 2, a range of different stakeholders may be interested in learning about and evaluating what you have found as a result of your project. These include your study centre or institution, the organisation(s) that have been involved in the research process, and in addition any professional institutes to which you may belong. Beyond this there may be others, such as other researchers or practitioners.

The most important and demanding of the various stakeholders are likely to be the tutors at the study centre who will assess your work, and any organisational sponsors or clients that have facilitated or authorised your enquiry. Although it is likely that you will have been communicating in a spoken form with them about the progress of your project, as it draws to a close they will also expect to receive a written project report from you.

ACTIVITY – KNOWING YOUR READERS

Draw up two short checklists. One list relates to your tutors at your study centre; the other relates to any organisation sponsor(s) or client(s) who will expect to read a report about your research. For each checklist identify:

- why those readers need to read your report
- their professional background and how this may influence what they expect to see in your report
- their attitude towards the research process
- what they really need to know about.

Feedback notes

The two lists that you have compiled may well have some similarities – but it is likely that there are also some differences. The tutor(s) at your study centre will be reading your report because they have to mark it and assess how well you have met the marking criteria. Their interest in the topic of your research is therefore a secondary reason for reading the report. Your sponsors or clients, on the other hand, will be reading it because they are interested in the topic of your research in the context of their organisation and its performance. It is likely that they will less interested in your knowledge of all the literature about your topic and possibly rather indifferent to the finer points of your methodological approach. They will, however, be very interested in knowing about your recommendations for action and the potential costs or other implications of any recommendations.

Assessors are interested in your level of knowledge and understanding, as well as your ability to apply a consistent and appropriate research methodology to investigate a defined HR issue, problem or opportunity. They are looking for analysis, critical evaluation different perspectives and synthesis of information from different sources. Your manager, client or sponsor, on the other hand, will look for a report that will communicate 'a clear way forward' that is affordable and implementable. Whereas your tutor will be looking for a report that is of significant length, your sponsors want something that is shorter and more action-oriented.

So different readers have very different sets of expectations. One report is therefore unlikely to satisfy the expectations of all those involved. You will probably produce one report for your tutors/assessors and another for the organisational stakeholders. Which report you tackle first depends on the different deadlines you have. Most people, however, prefer to tackle the longer report for the study centre first. The job of producing a punchier and shorter summary for the organisation is usually relatively straightforward once this has been achieved. (The shorter version might be a full executive summary, included as part of the management report submitted to the study centre, or it may be a stand-alone document.)

For these reasons the next sections in this chapter focus on meeting the requirements of academic tutors. Issues pertaining to the effective dissemination of your research, in organisations and more widely, are covered later in the chapter.

The academic report – clarifying institutional requirements

It is very important to remind yourself about the details of what your particular study centre is expecting. In particular, find out about:

Table 28 *A comparison of expectations for research reports at undergraduate and postgraduate levels*

	Undergraduate-level expectations	Postgraduate-level expectations
Knowledge and understanding	Comprehensive knowledge of topic area and an awareness of the provisional nature of that knowledge	Deep and systematic knowledge of topic area including theoretical and research-based knowledge at the forefront of HR practice
Ethical awareness	Awareness of personal responsibility and professional codes of conduct Can incorporate a critical ethical dimension into the project	Can recognise the implications of ethical dilemmas and work pro-actively with others involved in the project to formulate solutions
HR research methodologies	Can competently undertake reasonably straightforward research tasks with minimum guidance	Understanding of techniques and research methodologies in HR Can competently undertake research tasks with minimum guidance
Thinking skills	Can analyse data and situations without guidance, using appropriate HR techniques With minimum guidance can transform HR data and concepts towards a given purpose Can investigate contradictory information and critically evaluate evidence to support conclusions or recommendations	Can analyse complex, incomplete or contradictory areas of knowledge and communicate the outcomes effectively Can synthesise HR information utilising knowledge or processes from the forefront of HR practice Can critically evaluate HR research, advanced scholarship and methodologies and argue alternative approaches
Problem-solving	Can identify and define complex HR problems and apply appropriate knowledge, skills and methods to their solution	Can demonstrate initiative and originality in problem-solving Can make decisions in complex and unpredictable situations and can plan and implement tasks at a professional level

Source: adapted from SEEC (2002)

- length – What is the minimum and maximum wordcount?

- structure – What sections must be included?

- style – What conventions are expected with regard to, say, writing in the first or third person? What should be the standard tense (present or past)?

- format – Should it be presented in single-spaced, double-spaced, or some other format? What about the width of margins? How should the title page be laid out? What typeface and font size should be used?

- assessment criteria – All study centres will have an outline of the criteria by which they will be assessing the reports that are submitted. It is important to study these criteria at the beginning of the research process and then at regular intervals throughout it.

Management report or research report?

One cause of anxiety for some students when they approach the final stages of their research process are the extent of the differences between research reports associated with different levels of qualification. Some study centres, and qualifications, require the submission of a 'management report' (this is the general requirement for a CIPD postgraduate diploma-level qualification and for the Professional Assessment of Competence process). Other HR students undertaking research may, however, be submitting a dissertation as part of an undergraduate degree or for a taught master's-level qualification where the requirement may be for a 'research report'.

In making comparisons between the difference in expectations between undergraduate and postgraduate levels, the distinction – expressed in Table 28 – is essentially one of degree. Postgraduate-level researchers are expected to probe more deeply and work on a higher plane of uncertainty, achieving outcomes at a 'professional' grade, than are undergraduate students.

The difference in expectations between undergraduate- and postgraduate-level work is summarised in Table 28.

Exploring the difference between a management report and a research report/dissertation

The generic assessment criteria for CIPD management reports are shown below, followed by a statement of general marking criteria for a research report at Masters level.

GENERIC ASSESSMENT CRITERIA FOR CIPD PROFESSIONAL DEVELOPMENT SCHEME MANAGEMENT REPORTS

- clarity and relevance of proposal/terms of reference/aims and objectives
- demonstration of knowledge and understanding of literature at an appropriate level and of extent to which applicable
- justification and use of appropriate methods of data-collection
- focused and relevant discussion of organisational context, evidence of systematic data-collection, and clear presentation of findings
- comprehensive analysis and interpretation of findings in a holistic/integrated manner
- appropriateness of conclusions
- realistic, timely, cost-effective recommendations and action plan
- evidence that personal learning has been reviewed
- satisfactory presentation of material and argument, and clear and accurate referencing.

GENERAL MARKING CRITERIA OF A RESEARCH REPORT

- research objectives – Clear and relevant objectives, derived from an identification and definition of the area of investigation.
- research design – The research design and methodological approach and issues of access and co-operation are appropriate and justified to generate sufficient quality and quantity of data. An evaluation of issues of the reliability and validity of the data, taking the methodological approach into account.
- literature review – Relevant literature drawn from a range of appropriate sources is analysed and critically reviewed. Where appropriate, a clear and appropriate analytical framework is developed as a result of this evaluation.
- data-collection and analysis – Primary and/or secondary data that are relevant to the research objectives are gathered and presented. Data are analysed in a thorough and critical way, using (where appropriate) the analytical framework derived from the literature review.
- conclusions and recommendations – These are clearly expressed, supported by the evidence and derived logically from the analysis. They are practical, imaginative and relevant.
- presentation – Clear expression utilising a style, language and referencing that is appropriate to academic purposes.
- integration of academic knowledge – The research process demonstrates originality or use of initiative, and there is evidence of a learning process for the researcher.

Sources: adapted from Howard and Sharp (1994), Bowden (2002), CIPD (2002)

A comparison between these two sets of assessment criteria shows that there are more similarities than differences between the expectations of a CIPD management report at postgraduate diploma level, and those of a research report or dissertation that forms part of a taught master's-level qualification. Both sets of criteria emphasise the importance of clearly expressed and relevant research aims and objectives, a review of relevant literature, the use of appropriate methods to collect data, and the analysis of that data in an integrated and appropriate way. Although individual study centres operate slightly different assessment criteria, these components would be expected in any postgraduate-level project report. A diploma-level management report tends to be somewhat shorter (approx. 7,000 words) and there is greater emphasis on the use of the research to generate practical, costed, timely and realistic recommendations.

Bowden (2002) suggests that the assessment of a master's-level research report (or dissertation) would have more emphasis on:

- the analytical focus, scope and contribution of the literature review
- the evaluation of different research design and methodological issues and the skill with which methods of data-collection are undertaken
- the analysis of the data – particularly its thoroughness, the questioning nature of the approach used and the analytical links with the literature review
- the reasoning process behind the formulation of conclusions, and the links between the conclusions and the analysis of the literature and the primary data.

STRUCTURING AND ORGANISING YOUR WRITING
Getting started

ACTIVITY – BARRIERS TO WRITING

Think back to other pieces of writing you have undertaken as part or your studies.
Identify what hindered, inhibited, or made the writing process difficult.
What factors were important to you for getting the writing done?

Feedback notes
Most practitioners and academics feel somewhat daunted when faced with a 'writing job'. Common anxieties, which can result in delays in actually getting started, include reservations about not having enough information, or that the quoted optimum wordcount is too long (or too short). Levels of interruption and an inability to concentrate are common concerns – there are always other things that need to be done. Anxieties about the difficulty of meeting the deadline can add to a sense of delay, and often people complain that they suffer from writer's block.

Other delaying factors that may well affect you at some stage in your studies include those illustrated in Figure 36.

The factors illustrated in Figure 36 as well as the concerns you may have listed in response to the *Barriers to writing* Activity above are all valid and can be difficult to cope with or overcome. When considering the writing process it is important to try to deal with the things that are partly within your control so that you are better able to cope with those that are outside your control.

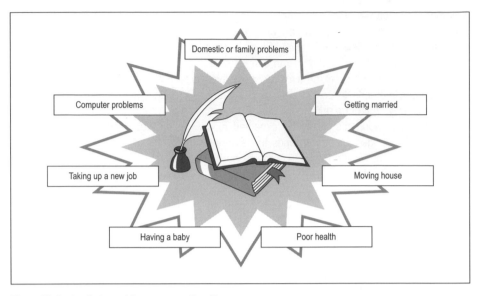

Figure 36 *Factors that can delay progress with writing*

In order to achieve the objective of completing the project, it is therefore important to overcome any tendency towards procrastination and to work through any feelings of writer's block. Common ways in which this can be achieved are shown in Table 29. No one will find all of these tips appropriate, so it is important to take what works for you and use it in your own way.

Safety first

If you can develop an approach that enables you to plan each section within the overall report and utilise personal strategies such that you maintain a habit of writing, then you should be able to achieve your objective of finishing and submitting your report in time for the submission date. However, there are other technical obstacles to be taken into account. These can seem trivial but can afflict anyone at any time and cause misery and devastation. Most tutors have had occasion to commiserate with a student whose computer has crashed less than a week before the submission date and who has no back-up copy of his or her work, or whose printer has failed for no apparent reason. *Writing is hard work*, and these technical problems are dispiriting at best, and can cause total despair – and failure to submit on time. The following suggestions (written from the heart) are therefore offered:

- Save your work every 1,000 words or every hour, whichever is the sooner.
- At the end of each session (or more frequently), back up your work to at least one other computer drive.
- If you are working at home, think about saving your work to your PC – but also e-mail it to yourself at work and then save it again there.
- Never trust your writing to a networked system – always back it up so you can continue outside of the network.
- Once each section is drafted, print off a hard copy as your ultimate back-up. This may be expensive but it is an insurance policy against more than one crisis occurring at any one time.
- Have in mind two alternative printers you can use when the time comes to print the final version. Ensure that you have a back-up copy of your work in a format that both printers can work from.

Table 29 *Making yourself write*

Planning to write	Divide up the wordcount and set limits for each of the chapters or sections. Set yourself a writing timetable and deadlines. Draft out the structure for the section of chapter you are about to write. Break down the main parts of the section or chapter into smaller parts – it is much less daunting to produce 200 words than 2,000. Use outlines, structures and plans to keep you focused.
When to write	Begin early – the closer you get to the deadline, the more the pressure mounts up. If you write something *now*, there will be time to improve on it. Create time ('prime time') for writing – put off other jobs so that you are not exhausted when you begin writing. Write regularly and develop a pattern or rhythm of work on the report. Try never to miss a writing session. If the going is getting tough, try writing at a different time of the day or time of the week. Write up a section as soon as possible.
Develop your own individual writing habits	Engage in your own personal writing rituals that might help you to get going (music in the background, sharpen your pencils, etc). Begin wherever it is easiest – start in the middle, if that is what it takes! Don't expect perfection – you are *drafting* something – you can improve on it later. Reduce interruptions – do what it takes to work for a defined period without distractions. Find a regular place for your writing (particularly if you are using a laptop). Familiarity with the surroundings means they won't distract you. Don't waste time getting everything out and putting it away again if you can avoid it. If you need to, start by speaking your ideas aloud, tape-recording them and then transcribing them. If you get stuck, take a short break and then come back to it after a walk/cup of tea, etc. Don't leave it for too long, however. Try not to stop mid-way if you can. If you can struggle through to the end of the troublesome section, you can revisit it another day, when you are fresh, and you will find that you can improve it then. Where possible, stop writing at a point from which it is easy to resume work again the next time.
Monitoring your progress	Set yourself a target for writing a given number of words each week or month. Reward yourself when you achieve significant wordcount targets. Allow someone else to oversee your writing progress (partner, child, colleague?). Get someone else to read what you have written. This is hard but well worth it because he/she can comment on how understandable your material is and can point out some easy ways of making your work much better. Ask you supervisor/tutor to read your drafts so that you can identify any writing problems early on and deal with them. Plan to finish – look forward to the day when you submit the project report and can then forget about it if you want to.

Sources: Blaxter *et al* (2001), Robson (2002), Neuman (2003), Jankowicz (2000)

Planning your writing

Students tend to adopt one of two approaches for their writing. Some plan the contents of each section to a greater or lesser extent and then work through their plan, amending it as necessary as they proceed. Although this is the approach recommended by almost every HR tutor and adviser in the UK, anecdotal evidence suggests that only a minority of students follow this advice. Many students, it appears, have a rough (often implicit) idea of where they mean to go in their writing and adopt the 'plunge in at the deep end' approach.

This 'deep end' approach is not for the faint-hearted. As noted in Table 29, the planning process enables you to break down what must be written into smaller parts which are less daunting to write. In addition, writing that is undertaken in a 'plunge in' way usually has to be significantly revised and restructured two or three times until it starts to take shape. Work that has been planned is still likely to need revision, but the process is less extreme and quicker to achieve.

There are a number of ways in which the planning process can be undertaken. All of them are techniques that many HR practitioners use in the course of their work. Each of them can be used in isolation, or they can be used in different combinations to facilitate the planning process.

- brainstorming – Use this technique (you could work with a colleague to do it) to generate a list of all the possible ideas or items you could include in the section you are concerned with. Then set about taking out the ideas that are not relevant, editing out repetitions and putting the remaining ideas into a logical order.
- mind mapping – Construct a mind map that represents the way in which different ideas or themes are linked together and branch out from one another. Use the 'shape' of the map to identify the main sections and the more detailed points to include within them.
- linear planning – Jot down the main themes you feel are relevant for the section you are planning. Under each one write down points that 'drop out' from it. Put the main themes into some kind of order (it might be chronological, by category, or by significance to the issue being researched).
- Post-Its – Write headings for all the different points you need to make onto different Post-It notes. Then under each heading list sub-points (rather like task analysis, if you are engaged in project planning). The sub-points also go onto Post-It notes, and you can organise and display your notes on the wall in front of your computer. This means that you can visually check your progress by removing Post-Its from the wall or flipchart when you have covered them in your writing.

Structuring your report

The process of structuring the report is closely linked with the planning of what you are writing. Your study centre may have particular requirements for the structure of the report, although most allow for some variation where it is appropriate to the nature of the topic and the research approach that has been utilised. The main areas to be incorporated within most project reports are:

- *title page* – title of the report; your name; date of submission; any other information required by the study centre

- *contents page*

- *summary or abstract* – a very short overview that indicates the issue being researched, the research questions, the approach taken to the investigation, the main findings and the conclusions

- *introduction* – an introduction to the topic and its significance for the organisation and/or HR practice more widely, as well as an explanation of the research objectives, aims, terms of reference, or the hypotheses to be examined. If you are required to make organisational recommendations, ensure that you include the making of recommendations as one of your objectives. There should also be a brief overview of the logic of the forthcoming sections or chapters

- *literature review* – This is where you set your enquiry in its wider context and indicate how your research builds on what is already known about the topic. Make sure you show how the review of the literature has informed your research questions as well as the research approach you have adopted. See Chapter 3 for an overview of what to include here

- *methodology* – an explanation of how the issue was investigated as well as a description of procedures undertaken in order to gather, record and analyse data. This section might also include a consideration of ethical issues you took into account as well as an evaluation of the strengths and weaknesses of your approach and the implications for the reliability and validity of the data you have collected. See Chapter 4 for more details about what to include here

- *data presentation/results* – the results of your data-gathering activities. The way this is presented will depend on the research approach you have adopted. This section is where you describe what you found (the facts) rather than your interpretation of it. Chapters 6 and 8 indicate different ways of presenting qualitative and quantitative data

- *analysis* – For some research approaches the analysis of the data may be integrated with its presentation, for others it is possible (and preferable) to differentiate between the presentation of data and its analysis. This section is where you answer the 'so what?' questions by interpreting your data in the light of the research objectives and questions. See Chapters 7 and 8 for what might be included in this section

- *conclusions* – a summary of the main features of the analysis and the implications of it for both theory and practice. Make sure your conclusions are clearly drawn from the evidence rather than from your opinions. Highlight any areas in which further research would be beneficial

- *recommendations (where appropriate)* – Where these are required (for example, for management reports), they should be action-oriented, indicating costs, timescales, accountabilities and contingencies. Whereas your conclusions are oriented to the past (they relate to what you have found out), the recommendations are future-oriented and are your views about what should happen now. It is important to show how the recommendations are based on the data and the analysis. The value of the report will be extremely limited if the reader feels that you could have made your recommendations without undertaking the enquiry in the first place

- *references* – See Chapter 3 for guidance on referencing using the Harvard approach. If you do not reference your work appropriately, you may be penalised for plagiarism, which is a serious form of cheating. It is wise to ask your supervisor for feedback about your referencing technique and obtain any necessary guidance in order to ensure that you are working within the conventions of your study centre

- *appendices* – These will include copies of your research instruments (questionnaires, interview schedules, etc) and other material that is relevant to an understanding of the main report. Research reports should make sense without having to refer to the appendices. Avoid using the appendices as a way around the wordcount.

Style and expression

Working out a structure for your report will help you clarify *what* to write. It is also important to develop an appropriate style to enable successful communication with your academic readers.

ACTIVITY – WRITING FOR DIFFERENT PURPOSES

Think back to all the letters and e-mails that you have received during the last week, at home and (if appropriate) at work. Try to classify them by:

- their purpose (why they were sent to you)
- the different styles used by the authors to communicate with you and achieve their purpose.

Feedback notes

Predicting the contents of someone's post and e-mail box is difficult, but it is likely that your mail has included:

- Junk mail – These communications (paper-based, texts, and electronic mail) encourage you to buy or pay for something (home-delivered pizza, credit-card facility, donation to a charitable cause, etc). They use a style that suggests you 'must' or 'should' respond in some way, or that you would be foolish (or churlish) not to respond. Although expressed in quite emotive terms, and often printed in full colour, these are not memorable and you may have forgotten about them already.

- Letters/cards/e-mails from family and friends – These may be to thank you for something, to wish you luck, to send birthday greetings, to send you news/gossip, to suggest a social gathering, etc. As well as giving some information they usually express feelings and are often written in a semi-humorous or 'flowery style'.

- Bank statements, insurance documents, payment reminders, pay-slips, etc – These are not at all flowery, and their purpose is to provide you with information on which you may want or need to take action. Their style is impersonal and official, and people rarely read all the information (the small print) that they provide.

- Everyday communications – These are often e-mails, notes on Post-Its or text messages. They provide snippets of information or suggestions and questions. They are partial and often only understandable by the people involved in the communication. They rely on participants' being able to 'read between the lines'.

The above Activity indicates in a very simplistic way how the purpose of different forms of writing influence the style that is appropriate for it. For your investigative enquiry, the purpose of producing a report is to provide a formal record of the research process as well as your findings. This enables others to evaluate what you have done and to learn from your enquiry. The appropriate style to achieve this purpose will be succinct and will imply some 'distance' from the subject matter. Research reports are not the place for language that moralises, is humorous or is 'flowery'. The purpose of the report is to inform rather than to entertain or to advocate a position. However, it is also important to produce a report that is more interesting that the small print on a gas bill. While adopting a formal style, therefore, it is also important to maintain the interest of the reader and to organise what you write in order to help the reader follow the logic of what you are communicating.

The report as a whole will have a 'storyline' something like the one illustrated in Figure 37. Each of the main sections of the report will also require a framework through which the purpose of the section can be explained and fulfilled, and the progression to the next section is indicated. A framework through which this might be achieved is shown as Figure 38.

The framework indicated in Figure 38 shows that it is likely to be necessary to subdivide each of the main chapters or sections, using subheadings, and to have an introduction and a conclusion to each of the sections, thus providing some form of 'signposting' to enable your reader to follow the logic of your report. Other stylistic hints and tips are included below (Robson, 2002; Saunders *et al*, 2003; Blaxter *et al*, 2001, Collis and Hussey, 2003).

- Write clearly and simply. Many students assume that academic language should be more complex and sophisticated than 'normal' writing. In fact, clear communication within the academic community is enhanced by the use of simple sentences. Where you have drafted a long sentence, check and see if you could rewrite it as two shorter ones.

- Avoid using too many direct quotations. You will get credit for your own thinking and your ability to express what is already known in your own words. Using other people's expressions too often makes the report look second-hand.

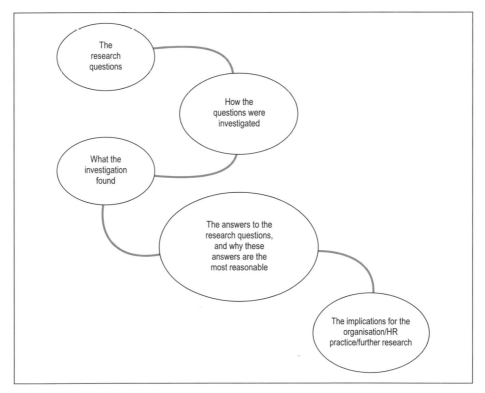

Figure 37 *Developing a project report storyline*

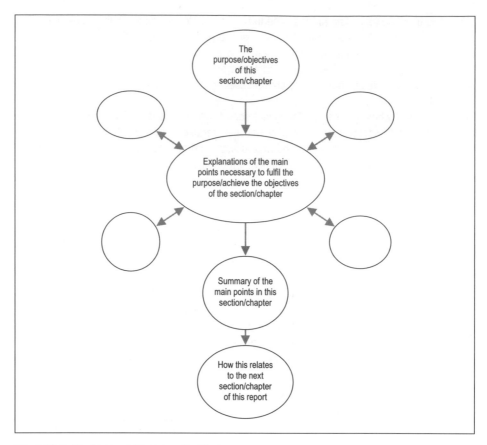

Figure 38 *Outline framework for each section/chapter*

■ Avoid using jargon, slang and abbreviations. Written communication is different from the spoken form. Abbreviations such as 'don't' should be written as 'do not', and avoid informal language such as 'the flip side of this is ...'. Use words that are precise rather than over-generalised. Where you have to use technical terms, include a glossary within the report.

■ Use a new paragraph for each new idea. Ideas cannot normally be expressed in one sentence. If you find you are using a new paragraph every one or two sentences, check that you are explaining your ideas fully or see whether two paragraphs really relate to the same idea and could be combined.

■ Avoid repetition. Make sure that you have not repeated yourself in two different sections. Look particularly carefully at the introduction to see if some expressions occur again in the same form in the literature review or in the conclusions. Where this is the case, redraft one of the passages in a different form.

■ Be consistent (and appropriate) with the grammatical 'voice', 'person' and tense. Different study centres have different protocols in respect of the 'person' in which you write. Most formal academic communication is written in the third person ('he', 'she', 'it' and 'they', as opposed to 'I' or 'you' or 'we') and may utilise the passive voice (at least as often as the active voice) as in the example below:

'The process undertaken for the research was as follows. First, a literature review was undertaken and key themes were identified. A questionnaire was then devised to ...'

Some research enquiries, particularly those adopting a more action-oriented and qualitative approach, can be appropriately written in the first person, provided that this is permitted within the regulations and preferences of your study centre. An example is shown below:

'At the beginning of the research process I reviewed the literature about ... In order to explore the key issues about ... I then organised a focus group consisting of ...'

Some study centres permit the use of the third person in some sections or chapters of the report, and the first person in others. Having decided what person to write in, however, it is important to maintain a consistent approach to it within each section or chapter. The same consistency is required with regard to the tense in which you write. The normal convention is to use the present tense when you are referring to work that has been previously published, as in the examples below:

'Jones (1993) highlights four key aspects of ... and these are briefly described now.

XYZ Ltd is a large employer situated in the north of England. The firm produces ... for high-street retail outlets.'

Where you are referring to primary data that you have gathered for your study, and the process by which you gathered it, however, the past tense may be more appropriate. (in active or – especially – passive voice):

'Questionnaires were issued to 78 people, and 62 completed returns were received.'

- Avoid discriminatory language. In order to maintain an objective stance within your writing it is necessary to avoid using language that can be interpreted as offensive or discriminatory. Such expressions are often unconsciously used by writers, so it is necessary to check your writing to eliminate them. Writing should be as 'gender-neutral' as possible. Some expressions that can occur within writing about HR, and that would always be better rephrased, are listed in Table 30.

Table 30 *HR language – remaining gender-neutral*

Try to avoid	Alternative expressions
businessman	businessperson, executive, business manager
committee chairman	chair, chairperson, the person who chairs/chaired the committee
manpower	staff, staffing, workforce, personnel
manpower planning	HR planning, personnel planning
manning levels	staff levels, staffing levels, workforce levels
spokesman	spokesperson, representative

Evaluating what you have written

Achieving perfection in one draft is not likely to occur. Once you have a draft report, it will be necessary to undertake a series of revision and editing processes. This will help you to clarify your thinking and communicate more effectively. You will need to 'clean up' or 'tighten up' your writing and undertake more significant revisions, such as inserting some new sections, deleting some material, and moving some material around within the structure. Key questions to be addressed, when evaluating your early drafts, therefore, are (Saunders, 2003; Bell, 2001):

- How clear and appropriate is the structure of the report and of each section?
- Are the research objectives or questions expressed clearly and consistently throughout the report? Have you achieved them?
- Is the meaning clear? What passages seem obscure or clumsy? Are all your terms clearly defined?
- Is there any evidence of biased, emotional or imprecise language?
- To what extent does the literature review inform the methodology and the data analysis?
- To what extent does your literature review describe what others have written, analyse the issues, and advance a line of argument?
- Where are the missing references?
- Have your presented and analysed your data in a way that the reader can follow?
- How close to the wordcount limit are you?

Honest answers to these questions should help you to prioritise your work as you set about revising what you have written. Your supervisor, tutor or adviser will also be able to provide a useful evaluation (but not at the last minute, however). Family and friends, although not technically knowledgeable, may also be able to spot the areas that need more careful explanation.

APPROACHING THE SUBMISSION DATE

Losing or finding more words

At the beginning of the project, most students think they will never find enough words to meet the required wordcount of their report. Once they begin drafting, however, they discover how difficult it is to stay within the wordcount limit. For most people, therefore, the process of revision involves losing words – which can be very painful, especially if it has been difficult to write some of them in the first place. For a minority of students, the problem is the reverse. They find that their report is too 'thin', or that some sections of it are not as long as they (and their supervisor) had been expecting. Some ideas about how to tackle these opposite areas of difficulty are provided in Table 31.

Describing and analysing

In writing your report it is important to minimise any simple description of the work of others and undertake more analysis of it. Description involves summarising what another person has written, more or less in the terms of the original author. Analysis, however, is a search for explanation and understanding.

Table 31 *Losing or adding words*

Making more into less	Making less into more
Check each sub-section in each section. Which ones are not central to your argument and analysis? Lose the 'nice to have' but make sure you retain the 'need to have' sub-sections.	Add new sections. Identify which section(s) might benefit from a fuller explanation or discussion.
Shorten lengthy descriptive passages by using tables, charts or diagrams.	Do you have a lot of appendices and not enough text? Consider working material from one or two of the appendices into the text (but don't engage in 'padding').
Take a good look at the quotations you have used. Do they repeat ideas you have already explained? Do you really need them? Could you express the ideas they articulate in a more concise way?	Look for more references or quotations on the subjects or issues you are writing about.
See if you can summarise the ideas in two or more sentences, or even turn a whole paragraph into one (shortish) sentence.	Are you making too many assumptions? Build up sentences into paragraphs by developing your argument or making your line of thinking more explicit.
Engage in 'word-weeding' (a form of literary gardening). Remove unnecessary qualifying or repetitive words from sentences.	Go further in your evaluation of different aspects of your methodology and how appropriate it was. (This section is often not discussed in enough length – particularly in management reports).

Source: Blaxter *et al* (2001)

If you are concerned that parts of your work are too descriptive (or your supervisor has indicated this to you), try the following steps.

1 For each theory, framework, concept or research procedure or method that you describe, write beside it the words 'Prove it'.

2 On a Post-It note try to note down possible objections to each 'Prove it' point where the opposite or a different situation might apply.

3 Redraft your work into a more critical and evaluative style by using this thinking process to highlight the limitations as well as the strengths of the ideas you are describing.

4 Read through your work again, and after each idea that you have evaluated write the words 'So what?'

5 Redraft your work again, attempting to answer the 'So what?' questions in the light of your research objectives or questions.

6 Read your work again. You may find that some of the answers to some of the 'So what?' questions are the same. If so, this means you are starting to identify some analytical themes.

7 Have a go at reorganising your work so that you tackle one theme at a time. This may mean considering more than one author's work at a time. There may also be implications here for the order in which you consider the data in your findings section. If this is the case, give yourself a reward, because it means you have probably started to think and write in a more analytical way.

Final checks

The process of drafting and revising your report can be both frustrating and rewarding. As the submission date approaches, however, there are some important final checks to make prior to printing the final draft. The aim at this stage is to arrive at a form of presentation that is as near to perfection as can be achieved. Close scrutiny of the text to ensure that spelling errors have been eradicated and that the punctuation is correct is vital. This is something that cannot be hurried. It is also necessary to check the formatting. Have all the section numbers, table numbers and labels for the appendices been consistently applied? Are all the font sizes consistent? Are there any glitches in the page layout? Are there still any missing references? Is the list of references at the back in the right order and listed in a consistent manner?

The first few pages of the report are crucial. Check the title page – does it have all the necessary information? Are all the pages numbered, and are the page numbers on the contents page still accurate? Have you listed the appendices on the contents page? Is the abstract or summary still appropriate, or does it require revision in the light of redrafting you have recently undertaken? Are the research objectives and questions explained clearly in the introduction?

Once you are satisfied, you can print your work. Before making any subsequent copies, make a final visual check to ensure that the printer has not inserted the odd blank page or the numbering system has not been disrupted by a section break. Then make sufficient copies and securely bind them ready for their journey to your study centre.

Once it has been submitted, you may feel as though you never want to hear another word or write another word about your topic. Yet it is likely that you will have to, or after a suitable break, may even want to disseminate what you have learned beyond your tutors. This is considered in the next section.

COMMUNICATING WHAT YOU HAVE LEARNED

The process of writing your research report provides a useful opportunity to reflect on what you have learned. Indeed, the assessment criteria for many study centres (and the CIPD) includes a requirement for a section dealing with 'Reflection on learning'. Additionally, if your HR project has been organisationally-based, it is likely that you will have to submit some form of report to the manager who has sponsored your project. This may take the form of an executive summary of what you have prepared for your study centre.

Before you begin writing your organisational report it is worth finding out from your sponsor-manager what is expected from you in terms of its format and length. Although you will be able to draw extensively on the material you are preparing, or have prepared, for your study centre, there are likely to be a number of differences in what you produce. These are indicated below:

- less detail in the content, suitable for a 'manager in a hurry' – You will need to write in a more accessible style, with less use of technical language. You may need to move some material from the main body to the appendices.

- well-thought-through recommendations – This is likely to be a key issue for the organisational sponsors of your research. Make sure that your recommendations are clearly derived from the data and expressed in direct and practical terms. Consider presenting recommendations as a set of options. Be clear about accountabilities, costs, timescales, priorities and contingencies.

Write persuasively. Indicate the benefits of implementing your recommendations.

Disseminating your research

Apart from the production of an organisational report (if one is required), most research undertaken by practitioner-researchers remains a well-kept secret, known only to them and a few other close friends. In spite of current interest in knowledge management, many HR professionals are strangely modest when it comes to sharing what they have learned from their investigative enquiries. This is regrettable for a number of reasons. Firstly, a lot of work will have gone into your project and it is a shame not to share what you have found out. Secondly, what you have investigated is likely to be valuable to others, to inform their thinking and their decision-making processes.

A variety of reasons may underpin this reticence. Fear that people will simply dismiss your work may be an inhibitor. Existing work commitments (there are never enough hours in the day) are another problem. However, there are a number of benefits from engaging in some form of 'knowledge transfer'. These include:

- personal recognition, both professionally and within your work organisation
- recognition for your organisation, if you disseminate your research externally
- an opportunity for the further clarification of your thinking by revisiting ideas and reflecting on them
- increasing your profile and (possibly) your promotion prospects.

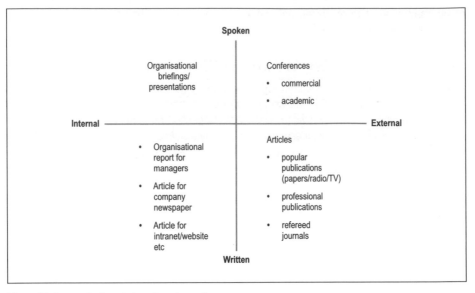

Figure 39 *Communicating what you have learned*

Dissemination practices can be as local as offering to make short departmental briefings about what you found out, or they may involve making a contribution to a conference or to some form of written publication (paper-based or electronic). Some of the options are illustrated in Figure 39, and some issues to bear in mind when preparing to disseminate are given below.

The main problem with disseminating what you have learned from your research is the need to write (and speak) more succinctly. Having spent a number of months learning to write in a relatively full way, you now have to reverse the process. The following steps can help you with this (Day, 1996).

1 Clarify the purpose, scope and value of what you did

It is important to be clear about your research problem and its context so that you can articulate it to those who will read your work or hear what you have to say. Useful questions to ask yourself include:

- What did I investigate, and why?
- How far did I decide to look, and why?
- What related issues did I *not* examine, and why?
- What constraints impacted on my work, and why?

In any dissemination that you undertake, you should communicate what you have found out and what this means for your readers/audience. Day (1996) suggests that a good way of preparing to communicate about your research is to write down an answer for yourself, in no more than 20 words, to the questions: 'What do I want to say, and why should anyone care?' This is a challenging thing to do, and will probably take at least five attempts. Having done it, however, you will find you have a useful focus to the preparation process of any dissemination about your research.

2 Summarise your work

Once you have clarified the purpose, scope and value of your research, you can go on to express the following aspects of your work, in no more than one paragraph each:

- findings – What did you find out? In what ways do your findings matter?
- literature – What did it say, and how did it affect your research?
- methodology – What did you do, and how did it affect the findings?
- analysis – How did the techniques you used to analyse the data affect your findings?
- implications – What are the implications of what you found for potential answers to your research problem? How far are you prepared to go, and why?

Writing these paragraphs enables you to establish what you have to communicate, and from this point you can develop presentations or write papers or articles to meet the expectations of the audience/readership. Some will be longer and fuller than others, but you have a basis on which to build.

Making presentations

You will find many opportunities to talk about your research on an informal basis, but the occasions on which you present your research more formally are likely to be talks to different groups of staff within the organisation, or a presentation made to a conference.

Conferences

Commercial conferences are advertised quite widely and take place in comfortable venues; delegates pay to hear from experts about good practice and research relating to particular topics, such as 'Flexible working', 'HR benchmarking', and so on. The format tends to involve a range of expert speakers making a 40–50-minute presentation, with short question-and-answer sessions following each of them. The emphasis is on the practical implications of the topic being presented, and delegates are interested in what it means for them and their organisations. Conference organisers usually source their speakers through a fairly extensive system of networking and 'colleague referral'. If they approach you, they will be fairly explicit about what is expected in terms of the length of the presentation and any supporting material they require . . . as well as any fee they may be prepared to pay.

It is likely that your presentation will be supplemented with some additional information. Copies of the OHPs or PowerPoint slides you have prepared will be expected. Whereas restricting your supplementary information to the OHPs may suffice for internal presentations within your own organisation, for any other external presentation this may be something of a lost opportunity. Provision of more detailed information, for which there was not enough time during the presentation, will enable you to disseminate your work more fully. Robson (2002) suggests that a 'pamphlet form' may be appropriate, using an uncluttered layout and use of photographs, tables and diagrams.

Other conferences are more academic in focus. These are usually less 'glossy', and delegates are likely to be academics undertaking research in similar areas. Here, a conference organiser will make a 'call for papers' about six months before the intended date of the conference. This 'call' may be published in relevant journal publications, through Internet databases and via university networks. Potential speakers submit a paper to the conference organisers, who will then decide whether to accept the contribution.

The audience at these conferences will be more interested in the academic as well as practical context of the research, the methodology, and the way in which data was analysed. If your paper is accepted, it is likely that the organisers will suggest that you submit a fuller version to them, which they will copy for all the participants at the conference. You will also make a presentation about your paper (usually about 20 minutes in length). Often these presentations are to smaller numbers of people (up to 50). There will be scope for questions at the time of your presentation, and it is possible that those who were interested in what you have to say will contact you later (either in person or via e-mail) for a further discussion of your work.

Although these presentations may be rather daunting, they are a useful way of clarifying your thinking, and for making contact with people who are also interested in similar areas. The feedback that you receive as a result of the process is also very valuable if you are thinking about going further and publishing your findings in a written form.

The content of presentations for different types of conferences therefore varies considerably, although the overall structure of the different presentations may be similar and is likely to involve:

- the objectives of the presentation
- the research purpose/problem/context
- methods of enquiry
- findings (data and analysis)
- the implications
- a final summary.

The final summary of any presentation is similar to the abstract or executive summary that you would produce for a written paper. It is quite a challenge to produce something punchy that encapsulates what you have done, but Day (1996) suggests the following approach to articulate your project in three sentences:

Sentence 1 – the purpose
Sentence 2 – the main points and methodology
Sentence 3 – the main conclusions.

Writing articles and papers

Written media of communication provide further opportunities to disseminate your findings. You might be tempted to write about your investigation in a popular publication, such as a newspaper or magazine (this could be a corporate publication or a local newspaper or radio station). Alternatively, you might feel that a short article in a professional journal such as *People Management* would be appropriate. Your organisational supervisor/mentor is a good source of advice about potential avenues for dissemination in popular media. If you wish to pursue academic means of dissemination, you may want to try to publish your work in a refereed journal. Here, your academic supervisor would be able to provide you with some guidance. Some ideas about how to go about these different forms of communication are given below:

News releases

These might be for a local intranet site, or directed at the editors of local media outlets (newspapers, radio and TV). Editors are always in a hurry and need to find the easiest ways possible to present topical news stories. A news release should be shorter than one side of A4 (or its electronic equivalent) and written in a lively style with a catchy heading. You should also provide a contact number for editorial enquiries. If your release is used, it is likely that the reporter, correspondent or subeditor will use some of your text on a word-for-word basis (hence the need to write in a topical and accessible way). However, you should be prepared also to read something that is not wholly familiar to you because the reporter/correspondent may also add his or her own 'spin'. It is very important, therefore, to check the PR policy of your organisation (if appropriate) before sending out any news releases, and to get the necessary authorisations. It is also important to render anonymous any organisations or participants in your research if there is even the slightest chance that they would object to media coverage.

Professional journals

Most professional and industry sector associations produce a monthly (or more frequent) journal publication which provides opportunities for the dissemination of your research findings. The wordcount limit here, for a feature article, is unlikely to be more than 2,000 words, and an accessible – rather than an academic – style is expected. If you are considering offering a contribution, it is worth writing to the editor with a short (500 words maximum) summary of your paper, explaining how it would be of interest to the readers of the publication. Useful headings, for such a summary would be:

- Target readership
- The aims of the paper/article
- The implications of the findings
- Treatment (style, etc)
- Contact details and arrangements (yours).

Use a your covering letter to make clear your name and the working title of your paper, providing a brief paragraph describing the contents and explaining why you chose this journal.

Often an editor will not respond for many weeks or months, if at all. If the editor does wish to go ahead, the deadline is likely to be fairly prompt. However, once agreement in principle is achieved, the article can be written quite quickly and may be structured in a similar way to a presentation.

Refereed journals

These are the most demanding articles to write. If you think you would like to submit your work to a refereed journal (such as the *Human Resource Management Journal*), you should first find and read the guidance for authors that is provided in each copy of the journal. This indicates the sort of articles that are expected. If you wish to proceed, you should draft your paper and submit two or three copies to the editor. If the editor believes the paper may be acceptable, it will be sent – without the details of the author(s) – to a number of 'referees' whose job is to critically evaluate the article and to say whether it might be worth publishing, as well as how or where it could be improved. This is a lengthy process, rarely taking less than three months. Only seldom is an article accepted without revisions, and the process of further enhancing the paper means that many articles are not accepted for publication for at least a year from the date of their original submission. There is also likely to be a further delay of three to 12 months before the paper appears in print.

The process is quite daunting, therefore, but it can be hugely rewarding when your paper finally appears in a refereed publication. Most first-time researchers who decide to attempt publication in such a journal find it helpful to team up with a more experienced academic writer – often their supervisor or someone recommended by them.

SUMMARY

- The process of writing about your research underpins the learning process. It enables you to reflect on what you have found, clarify your thinking, and communicate more effectively about your research.

- Readers in different contexts have different expectations of what they read. Academic readers expect a formal and objective written style and a demonstration of your knowledge and understanding of your subject area. They will want to evaluate how you have applied and evaluated an appropriate research methodology for your enquiry. Managers and other organisational sponsors expect a more persuasive and accessible written style and a report that focuses on implementable recommendations that can contribute to the resolution of HR problems, issues or opportunities.

- All research reports, whatever level or type of qualification they are associated with, should clearly express the research aims and objectives, review relevant literature, report the use of appropriate methods of data-collection, and analyse data in an integrated and objective way. Management reports have more emphasis on the generation of practical, costed, timely and realistic recommendations. Master's-level dissertations or research reports have more emphasis on the analytical focus, scope and contribution of the literature review, the evaluation of different research design and methodological issues, the analysis of data, and the reasoning process that links conclusions with analysis of the literature and other data.

- To overcome factors that inhibit the writing process it is important to develop writing habits, to write regularly, to plan your writing, to reward yourself when you achieve your writing targets, and to ensure that everything you write is regularly backed up.

- Planning can reduce the stress of writing. Useful techniques that can enhance the planning process are: brainstorming, mind mapping, linear planning, and making lists on Post-It notes in a structured way.

- It is important that readers of any report can follow its logic through its structure and the style and expression that is used. Effective writing is expressed clearly and simply with appropriate paragraphing and a consistent system of headings and subheadings. Jargon, slang, abbreviations, informal and discriminatory language are not appropriate.

- Involving others in evaluating your draft report, or sections of it, will enable you to prioritise the revisions that are required to ensure that it meets the assessment criteria by which it will be judged.

- Dissemination of what you have learned, beyond the submission of a report to your study centre, can benefit you and the organisation(s) in which your research was undertaken. Dissemination can occur within the organisation through internal briefings or presentations and papers, as well as externally through conferences and papers or articles aimed at academics and/or professionals and via more popular media.

Questions for review/reflection

These questions are designed to enable you to identify key areas for development with your project that you should discuss with your project tutor, supervisor or adviser if possible. The responses to them can also form part of a Continuing Professional Development log or portfolio. This is required by the CIPD from those who wish to upgrade their membership status.

Taking stock

1   What written reports about your research are required by your study centre, employer, or other sponsor or client? How clear are you about the required length, format and content required by these different readers?

2   What time do you have before the submission date for your research report? Draw up a writing schedule that will enable you to submit on time. Who will you approach to help you to evaluate your draft sections? What lead-time will they require to review your work and offer feedback?

3   Where will you undertake your writing? Whose help might you need in order to ensure that you have a computer and can have the space to write without distractions? What other organisational arrangements will you need to make to ensure that you are able to keep to your writing schedule?

4   What arrangements will be necessary to ensure that your work can be printed, copied and bound when the time comes?

Strengths and weaknesses

1   Look back at previous written coursework assignments that you have submitted. What comments have your tutors made? What improvement areas have they highlighted with your writing, and how might you develop the skills that you need?

2   Consider your strengths as a writer. What sections or chapters of your report or dissertation are likely to cause fewer problems for you? Which ones worry you most? What steps can you take to ensure that you tackle the difficult sections in an effective way?

Being a practitioner-researcher

1   What writing conventions or styles are prevalent at your organisation? How compatible are they with the expectations for academic writing? What are the implications of this for the way that you draft your report and the way you make use of feedback on any draft sections you produce?

2   What opportunities for the dissemination of your research might there be within your organisation? How might you explore these opportunities? What constraints are there on dissemination? Are any details from your research particularly sensitive? How will you establish the limits to what you can communicate?

3   In what ways might your organisation or department benefit from the wider dissemination of your research? Do you already participate in benchmarking or special-interest groups? Are there other companies within your wider organisation, or within the supply chain, that might benefit from hearing about what you have learned? To what extent might articles for local media, professional publications or academic journals be appropriate as means of disseminating your learning? How might you find out about such opportunities? What skills would you need to develop, and how might you go about developing them?

4   Which individuals or groups might wish not to be identified through any dissemination process? What steps could you take to ensure that appropriate anonymity and confidentiality are maintained?

FURTHER READING

It is very difficult to read about writing. The best way to learn to do it is by writing yourself and by critically evaluating the writing of others. In this way, the very process of reviewing the literature will help you to learn to write. It is also worth reading the projects submitted by past students at your study centre and trying to identify why some reports seem to communicate in a more objective and reasonable way than others. The following publications offer useful advice when writing for different audiences.

COGHLAN, D. and BRANNICK, T. (2001) *Doing Action Research in Your Own Organisation*. London, Sage.

DAY, A. (1996) *How to Get Research Published in Journals*. Aldershot, Gower.

MARSEN, S. (2002) *Professional Writing*. London, Palgrave.

RAWLINS, K. (1993) *Presentation and Communication Skills: A handbook for practitioners*. London, Emap Healthcare Ltd.

RUDESTAM, K. and NEWTON, R. (1992) *Surviving Your Dissertation*. London, Sage.

WINKLER, A. and MCCUEN, J. (1994) *Writing the Research Paper: A handbook*. Orlando, Harcourt Brace.

Final reflections

CHAPTER 10

Chapter outline
How to use this chapter
HR research – why bother?
The future of HR research
Developing practitioner-researchers in HR
Summary

LEARNING OUTCOMES

This chapter should help you to:

- **think about the relationship between HR research and HR practice**

- **debate how research in HR could make more of an impact on organisational change**

- **explore key issues for the future of HR research and for HR practitioner-researchers.**

HOW TO USE THIS CHAPTER

This chapter promotes the view that effective HR practice should be underpinned by rigorous enquiry activity, and considers the key skills and competences that HR practitioners can develop by engaging with this process. If you have worked your way through this book, then this chapter can help you to pull together your reflections within any Continuous Professional Development process you may be involved with. Hopefully, you will also reflect on ways in which you can make use of your investigative skills in new contexts and situations in the workplace as well as in any further study you choose to undertake.

Case illustration

Why do we clutch at academic musings?

After more than 20 years as an HR practitioner, one thing that has always struck me as odd is why we so often look to academics for new ideas. Our profession is fundamentally a job of dealing with everyday issues, with people in real situations, so why do we look to HR academics and their research as a means of legitimising our methodologies?

Rather than formulate new HR strategies in the crucible of the workplace – where theoretical shortcomings and implementation problems are readily apparent – we still seem to clutch at the musings of academics as a foundation for the next big initiative.

Don't get me wrong, HR academics have their place – but it is called a university rather than a workplace. Beware of ever letting them loose in the real world. After all, academic research was quite clearly to blame for the plague of competence frameworks in the 1990s that infected so many HR initiatives and rendered them ineffective.

One piece of beloved research by HR academics is the Sears-Roebuck employee satisfaction/customer service/profit chain case study that everybody seems to be quoting these days. It is popular because it appears to support what all good HR people want to believe: good HR practices lead to good business.

One little-quoted aspect of this study is that Sears employed econometricians to prove the correlation. Why? Is it not that obvious to the naked eye? As an economist myself I must say that I have never felt such techniques were designed or appropriate for the HR field.

Senior HR professionals who understand the real strategic issues have been agreeing for some years now that there has to be a paradigm shift in HR thinking. This is partly why the whole debate about harnessing human capital has moved to the front of the new concept queue. Yet, if there has to be a shift from existing models, what use is academic research based on existing organisational practices?

When such HR professionals are asked which HR paradigm they want to move to, they invariably refer to Dave Ulrich's change agent/business partner model. But does this particular paradigm have a solid theoretical foundation? Has it been proven? The 'HR Scorecard' (Becker, Huselid, Ulrich, Harvard Business School, 2001) which tries to show HR how to align itself strategically appears to be trying to move HR further down the road to complex answers based on arcane regression analyses, rather than common sense solutions to difficult HR issues.

Do we really need academics to tell us how to get the best out of people? . . .

Extracts from: P. Kearns, *Personnel Today*, 4 June 2002.
Reproduced by permission of *Personnel Today*

This article encapsulates many of the views of those who question the value of 'research' in the everyday business of undertaking HR activities. The following article argues for more HR research as a basis for decision-making.

Case illustration

Burning questions

How do we create knowledge within the HR community? How can we ensure that our ideas are as near to the truth as possible, rather than being based on superstition, prejudice or naive notions of causality?

There is a story much loved in the academic world that goes something like this. One day in an ancient forest in a far-off land, a hut, in which a hog was sheltering from the storm, is hit by lightning. The hut is instantly engulfed in flames. As the embers die down the wonderful smell of roast pork wafts through the small settlement, and delighted by the smell, the hungry villagers eat the roasted hog. Observing the burnt-down hut, the villagers from that day on wait until a storm is approaching, entice a hog into a hut and then burn it down. . . .

How many of us are like the ancient villagers – with little idea of causality, endlessly attempting to reproduce a situation that appeared to work, rather than understanding the precise mechanisms of its success? . . .

Perhaps now is the time to begin the hard march to 'good theory', to build a profound understanding of how we can sustain the performance of companies and create places in which people flourish. . . .

At BT, for example, a team of people have been studying the impact of flexible working with as much rigour as you will find in any university. Their initial hypothesis was that those employees who worked flexible hours would be more productive.

The team began testing their hypothesis in 1998 by taking the classic four-step experimentation process. They identified a pilot site (in the Cardiff Engineering Centre) and established baseline measures for productivity, turnover and employee engagement.

Next they designed a series of interventions introducing flexible working. Then they observed productivity, turnover and employee engagement in the pilot site at frequent intervals over a three-year period. Lastly, they examined the relationship between productivity and flexibility.

The research showed a significant increase in productivity, a substantial reduction in turnover and a notable increase in employee engagement. . . .

Significant progress in our profession can occur only if collectively we create good theory. And this means more than burning huts. . . .

Extracts from: L. Gratton, *People Management*, 24 July 2003.
Reproduced by permission of Lynda Gratton

DISCUSSION QUESTION
What are the main arguments raised in these articles for and against HRM research?

Feedback notes

These two articles represent fundamentally different understandings of what constitutes research in HR and its value for management and HR practice. The first article characterises HR research as being remote from the real world and irrelevant to the day-to-day business-focused perspective of HR practitioners. The second article depicts HR research as the only sensible way forward in making decisions about the most appropriate way to manage people in work organisations. It is interesting that both commentators feature illustrations of large-scale and long-term research projects.

The purpose of this chapter – written from within a perspective that advocates the application of systematic research processes within HR practice and thinking – is to explore why it is that so many HR practitioners are suspicious of 'research'. On the basis of this discussion, different ways in which HR research might be able to contribute more consistently and openly to organisational performance are highlighted. The implications for practitioner-researchers are then outlined.

HR RESEARCH – WHY BOTHER?

The premise from which this book has been written is that HR research involves systematically enquiring into people management and development issues to increase knowledge and underpin effective action. In this sense, HR research is inevitably involved with the 'real world' and is initiated as a result of the need of practitioners to solve problems, to evaluate innovative practices, and to develop and implement new forms of HR intervention. In this way, HR research has value for a range of different individuals and groups who are involved with the employment relationship, including employees, employers, managers, employee representatives, business associations and policy-makers within the business environment. HR research therefore has the potential to help organisations change and, at the same time, to generate knowledge (Coghlan, 2002).

Robson (2002) argues that systematic enquiry is a more effective basis from which to make decisions and take action than many other commonly-used starting points – such as political preference, managerial edict, bandwagon-jumping or personal whim. However, as the first case illustration suggests, many people believe that HR research does not have any meaningful impact on HR practice. It is important to explore some of the reasons for this antipathy towards research, some of which are summarised below.

Hard-pressed HR managers

One reason those in organisations may be suspicious of HR research stems from the nature of the work of many HR managers. The process of management rarely, if ever, occurs as an idealised one of logical planning, control, communication and co-ordination, etc. In reality, managerial work – in HR as elsewhere in the organisation – is fragmented, and characterised by the need to deal with many different issues at the same time (Stewart, 1983; Whitley, 1984). When 'important and urgent' operational issues are constantly pressing, it is not surprising that managers do not find time to seek out and evaluate the products of systematic HR research projects. Where 'new' findings and ideas are desired, the pressures of managerial work can also, perhaps, foster a preference for those that are strikingly packaged and well publicised. The very nature of this packaging may mean that research is communicated and understood in an over-simplified and naive way. Indeed, it is possible that striking findings may stem from research of limited value, in terms of its methods, reliability and validity. Publicity can influence managers, however, if they are hoping for an easily applied solution, or to try out the latest fad without first evaluating its credibility. The application of such research in these circumstances, though, is likely to have a limited impact on organisational performance.

The separation of HR research from HR practice

A further factor that inhibits the impact of HR research in practice may be a separation of roles within the HR community. Large-scale research, for example, tends to be undertaken by and in university departments by those who specialise in it. Policy decisions that might be informed by such large-scale research are made by a different group of people, such as those working in government departments or those in strategic decision-making roles in large organisations. The communication and implementation of those policy decisions is the responsibility of yet another group of HR practitioners and managers. Although there is a logic to this separation of roles, the effect of the lack of 'ownership' of the initial investigative activity may be to diminish the impact of the implementation of the research.

The 'mystification' of research

Another factor that may inhibit the impact of HR research is the fear of the 'mysteries' and jargon of the research process itself. Research can seem to be a complex and difficult process involving computers, statistical packages, vast quantities of information and huge investments of time and other resources. It is not. Bell and Opie (2002; p.2) comment that research is no more and no less than identifying a topic that is worth investigating, planning and designing a suitable methodology, designing appropriate research instruments, and gaining access to data. Although there are no short cuts or quick fixes in research, the process itself is not mysterious. Fear of it is probably based on a misunderstanding of its nature and purpose.

Yet research is important and HR practice can be more effective if HR practitioner-researchers are better equipped to articulate the development of their understanding and learning so that those not directly involved in an enquiry can take something from it. What can HR practitioners, and the profession as a whole, do to encourage the use of good research as a basis for action and professional practice?

First, it is important to value the activity of systematic enquiry within the role of HR practitioners at all levels and within all types of employing organisation. All HR practitioners should be prepared, following Schon (1983), to surface and question intuitive understandings of HR issues and to test new understandings. A reflective approach to the diagnosis of HR issues is thus required.

Second, it is important to see the research or enquiry process as a routine part of the HR toolkit, applicable to problems and issues at individual, team, or organisational levels. It is important to recognise that the distinction between HR researcher and HR practitioner is a false one. Some professionals may engage more with 'research', others may engage more with 'practice', but it is only when the role of 'practitioner-researcher' is accepted as valid that the research process itself will be demystified.

This book therefore seeks to celebrate and encourage the contribution of small-scale research enquiries undertaken by practitioner-researchers, in which 'local theory' (Coghlan, 2002) relevant to particular organisations can be developed, evaluated and revised as appropriate. Where practitioner-researchers, and those who work with them, have been involved in gathering and analysing data relevant to organisational problems or issues, there is more chance of effective implementation of the solutions that their work suggests. Similarly, involvement in planning and implementing interventions that are based on systematic enquiries and observing, evaluating and questioning the impact of the actions will enable a fuller HR contribution to organisational effectiveness. As practitioner-researchers reflect on and learn from the process, there is also more chance that the benefits of the process will be realised to the advantage of the individuals involved and of the organisation(s) in which the research took place.

If HR practitioner-researchers are prepared to reflect on and disseminate their findings more widely, there is more of an opportunity for their work to have more impact within the profession as a whole. Equally, those who undertake enquiry processes after them can develop both thinking and practice in an incremental and credible way. Although most small-scale projects are essentially local, the dissemination of what has been learned can allow others, who are not so local, to benefit from it and take something for their own professional practice.

THE FUTURE OF HR RESEARCH

If the premise of this book – that systematic research enquiries are a valuable process – is accepted, it is also worth considering how HR research may develop in the future. One of the major themes of this book has been a discussion about the usefulness of both positivist and interpretivist approaches to research in business and the social sciences more widely. Will HR research tend to develop within the assumptions of an objective 'scientific' approach, or will it involve trying to access and understand individuals' perceptions of the world of work from more of an interpretevist perspective?

The answer, of course, is 'both'. There will always be a need for systematically-obtained data, gathered from within both understandings of the nature of research enquiry, to fulfil different purposes in HR. So HR research that describes current practices and phenomena is valuable to HR practitioners as an influence on their decision-thinking. Additionally, research that explores the dimensions of HR issues and problems will also be required. Research that seeks to identify causes or to explain phenomena is also indispensable as a basis for problem diagnosis and action planning. Interpretivist and positivist approaches *both* contribute to the achievement of these purposes. Equally, if practitioner-researcher enquiries, which are advocated in this book, become more integrated within professional practice, then it is likely that a sensible use of both quantitative and qualitative data will become a feature of organisational enquiries (Gill and Johnson, 2002).

DEVELOPING PRACTITIONER-RESEARCHERS IN HR

Finally, it is important to explore the characteristics, or competences, that might underpin an effective practitioner-researcher. The advantages and disadvantages of this role are considered in Chapter 1. Having explored the different features of the research process in the main body of this book, it is worth a consideration of the qualities of an effective practitioner-researcher. Coghlan and Brannick (2002) suggest four such qualities for those engaged in action research:

Being critical and committed

Implicit preconceptions about issues and situations are inevitable if you are part of the organisation being researched. The effective practitioner-researcher will therefore be able to critically evaluate and question received wisdom at the same time as maintaining and communicating a commitment to the development of the organisation.

Having aspirations and being realistic about limits

Organisational realities may make it difficult for investigative enquiries to be taken seriously. It is important, therefore, to aim high but, at the same time, to be prepared and able to work within the limits of organisational realities.

Being independent and working well with others

As a part of the organisation, practitioner-researchers have access to a range of contacts and sources of information. At the same time it is important to retain an independence as a grounding for the investigative enquiry.

Being proactive and reflective

As well as being action-oriented, the effective practitioner-researcher must reflect on the wider context of the problem or issue that is being researched, both within the organisation and with regard to practice and developments outside the organisation. It will also involve promoting the dissemination of the findings of studies so that they can inform the development of practice and understanding in other organisations and contexts.

SUMMARY

- HR research is valuable for a range of different individuals and groups who are involved with the employment relationship, including employees, employers, managers, employee representatives, business associations and policy-makers within the business environment.

- Much HR work in the 'real world' is fragmented and characterised by the need to deal with many issues at the same time. As a result, managers tend not to access and evaluate the findings of many HR research projects.

- Within the HR profession the processes of 'research', 'policy formulation' and 'action and implementation' are undertaken by different groups of professionals. The lack of involvement in the process as a whole can limit the impact of research findings in HR.

- Many HR practitioners are reluctant to engage in research because they believe it is complex, difficult and mysterious.

- A key skill for all HR practitioners is to make explicit and question implicit understandings of HR issues within their organisation. In addition the research or enquiry process should be part of their HR contribution to the employing organisation.

- As more HR professionals engage with the role of practitioner-researcher in organisations, so the research process itself can become demystified.

- As practitioner-researchers reflect on and disseminate the outcomes of their enquiries more widely, their work can have more impact within the profession as a whole and contribute to the development of HR practice in an incremental and credible way.

■ Positivist and interpretivist approaches to research are valuable in systematically enquiring into people management and development issues to increase knowledge and underpin effective action.

■ Qualitative and quantitative data is valuable in organisational studies and can contribute to inductive and deductive analysis processes.

■ Effective practitioner-researchers have to be both critical and committed, independent and collaborative, ambitious and realistic, proactive and reflective.

Final review/reflection

Reports submitted to the CIPD as part of professionally-accredited qualification routes must include some reflection by the author about the contribution of the enquiry process to their personal and professional development. The expectations of many other study centres where a research project or dissertation is required also include a requirement for some critical reflection at the end of the research process.

Reflecting on the following questions can underpin the process of identifying development that has been achieved as well as considering future development needs.

Looking back – reflecting on the enquiry process

1 What features of the enquiry process that you have undertaken have benefited from your involvement with the organisation(s) in which the project has been undertaken?

2 To what extent have you been able to achieve an independent and critically reflective analysis of the organisational context(s)? What factors have helped and what have hindered this? What have you learned about the organisation that you might not otherwise have been able to learn?

3 What relationships have you developed in order to achieve your project objectives? What factors have helped you to achieve this?

4 At what times during the process of undertaking your project have you had to act in a proactive way? What have you learned about working as an 'independent learner' and practitioner-researcher?

Where now?

1 What would you seek to do differently if you were starting a new investigative enquiry from scratch?

2 What skills and qualities, relevant to being a practitioner-researcher, would you like to further develop in the future? How might you go about developing in these areas?

3 What opportunities might there be to disseminate the findings from your project? What skills will you need in order to share what you have learned more widely?

References

ADAM-SMITH, D. and GOSS, D. (1993) 'HIV/AIDS and hotel and catering employment: some implications of percieved risk', *Employee Relations*, 15 (2) 25–32.

ADELMAN, C. (1989) 'The practical ethic takes priority over methodology', in W. Carr (ed.) *Quality in Teaching: Arguments for a reflective profession*. London, Falmer.

ALLEN, B. (2003) 'Accidental costs', *People Management*, 23 January, 65.

AL-KHALIFA, E. (1988) 'Pin-money professionals? Women in teaching', in A. Coyle and J. Skinner (eds) *Women at Work: Positive action for change*. Oxford, Macmillan Education.

ANALOUI, F. and KAKABADSE, A. (1992) 'Unconventional practices at work: insight and analysis through participant observation', *Journal of Managerial Psychology*, 7 (5).

ANDERSON, V. and SKINNER, D. (1999) 'Organisational learning in practice: how do small businesses learn to operate internationally?', *Human Resource Development International*, 2 (2) 235–258.

ANDERSON, V., BOOCOCK, G., GRAHAM, S. and LAWRENCE, P. (1999) 'International business: experiences and outcomes', unpublished.

ARGYRIS, C., PUTNAM, R. and MCLAIN SMITH, D. (1984) *Action Science*, Jossey Bass, SF.

ARMSTRONG, M. and BARON, A. (1998), 'Out of the tick box', *People Management,* 23 July.

BABAKUS, E., CRAVENS, D. W., JOHNSTON, M. and MONCRIEF, W. C. (1996) 'Examining the role of organizational variables in the salesperson job satisfaction model', *Journal of Personal Selling and Sales Management*, 16 (3) 33–46.

BAGGULEY, P. (1991) 'The patriarchal restructuring of gender segregation: a case study of the hotel and catering industry', *Sociology*, 25 (4) 607–25.

BARBER, T. X. (1976) *Pitfalls in Human Research*. Oxford, Pergamon.

BEARDWELL, J. and BRITTON, C. (2003) 'Look who's talking: the impact on workplace communication and information sharing', Paper presented to the CIPD Professional Standards Conference, Keele University, 1 July 2003.

BEER, M., SPECTOR, B., LAWRENCE, P., QUINN MILLS, D. and WALTON, R. (1985) *Human Resource Management: A general management perspective*. Glencoe, Free Press.

BEHRMAN, D. N. and BEREAULT, W. D. (1984) 'A role stress model of the performance and satisfaction of industrial salespersons', *Journal of Marketing*, 48, 9–21.

BELL, J. (2001) *Doing Your Research Project: A guide for first-time researchers in education and social science*. Buckingham, Open University Press.

BELL, J. and OPIE, C. (2002) *Learning from Research*: *Getting more from your data*. Buckingham, Open University Press.

BISWAS, R. and CASSELL, C. (1996), 'Strategic HRM and the gendered division of labour in the hotel industry: a case study', *Personnel Review*, 25 (2) 19–34.

BLACK, T. B. (1993) *Evaluating Social Science Research*. London, Sage.

BLAXTER, L., HUGHES, C. and TIGHT, M. (2001) *How to Research*. Buckingham, Open University Press.

BOELLA, M. J. (1996) *Human Resource Management in the Hospitality Industry*. Bolton, Stanley Thornes Publishers.

BOWDEN, J. (2002) *Project Guide: MA in Personnel and Development*. University of Westminster, unpublished.

BRESNAN, M. J., WRAY, K., BRYMAN, A., BEARDWORTH, A. D., FORD, J. R. and KEIL, E. T. (1985) 'The flexibility of recruitment in the construction industry: formalization or recausalization?', *Sociology*, 19, 108–124.

BROWN, S. P. and PETERSON, R. A. (1993) 'Antecedents and consequences of salesperson job satisfaction: meta-analysis and assessment of causal effects', *Journal of Marketing Research*, 30, 63–77.

BROWN, S. P. and PETERSON, R. A. (1994) 'The effect of effort on sales performance and job satisfaction', *Journal of Marketing*, 58 (2) 70–80.

BRYMAN, A. (1988), *Quality and Quantity in Social Research*. London, Unwin.

BRYMAN, A. and CRAMER, D. (1997) *Quantitative Data Analysis for Social Scientists*. London, Routledge.

CARR, F. (1999) 'Local bargaining in the National Health Service: new approaches to employee relations', *Industrial Relations Journal*, 30 (3) 197–211.

CARR, W. and KEMMIS, S. (1986) *Becoming Critical*. London, Falmer.

CHALLAGALLA, G. N. and SHERVANI, T. A. (1996) 'Dimensions and types of supervisory control: effects of salesperson performance and satisfaction', *Journal of Marketing*, 60, 89–105.

CHURCHILL, G. A., FORD, N. M., HARTLEY, S. W. and WALKER, O. C. (1985) 'The determinants of salesperson performance: a meta-analysis', *Journal of Marketing Research*, 22, 103–18.

CIPD (2002) *Generic Assessment Criteria for CIPD Professional Development Scheme Management Reports*.

COFFEE, A. and ATKINSON, P. (1996) *Making Sense of Qualitative Data*. London, Sage.

COGHLAN, D. (2002) 'Putting "research" back into OD and action research: a call to OD practitioners', *Organization Development Journal*, 29 (1) 62–65.

COLLIS, J. and HUSSEY, R. (2003) *Business Research: A practical guide for undergraduate and postgraduate students*. London, Palgrave.

COTTON, J. L. and TUTTLE, J. M. (1986) 'Employee turnover: a meta-analysis with review and implications for research', *Academy of Management Review*, 11 (1) 55–70.

COUPAR, W. and ALLEN, M. (1998) 'Towards a new model of industrial partnership: beyond the HRM versus industrial relations debate', in P. Sparrow and M. Marchington (eds) *Human Resource Management: the new agenda*. London, *Financial Times*/Pitman.

CRABB, S. (2001) 'Deutsche Bank detects feelgood factor', *People Management*, 8 March.

CREAGH, M. and BREWSTER, C. (1998) 'Identifying good practice in flexible working', *Employee Relations*, 20 (5) 490–503.

CRESSWELL, J. W. (1994) *Research Design: Qualitative and quantitative approaches*. Thousand Oaks, Sage.

CROUCHER, R. and BREWSTER, C. (1998) 'Flexible working practices and the trade unions', *Employee Relations*, 20 (5) 443–52.

DAINTY, A. R. G., BAGILHOLE, B. M. and NEALE, R. H. (2000) 'The compatibility of construction companies' human resource development policies with employee career expectations', *Engineering, Construction and Architectural Management*, 7 (2) 169–78.

DAY, A. (1996) *How to Get Research Published in Journals*. Aldershot, Gower.

DECARLO, T. E. and LEIGH, T. W. (1996) 'Impact of salesperson attraction on sales managers' attibutions and feedback', *Journal of Marketing,* 60, 47–66.

DELBRIDGE, R. and KIRKPATRICK, I. (1994) 'Theory and practice of participant observation', in V. Wass. and P. Wells (eds) *Principles and Practice in Business and Management Research*. Aldershot, Dartmouth.

DEY, I. (1993) *Qualitative Data Analysis*. London, Routledge.

DIAMANTOPOULOS, A. and SCHLEGELMILCH, B. (1997) *Taking the Fear out of Data Analysis*. London, Dryden.

DRUKER, J. and WHITE, G. (1996) *Managing People in Construction*. London, IPD.

DRUKER, J., WHITE, G., HEGEWISCH, A. and MAYNE, L. (1996), 'Between hard and soft HRM: human resource management in the construction industry', *Construction Management and Economics*, 14, 405–16.

DUBINSKY, A. J. and MATTSON, B. E. (1979) 'Consequences of role conflict and ambiguity experienced by retail salespeople', *Journal of Retailing*, 55, 70–86.

EASTERBY-SMITH, M., THORPE, R. and LOWE, A. (2002) *Management Research: An introduction*. London, Sage.

EGAN, J. (1998) *Rethinking Construction. The Report of the Construction Task Force*. London, DETR.

EISENHARDT, K. M. (1989) 'Building theories from case study research', *Academy of Management Review*, 14 (4) 532–50.

ELDEN, M. and CHISHOLM, R. (1993) 'Emerging varieties and action research: introduction to the Special Issue', *Human Relations*, 46 (2) 121–42.

ERICKSON, B. H. and NOSANCHUCK, T. A. (1992) *Understanding Data*. Buckingham, Open University Press.

FALUDI, S. (1991) *Backlash: The undeclared war against women*. New York, Chatto & Windus.

FLATHER, S. (2003) 'Losing out to inflation', *People Management,* 12 June.

FINE, G. A. (1987) 'One of the boys: women in male-dominated settings', in M. S. Kimmel (ed.) *Changing Men: New directions in research on men and masculinity.* Thousand Oaks, Sage.

FIRTH-COZENS, J. and WEST, M. A. (1991) *Women at Work: Psychological and organizational perspectives*. Buckingham, Open University Press.

FOMBRUN, C., TICHY, N. and DEVANNA, M (eds) (1984) *Strategic Human Resource Management*. New York, Wiley.

GALL, M. D., BORG, W. R. and GALL, J. P. (1996) *Educational Research: An introduction*. New York, Longman.

GENNARD, J. and JUDGE, G. (2002) *Employee Relations*. London, CIPD.

GIBBONS, M. L., LIMOGES, H., NOVOTNY, S., SCHWARTMAN, P., SCOTT, P. and TROW,

N. (1994) The New Production of Knowledge: The Dynamics of Science and Research in Contemporary Societies. London, Sage.

GILL, J. and JOHNSON, P. (2001) *Research Methods for Managers*. London, Paul Chapman.

GLASER, B. J. and STRAUSS, A. (1967) *The Discovery of Grounded Theory*. Chicago, Aldine.

GLASSNER, B. and MORENO, J. D. (eds) (1989) *The Qualitative–Quantitative Distinction in the Social Sciences*. Dordrecht, Kluwer.

GLASSNER, B. J. (1992) *The Basics of Grounded Theory*. Mill Valley, CA, Sociology Press.

GRATTON, L. (2003) 'Burning questions – it's time to abandon superstition for good, solid theory', *People Management*, 24 July.

GROVES, R. M. (1996) 'How do we know what we think they think is really what they think?', in N. Schwarz and S. Sudman (eds) *Answering Questions*. San Francisco, Jossey Bass.

GUERRIER, Y. (1992) 'Hotel manager: an unsuitable job for a woman?', *The Service Industries Journal*, 6, 227–40.

GUEST, D. and PECCEI, R. (2001) 'Partnership and work: mutuality and the balance of advantage', *British Journal of Industrial Relations*, 39 (2) 207–36.

GUMMESSON, E. (1991) *Qualitative Methods in Management Research*. Newbury Park, Sage.

HACKMAN, J. R. and OLDHAM, G. R. (1975) 'Development of the job diagnostic survey', *Journal of Applied Psychology*, 60 (2) 159–70.

HAMMOND, V. (1992) 'Women managers: developing their full potential', in M. Syrett and C. Hogg (eds) *Leadership: An essential reader*. Oxford, Blackwell.

HANSARD SOCIETY COMMISSION (1990) *Women at the Top*. London, Hansard Society.

HARRIS, M. and HARRIS, J. (2002) 'Achieving organisational collaboration in the non-profit sector: an action research approach', *Organization Development Journal*, 20 (1) 28–35.

HART, E. and BOND, M. (1995) *Action Research for Health and Social Care*. Buckingham, Open University Press.

HARTLEY, J. F. (1994) 'Case studies in organizational research', in C. M. Cassell and G. Symon (eds) *Qualitative Methods in Organizational Research: A practical guide*. London, Sage.

HAYNES, P. and ALLEN, M. (2001) 'Parternship as union strategy: a preliminary analysis', *Employee Relations* , 23 (2) 164–87.

HEDRICK, T. E., BICKMAN, L. and ROG, D. J. (1993) Applied Research Design, Newbury Park. CA, Sage.

HENDRY, C. (1995) *Human Resource Management: A strategic approach to employment*. Oxford, Butterworth-Heinemann.

HICKS, L. (1990) 'Excluded women: how can this happen in the hotel world?', *The Service Industries Journal*, 4 (4) 44–62.

HIGGINBOTTOM, K. (2002) 'Disability sidelined in firms social reports', *People Management*, 11 July.

HIGGINBOTTOM, K. (2002) 'Profits rise with a written HR strategy', *People Management*, 26 December.

HILL, R. and STEWART, J. (2000) 'Human resource development in small organizations', *Journal of European Industrial Training*, 24 (2/3/4) 105–17.

HIRSCH, W. and JACKSON, C. (1989) 'Women into management: issues influencing the entry of women into managerial jobs', Paper 158, Institute of Manpower Studies, University of Sussex.

HODGKINSON, G. P., HERRIOT, P. and ANDERSON, N. (2001) 'Re-aligning the stakeholders in management research: lessons from industrial, work and organizational psychology', *British Journal of Management*, 12 (special edition), 41–8.

HOSPITALITY TRAINING FOUNDATION (HtF) (2000) *Skills and Employment Forecasts 2000*. London, Hospitality Training Foundation.

HOWARD, K. and SHARP, J. A. (1994) *The Management of a Student Research Project*. Aldershot, Gower.

HUANG, Z., OLOMALAIYE, P. O. and AMBROSE, B. (1996) 'Construction company manpower planning', in A. Thorpe (ed.) *Proceedings of the 12th Annual ARCOM Conference*, Sheffield Hallam University, UK, September 1996, Vol. 1, 17–26.

ILGEN, D. R. and FELDMAN, J. M. (1983) 'Performance appraisal: a process focus', *Research in Organizational Behavior*, 5, 141–97.

JACKSON, D. W., SCHLACTER, J. L. and WOLFE, W. G. (1995) 'Examining the bases utilized for evaluating salesperson's performance', *Journal of Personal Selling and Sales Management*, 15, 57–65.

JANKOWICZ, A. D. (2000) *Business Research Projects for Students*. London, Chapman & Hall.

JAWORSKI, B. J. and KOHLI, A. K. (1991) 'Supervisory feedback: alternative types and their impact on salesperson's performance and satisfaction', *Journal of Marketing Research*, 28, 190–201.

JAWORSKI, B. J., STATHAKOPOULOS, V. and KRISHNAN, H. S. (1993) 'Control combinations in marketing: conceptual framework and empirical evidence', *Journal of Marketing*, 57, 57–69.

KAHN, T. (1995) 'Managing people in built environment organizations', in M. Waterhouse and G. Crook, (eds) *Management and Business Skills in the Built Environment*. Oxford, Spon.

KEARNS, P. (2002) 'Why do we clutch at academic musings?', *Personnel Today*, 4 June.

KEMMIS, S. and MCTAGGART, R. (1981) *The Action Research Planner*. Victoria, Deakin University Press.

KING, N. (1994) 'The qualitative research interview', in C. M. Cassell and G. Symon (eds) *Qualitative Methods in Organizational Research: A practical guide*. London, Sage.

KING, N. (1998) 'Template analysis', in G. Symon and C. Cassell (eds) *Qualitative Methods and Analysis in Organisational Research*. London, Sage.

KNIGHTS, D. and WILMOTT, H. (1986) *Gender and the Labour Process*. Cambridge, Cambridge University Press.

KODZ, J. and HARPER, H. (2002) *Work-Life Balance: Beyond the Rhetoric*. London, Institute for Employment Studies.

KOLB, D. A.. RUBIN, I. M. and MCINTYRE, J. M. (1979) *Organizational Psychology: An experiential approach*. London, Prentice Hall.

LANDSBERGER, H. A. (1958) *Hawthorne Revisited*. Ithaca, Cornell University Press.

LANGFORD, D., HANCOCK, M. R., FELLOWS, R. and GALE, A. W. (1995) *Human Resources Management in Construction*. Harlow, Longman.

LARSON, J. R. (1984) 'The performance feedback process: a preliminary model', *Organizational Behaviour and Human Performance*, 33, 42–76.

LASHLEY, C. (2000) *Hospitality Retail Management: A unit manager's guide*. Oxford, Butterworth-Heinemann.

LASHLEY, C. and BEST, W. (2002) 'Employee induction in licensed retail organisations', *International Journal of Contemporary Hospitality Management*, 14 (1) 6–13.

LATHAM, G. P., SKARLICKI, D., IRVINE, D. and SIEGEL, J. P. (1993) 'The increased importance of performance appraisals to employee effectiveness in organisational settings in North America', in C. L. Cooper and J. T. Robertson, *International Review of Industrial and Organizational Psychology*. New York, John Wiley & Sons.

LAZIER-SMITH, L. (1989), 'Advertising: women's place and image', in P. Creedon (ed.) *Women and Mass Communication: Challenging gender values*. Thousand Oaks, Sage.

LEGGE, K. (1995) *Human Resource Management: Rhetorics and realities*. London, Macmillan.

LEININGER, M. (1994) 'Evaluation criteria and critique of qualitative research studies', in J. M. Morse (ed.) *Critical Issues in Qualitative Research Methods*. Thousand Oaks, Sage.

LEWIN, K. (1946) 'Action research and minority problems', *Journal of Social Issues*, (2) 34–6.

LINCOLN, Y. S. and GUBA, E. G. (1985) *Naturalistic Enquiry*. London, Sage.

LOWE, A. (1995) 'The basic social processes of entrepreneurial innovation', *International Journal of Entrepreneurial Behaviour and Research*, 1 (2) 54–76.

LUNDY, O. and COWLING, A. (1996) *Strategic Human Resource Management*. London, Routledge.

MABEY, C., SALAMAN, G. and STOREY, J. (eds) (1998) *Strategic Human Resource Management: A reader*. London, Sage.

MAHONEY, C. (2003) 'UK firms need more innovation', *People Management,* 15 May.

MARCHINGTON, M. (1995) 'Employee relations', in S. Tyson (ed.) *Strategic Prospects for HRM*. London, IPD.

MARCHINGTON, M. and WILKINSON, A. (2002) *People Management and Development: Human resource management at work*. London, CIPD.

MARKOWICH, M. M. (1994) 'We can make performance appraisals work', *Compensation and Benefits Review*, 26 (3) 25–8.

MARS, G. (1985) 'Hotel pilferage: a case study in occupational theft', in C. R. Littler (ed.) *The Experience of Work*. London, Gower.

MASLOW, A. H. (1943) 'A theory of human motivation', *Psychological Review*, 50 (4) 370–96.

METCALF, H. and LEIGHTON, P. (1989) *The Under-utilization of Women in the Labour Market*. IMS Report 172, Institute of Manpower Studies, Brighton.

MICHAELS, R. E., CRON, W. L., DUBINSKY, A. J. and JOACHIMSTHALER, E. A. (1988) 'Influence of formalization on the organizational commitment and work alienation of salespeople and industrial buyers', *Journal of Marketing Research*, 25 (4) 376–83.

MILES, M. and HUBERMAN, A. (1994) *Qualitative Data Analysis*. Thousand Oaks, Sage.

MOHRMAN, A. M., RESNICK-WEST, S. M. and LAWLER, E. E. (1989) *Designing Performance Appraisal Systems*. San Francisco, Jossey Bass.

MORRIS, M. H., DAVIS, D. L., ALLEN, J. W., AVILA, R. A. and CHAPMAN, J. (1991) 'Assessing the relationships among performance measures, managerial practices, and satisfaction when evaluating the salesforce: a replication and extensions', *Journal of Personal Selling and Sales Management*, 9, 25–35.

MORTON, C. (1998) 'Water proof', *People Management,* 11 June.

MOUNT, M. K. (1983) 'Comparisons of managerial and employee satisfaction with a performance apraisal system, *Personnel Psychology*, 36 (3) 99–110.

MOWEN, J. C., FABES, K. J. and LAFORGE, R. W. (1986) 'Effects of effort, territory situation, and rater on salesperson evaluation', *Journal of Personal Selling and Sales Management*, 1–8.

NEUMAN, W. (2003) *Social Research Methods: Qualitative and quantitative methods*. Boston, Wiley.

OLIVER, R. L. and ANDERSON, E. (1994) 'An empirical test of the consequences of behavior- and outcome-based sales control systems', *Journal of Marketing*, 58, 53–67.

OLIVER, R. L. and ANDERSON, E. (1995) 'Behavior- and outcome-based sales control systems: evidence and consequences of pure-form and hybrid governance', *Journal of Personal Selling and Sales Management*, 15, 1–15.

PATTON, W. E. and KING, R. H. (1985) 'The use of human judgement models in evaluating sales force performance', *Journal of Personal Selling and Sales Management,* 1–14.

PEKARNE, B. and VON ARNOLD, J. (1991) 'Output vs. input', *Sales and Marketing Management*, 10, 12.

PEOPLE MANAGEMENT (2000) 'Managers fail to blow whistle on fraud', 28 December.

PETTIJOHN, L. S., PARKER, R. S., PETTIJOHN, C. E. and KENT, L. (2001) 'Performance appraisals: usage, criteria and observations', *Journal of Management Development*, 20 (9) 754–71.

PFEFFER, J. (1998) *The Human Equation: Building profits by putting people first*. Boston, Harvard Business School Press.

PINNINGTON, A. and HAMMERSLEY, G. (1997) 'Quality circles under the new deal at Land-Rover', *Employee Relations*, 19 (5) 415–29.

PUBLICAN (2000) *The Pub Industry Handbook*. Croydon, Quantum Publishing.

PURCELL, J. (1995) 'Corporate strategy and its link with human resource management strategy', in J. Storey (ed.) *Human Resource Management: A critical text*. London, Routledge.

PURCELL, K. and ELIAS, P. (2003) 'On higher ground', *People Management*, 29 May.

RAE, D. and CARSWELL, M. (2000) 'Using a life-story approach in researching entrepreneurial learning: the development of a conceptual model and its implications in the design of learning experiences', *Education and Training*, 42 (4/5) 220–8.

RAGIN, C. and BECKER, J. (1992) *What is a Case? Exploring the Foundations of Social Enquiry*. Cambridge, Cambridge University Press.

RAPOPORT, R. N. (1970) 'Three dilemmas in action research', *Human Relations*, 23, 499–513.

REEVES, T. K. and HARPER, D. (1981) *Surveys at Work: Student project manual.* London, McGraw-Hill.

REMENYI, D., WILLIAMS, B., MONEY, A. and SWARTZ, E. (1998) *Doing Research in Business and Management: An introduction to process and method.* London, Sage.

RILEY, M., WOOD, R. C., CLARK, M. A., WILKIE, E. and SZIVAS, E. (2000) *Researching and Writing Dissertations in Business and Management.* London, Thomson.

ROBSON, C. (2002) *Real World Research: A resource for social scientists and practitioner-researchers.* Oxford, Blackwell.

ROETHLISBERGER, F. J. and DICKSON, W. J. (1939) *Management and the Worker.* Boston, Harvard University Press.

SAPPAL, P. (2003) 'Cultural evolution', *People Management*, 17 April.

SAUNDERS, M., LEWIS, P. and THORNHILL, A. (2003) *Research Methods for Business Students.* London, *Financial Times*/Pitman.

SCARNATI, J. T. (1999) 'Beyond technical competence: the fundamentals of flexibility', *Participation and Empowerment: An international journal*, 7 (7) 194–200.

SCHON, D. A. (1983) *The Reflective Practitioner.* London, Temple Smith.

SCOTT, J. (1990) *A Matter of Record.* Cambridge, Polity Press.

SEEC [Southern England Consortium for Credit Accumulation and Transfer] (2002) *SEEC Credit Level Descriptors.*

SHARP, J. and HOWARD, K. (1996) *The Management of a Student Research Project.* Aldershot, Gower.

SHERIDAN, A. (1994) 'Managers in cartoons: they are still men in the Harvard Business Review', *Women in Management Review*, 9 (4) 20–4.

SHERIDAN, A. and CONWAY, L. (2001) 'Workplace flexibility: reconciling the needs of employers and employees', *Women in Management Review*, 16 (1) 5–11.

SIMS, B. P. (1993) 'The formation of top managers: a discourse analysis of five managerial autobiographies', *British Journal of Management,* 4, 57–68.

SMITH, J. K. (1983) 'Quantitative v qualitative research: an attempt to clarify the issue', *Educational Research*, March, 6–13.

SPENCER, A. and PODMORE, D. (1987) *In a Man's World: Essays on women in male-dominated professions.* London, Tavistock.

STARKEY, K. and MADAN, P. (2001). 'Bridging the relevance gap – aligning stakeholders in the future of management reasearch'. British Journal of Management, 12, 3–26

STEVENS, P., SCHADE, A., CHALK, B. and SLEVIN, O. (1993) *Understanding Research: A scientific approach for health care professionals.* Edinburgh, Campion Press.

STEWART, D. W. and SHAMDASANI, P. M. (1990) 'Focus groups: theory and practice', *Applied Social Research Methods Series*, 20. New York, Sage.

STEWART, R. (1983) 'Managerial behaviour: how research has changed the traditional picture', in M. J. Earl (ed.) *Perspectives on Management: A multidisciplinary analysis.* Oxford, Oxford University Press.

STOREY, J. (1992) *Developments in the Management of Human Resources*. Oxford, Blackwell.

STOREY, J. (ed.) (2001) *Human Resource Management: A critical text*. London, Thomson Learning.

STRAUSS, A. and CORBIN, J. (1988) Basics of Qualitative Research. Thousand Oaks, CA, Sage.

STUART, M. and MARTINEZ-LUCIO, M. (eds) (2004) *Partnership and Modernisation in Employment Relations*. London, Routledge.

TINKER, T. and LOWE, T. (1982) 'The management of science of the management sciences', *Human Relations*, 35 (4) 331–47.

TREMBLAY, M. A. (1982) 'The key-informant technique: a non-ethnographic technique', in R. Burgess (ed.) *Field Research: A source book and field manual*. London, Allen & Unwin.

TYSON, S. (1995) *Human Resource Strategy*. London, Pitman.

US BUREAU OF THE CENSUS (1992) *112th Statistical Abstract of the United States*. Washington DC, US Government Printing Office.

VERMA, G. K. and BEARD, R. M. (1981) *What is Educational Research? Perspectives on Techniques of Research*. Aldershot, Gower.

VINTEN, G. (1994) 'Participant observation: a model for organizational investigation?', *Journal of Managerial Psychology*, 9 (2) 30–8.

WALLIMAN, N. (2001) *Your Research Project: A step by step guide for the first-time researcher*. London, Sage.

WANGURI, D. M. (1995) 'A review, an integration, and a critique of cross-disciplinary research on performance appraisals, evaluations, and feedback: 1980–1990', *The Journal of Business Communication*, 32 (3) 267–93.

WELLS, P. (1994) 'Ethics in business and management research', in V. J. Wass and P. E. Wells (eds) *Principles and Practice in Business and Management Research*. Aldershot, Dartmouth.

WERNER, O. and SCHOEPFLE, G. (1987) *Systematic Fieldwork: Foundations of ethnography and interviewing*. Newbury Park, Sage.

WHITLEY, R. (1984) 'The fragmented state of management studies: reasons and consequences', *Journal of Management Studies*, 21 (3) 331–48.

WHYTE, W. F. (1948) *Human Relations in the Restaurant Industry*. Ann Arbor, MI, University of Michigan Press.

YIN, R. K. (2003) *Case Study Research: Design and methods*. London, Sage.

ZIKMUND, W. (2000) *Business Research Methods*. Fort Worth, TX, Dryden.

Index

Also from CIPD Publishing . . .

Developing and Applying Study Skills:

Writing assignments, dissertations and management reports

Donald Currie

Having trouble writing your assignment?

Do you want to improve your study skills and write successful reports?

Help is at hand with this latest title from CIPD Publishing. A practical guide to help you prepare, write and complete assignments, dissertations and management reports. This text looks at the skills required to produce successful documents, how to gain these skills and how and when to use them. Taking a straight forward, hands-on approach, you can use this book as an ongoing tool to aid you in your studies. It offers guidance on getting the best from lectures, tutorials, seminars, structured learning sessions and group work. Included throughout the book are exercises, case studies and self-test questions that can help you increase your experience of tackling organisation-based problems, addressing issues, increasing your academic understanding and monitoring your progress.

Order your copy now online at www.cipd.co.uk/bookstore or call us on 0870 800 3366

Donald Currie worked as a personnel officer for more than 15 years before joining the Southampton Institute as a Lecturer in personnel management. In 1990 he was appointed Fellow In Human Resource Management and for more than 10 years led the CIPD Professional Education Scheme. Donald continues to work as a consulatnt to the Southampton Business School, and has been running the CIPD CPP course since 1995.

| Published 2005 | 1 84398 064 9 | Paperback | 240 pages |

The Chartered Institute of Personnel and Development is the leading publisher of books and reports for personnel and training professionals, students and all those concerned with the effective management and development of people at work.

Also from CIPD Publishing . . .

Personal Effectiveness

Diana Winstanley

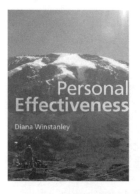

Written by a leading author in this field, this new text on Personal Effectiveness is designed to give students a basic understanding of study skills and management skills, and to give context to other studies.

Suitable for use on a range of undergraduate and postgraduate modules, including those relating to self development, personal skills, learning and development, management skills, study skills and coaching modules, and as part of general business or HR degrees, this text seeks to be both comprehensive and accessible through the use of learning aids.

Each chapter includes:

- learning objectives and a synopsis of content;
- vignette examples to illustrate key points;
- exercises with feedback;
- a self-check exercise and synopsis at the end of the chapter; and
- references and further sources of information.

Order your copy now online at www.cipd.co.uk/bookstore or call us on 0870 800 3366

Diana Winstanley has over 15 years experience of training staff, students and managers in personal effectiveness, as well as in human resource management, and is already a well respected author of a number of books and articles. She has also led, designed and supported a number of PhD and postgraduate programmes in transferable skills and personal effectiveness, and is currently Professor of Management and Director of Postgraduate Programmes at Kingston Business School. Previously she has been Senior Lecturer in Management and Personal Development, Deputy Director of the full-time MBA programme and Senior Tutor at Tanaka Business School, Imperial College London. She also has professional qualifications as a humanistic counsellor.

| Published 2005 | 1 84398 002 9 | Paperback | 256 pages |

The Chartered Institute of Personnel and Development is the leading publisher of books and reports for personnel and training professionals, students and all those concerned with the effective management and development of people at work.